A JOURNAL OF
CONSCIOUSNESS AND TRANSFORMATION

ReVision

CONTENTS

Earth Dreaming
Karen Jaenke, Editor

1	Earth Dreaming, World Awakening *Lee Irwin*
7	Poem: Daughter of mine *Arti Punj Singh*
9	Shamans, Sacred Places and the Healing Earth *Stanley Krippner*
14	Dreaming with the Earth *Karen Jaenke*
25	Myth of the Earth *Lorraine Almeida*
31	Ecological Complexes *Craig Chalquist*
42	TerraPlaces *Katrina Martin Davenport*
49	From Pet to Planet *Lesley Osman*
54	Poem: I dreamt the earth was dying *Darlene Cimino-DeRose*
55	Sustaining Wellness *Jay Rice*
62	Dreams Are Pure Nature *Meredith Sabini*
69	Giving Voice to the Earth Dreaming *Kimmy Johnson*
71	Spiritual Intelligence and the Body *Karen Jaenke*
83	Poetry at the End of the World *Leny Strobel*

Book Reviews

84	Rebearths: Conversations with a World Ensouled *Craig Chalquist*

Cover art by Lorraine Almeida

Fall 2019/Winter 2020 • Volume 32-4/ Volume 33-1

What Is ReVision?

For over forty years ReVision has explored the transformative and consciousness-changing dimensions of leading-edge thinking. Since its inception ReVision has been a vital forum, especially in the North American context, for the articulation of contemporary spirituality, transpersonal studies, and related new models in such fields as education, medicine, organization, social transformation, work, psychology, ecology, and gender.

With a commitment to the future of humanity and the Earth, ReVision emphasizes the transformative dimensions of current and traditional thought and practice. ReVision advances inquiry and reflection especially focused on the fields presently identified as philosophy, religion, psychology, social theory, science, anthropology, education, frontier science, organizational transformation, and the arts. We seek to explore ancient ways of knowing as well as new models of transdisciplinary, interdisciplinary, multicultural, dialogical, and socially engaged inquiry. It is our intention to bring such work to bear on what appear to be the fundamental issues of our times through a variety of written and artistic modalities. In the interests of renewal and fresh vision, we strive to engage in conversation a diversity of perspectives and discourses which have often been kept separate, including those identified with terms such as Western and Eastern; indigenous and nonindigenous; Northern and Southern; feminine and masculine; intellectual; practical, and spiritual; local and global; young and old.

Dream Web. (Photo by Karen Jaenke)

Volume 32 (4) and 33(1) (ISBN 978-0-9819706-9-1)

ReVision (ISSN 0275-6935) is published by
The Study of Shamanism, Healing, and Transformation.

Copyright © 2020 ReVision Publishing.
Copyright retained by author when noted. The views expressed are not necessarily those of ReVision or its editors.

ReVision provides opportunities for publishing divergent opinions, ideas, or judgments.

Manuscript Submissions

We welcome manuscript submissions.
Manuscript guidelines can be found on our webpage:
http://revisionpublishing.org.

POSTMASTER: Send address changes to
ReVision Publishing,
P.O. Box 1855,
Sebastopol, CA 95473.

Subscriptions

For subscriptions mail a check to above address or go to
www.revisionpublishing.org.

Individual Subscriptions

Subscription for one year: $36 online only,
$36 print only (international $72),
$48 print and on-line (international $84).

Subscription for two years: $60 online only,
$60 print only (international $96),
$79 print and online (international $115).

Subscription for three years: $72 online only,
$72 print only (international $108),
$96 print and online (international $132).

Institutional Subscriptions

$98 online only (international $134),
$134 print and online (international $191).

Please allow six weeks for delivery of first issue.

Editorial Board

Editor
Jürgen Werner Kremer, PhD
Santa Rosa Junior College, Santa Rosa, CA

Associate Editor
Karen Jaenke, PhD
John F. Kennedy University, Pleasant Hill, CA

Editorial and Production Management Team

Denita M. Benyshek
Art Editor

Cristina Kaplan
Poetry Editor

Gary Newman
Book Designer/Production Specialist

Samuel A. Malkemus
Book Review Editor

Consulting Editors

John Adams, PhD
Saybrook University, San Francisco, CA

Sally Atkins, EdD
Appalachian University, Boone, NC

Caroline L. Bassett, PhD
The Wisdom Institute, Minneapolis, MN

Adam Blatner, MD
Senior University Georgetown, Georgetown, TX

Matthew C. Bronson, PhD
O'Reilly Scool of Technology, UC Davis, Davis, CA

Allan Combs, PhD
California Institute of Integral Studies, San Francisco, CA

Apela Colorado
Worldwide Indigenous Science Network

Jorge Ferrer, PhD
California Institute of Integral Studies, San Francisco, CA

Mary Gomes, PhD
Sonoma State University, Rohnert Park, CA

Stanislav Grof, MD
California Institute of Integral Studies, San Francisco, CA

Irene Karpiak, PhD
University of Oklahoma, Norman, OK

Nancy Kolenda
Center for Frontier Sciences, Philadelphia, PA

Stanley Krippner, PhD
Saybrook University, San Francisco, CA

Joan Marler, MA
California Institute of Integral Studies, San Francisco, CA

Laurel McCabe, PhD
Sonoma State University, Rohnert Park, CA

Alfonso Montuori, PhD
California Institute of Integral Studies, San Francisco, CA

Joseph Prabhu, PhD
California State University Los Angeles, CA

Donald Rothberg, PhD
Spirit Rock Meditation Center, Woodacre, CA

Meredith Sabini
The Dream Institute of Northern California, Berkeley, CA

Elenita Strobel, Ed.D
Sonoma State University, Rohnert Park, CA

Robin Voetterl, Ed.D
Portland State University, Portland, OR

ReVision Abstracts

Vol. 32 No. 4/Vol. 33 No. 1 • Fall 2019/Winter 2020

Almeida, L. (2020). Myth of the Earth. *ReVision*, *32*(4), 25-30. doi:10.4298/REVN. 32(4)/33(1) 25-30

"Myth of the Earth" succinctly tells the story - in paintings and words - of our planet's inception, evolution and possible future return to the source through involution and depicts the different stages of our planet's evolution as seen from outer space. The cyclical reality of life is highlighted through the series of images of the changing planet. The paintings were completed parallel to the artist's giving birth to a child who would also grow to capacity and someday die, just as she would. Like Earth, we are part of Nature's cycles. Acceptance of death and the return of matter to energy is viewed as another stage in the cycle of life's maturation.

Chalquist, C.. (2020). Ecological Complexes: Wounded Places, Wounded People. *ReVision*, 32(4)/33(1), 31-41. doi:10.4298/REVN.32.4.31-41

Although Jung brought discussion of the anima mundi (World Soul) back into depth psychology, we still tend to see the lands we live on as inanimate. Nor has depth psychology focused much on the psychic impact of environmental destruction of the type now ravaging so much of Earth's surface. Introduced is the concept of ecological complexes: points of deep environmental wounding that resonate into the human psyche. Methods for tracing human sufferings back to the pain of place are now being assembled and used in the field. Sensitivity to ecological complexes offers a new understanding of how intimately we interact with land and place and suggests an ecology of the heart that moves beyond considerations of sustainability.

Davenport, K. M. (2020). TerraPlaces: Enlivening Relationship with Place. *ReVision* 32(4)/33(1), 42-48. doi:10.4298/REVN.32.4.42-48

Regular, sustained, and intimate contact with natural places, combined with increased awareness of and attention to place, leads to shifts in consciousness. These shifts can be subtle or pronounced depending on the level of contact and depth of awareness. The TerraPlaces project invited participants to spend regular time in a self-selected place in nature and to keep a journal and share in an online forum about their experiences. During the first five months of the TerraPlaces project, participants demonstrated rapid shifts (both inner and outer), increased intimacy, a change in their levels of attention, and increased community.

Irwin, L. (2020). Earth Dreaming, World Awakening. *ReVision*, 32(4)/33(1), 1-5. doi:10.4298/REVN.32.4.1-5

An overview of the core idea of Earth Dreaming and Earth Awakening as seen from a transpersonal perspective. I address the issues of future dreaming as both an individual and collective phenomenon whose consequences depend on a capacity to mobilize action based on dream reflection and participant knowing. I also address the moral aspects of dreaming and issues of diversity on a global scale. I see Earth Dreaming as an expression of a global, evolutionary process which requires every dreamer to be a conscious agent of transformation.

Jaenke, K. (2020). Dreaming with the Earth. *ReVision*, 32(4)/33(1), 14-24. doi:10.4298/REVN.32.4.14-24

Dreams carry the wisdom of the natural mind, capable of restoring humanity's psychic kinship with the earth. Considering the earth-human relationship through the lens of dreams provides an approach to the global ecological crisis rooted in human subjectivity and evolutionary psychology. A series of the author's significant earth dreams are explored and grouped into three categories: earth communing, earth destruction, and earth healing. The dreams point first to the necessity of recovering a numinous feeling connection with the earth; second, to the importance of engaging images of elemental destruction; and third, to healing the human-earth relationship through balancing opposites. Altogether these earth dreams illustrate the process of restoring humans to a participatory relationship with the earth.

Jaenke, K. (2020). Spiritual Intelligence and the Body. *ReVision*, 32(4)/33(1), 71-82. doi:10.4298/REVN.32.4.71-82

Spiritual intelligence has been conceptualized with different degrees of neglect or attention given to the role of the body in spiritual intelligence. Definitions of spiritual intelligence are compared, along with their accompanying skillsets. Strikingly, most authors do not address the mind-body connection as an aspect of spiritual intelligence. Literature on spiritual intelligence reflects the longstanding bias in Western culture for mind over body, a distortion writ large in our global ecological crisis, which is a manifestation of mind-matter and human-nature splits. Calling for an expansion of the theory of spiritual intelligence to explicitly include the body, this article offers four bodily-based abilities that contribute to holistic spiritual intelligence: body awareness; tracking expansion and contraction in the body; accessing, clearing and balancing body energies through the chakras; and accessing external and internal flow states.

Johnson, K. (2020). Giving Voice to the Earth Dreaming. *ReVision*, 32(4)/33(1), 69-70. doi:10.4298/REVN.32.4.69-70

The Earth speaks to us in dreams. By listening to the voice of the Earth, we open to a knowing that encompasses past, present and future, a knowing that offers wisdom and depth. In "Giving Voice to the Earth," the experience of listening to this knowing is presented through two dreams that extend far beyond one human life. The dreamer's life journey is embedded in, and an expression of these dreams. Releasing power, mystery and grief, these dreams enfold the dreamer's personal destiny into larger cycles of the earth's memory and future.

Osman, L.. (2020). From Pet to Planet: Our Attachment to Companion Animals as a Portal into Grief and Loss. *ReVision*, 32(4)/33(1), 49-53. doi:10.4298/REVN.32.4.49-53

Prompted by the loss of a beloved pet, this essay provides a mirror into our relationship and connection to the non-human world and the tenuous attachment we have to our own wild natures. Civilized out of wildness with the imperative that all that is not human is of lesser intrinsic value, the essay touches on the human-animal relationship, attachment theory and the ecological self, the grief and loss cycle, and our growing awareness of a greater planetary loss. The essay takes a very personal experience and attempts to weave larger understandings concerning the interconnected web of life using eco-psychological theory.

Rice, J. S. (2020). Sustaining Wellness: Drawing from the Roots of Horticultural Therapy. *ReVision*, 32(4)/33(1), 55-61. doi:10.4298/REVN.32.4.55-61

Horticultural therapy is a treatment modality used with physically, psychologically, socially and economically challenged populations. The applicability of horticultural therapy for preventative wellness engenders an examination of human well-being amidst growing ecological peril, cultivating a larger understanding of our experience within the cycles of nature. Utilizing fear as a teacher and venturing into the experience of isolation and loss, we discover how plants bestow the evolutionary wisdom of interdependence and cocreation. Mythology, Jung's archetypal theory, nature based wisdom traditions, Jewish mystical teachings, and contemporary ecology illuminate horticultural therapy's unique contribution to sustaining wellness, both individually and collectively, as we move through an "end of days" phase in our human evolutionary cycle.

Sabini, M. (2014). Dreams Are Pure Nature. *ReVision*, 32(4)/33(1), 52-68. doi:10.4298/REVN.32.4.62-68

Dreams are a natural phenomenon with a long evolutionary history and serve survival functions for the individual as well as the species. At times when the stability of life systems is threatened, helpful dreams about the earth may occur. An example given is the prophetic dream of eighteenth-century philosopher/scientist Georg Lichtenberg, who was advised to view the earth as a book to be read rather than an object to be dissected; another were the visionary dreams of Harriet Tubman, which showed specific routes to take escaping slaves. Contemporary dreams seem to emphasize the vitality of life processes to renew themselves autonomously.

Earth Dreaming, World Awakening

Lee Irwin

Winter moon. (Photo by Gary Newman)

We live in a time of change and great challenge, a time between dreams and paradigms, a time of contestation and emergence. The ground where we stand is not the same, it holds the quality of the abyss; each dreamer perceives only a portion of what is emerging. But this shifting ground is also a time of opportunity, a phase of creative intersection with what is possible for the sacred human. We each hold within us a visionary depth, a prophetic capacity, within which our unrealized spiritual potential can spontaneously foster a new wholeness. What inhibits us is our fears, alienation, skepticism, and denials that we can, as conscious and dedicated agents, actualize our deep spiritual

---

Dr. Lee Irwin is a full Professor in the Religious Studies Department at the College of Charleston where he teaches world religions with an emphasis on Native American traditions, western esotericism, hermeticism, contemporary spirituality, mystical cosmology, and transpersonal religious experience as related to dreams and visions. He is the Vice President of the Association for the Study of Esotericism (ASE) and a board member of the Sophia Institute; he is also a Guiding Voice for the Seven Pillars House of Wisdom (Sufi Inayati Order) program. He is the author of nine books and over 60 scholarly articles.

capacities. In a time of great change and contestation, it is inevitable that the harsh or destructive aspects stand forth as illustrating our lack of care or concern, our indifference toward the well-being of the earth and all its inhabitants. And yet, if we have any hope of attaining to the sacred human, it is visions that heal that are most needed, visions of hope whose actualization is possible and necessary for the health of all.

Are these healing visions based in individual capacity or is it possible that our visionary ability, our creative intentions, require the creativity of others? We are not each an island, but we do inhabit unique ecologies of mind and spirit. What we shape and what shapes us is not only the immediate, shared mentalities of local island culture but also the deep surrounding currents of our time as they circulate through the global ocean of cross-cultural intersections, spiritual alternatives, and scientific challenges. Our creativity as individuals is inseparable from these currents and from the influences of others as they impact our thinking, imagining, and dreaming. The transformation is not just personal, but also deeply shared and global; our creativity emerges from our individual ability to participate in shared dreaming and to offer our psychic support for those themes and concerns that best reflect the ideals we hope to realize. While our dreams are shared, they are not simply determined by a collective mentality, but emerge through the interactive media of dreaming and visionary perception as they contribute to collective transformation.

If we envision the collective as a psychonoetic field, that is as constituted by psychic and emotional capacities infused with reflective thought, then such a field must be highly dynamic as we ourselves our engaged in constant processes of feeling and reflection. In so far as this field is dynamic, its psychonoetic contents are interactive, that is, my thoughts and feelings impinge on and are impinged on by the thoughts and feelings of others. If I read a book that is 300 years old, written by an esoteric master, through a careful, attentive reading I may find psychonoetic resonance with specific ideas or beliefs in the book. Those ideas or beliefs are then taken in, processed, and reconstituted through a visionary process, one that is also influenced by the current dreaming and envisioning of others in my own time. This reconstitution is not only done in a waking state, but also in imaginative day dreaming, in night dreams, and in the spontaneous processes of syntegration - that is, on the boundary and through the abyssal ground - where psychic influences are not limited to individual mentality. The shared psychonoetic field is alive with the currents of past and present and may well include within it, future influences that exceed the normative boundaries of the current temporal order.

If we unbind the present, liberating psychic energies through a process of gradual awakening to deep potential, then the temporal order can shift, can realign and open to a vast horizon of shared perceptions. It is in this unbound present that we encounter the Dreaming Earth, the living consciousness of our shared planetary being, the living Heliocosm of which we are all part. In the limited mentality of a dreaming individual, often only the surface of the dream appears, like a mirror image reflecting the dreamer, but in the shared mentality of the full psychonoetic field, the dream explodes into the "jewel net" of unlimited multiple dreamers and visionaries. And every jewel offers a unique reflection of the whole, both as a mirror and as a kaleidoscope of reflected possibility. In this gallery of visionary images, the Dreaming Earth, like the image of earth seen from the moon, is a rich psychonoetic syntegration, suggesting all manner of possible futures and outcomes. The beauty and vibrancy of the image, the earth as a single planetary being, filled with life and luxurious with diversity and ecological distinctiveness, is a beckoning promise for all dreamers. But the reality of the positive dream can only manifest if there is a convergence of dreaming intent.

The dynamic processes of atemporal dreaming must be anchored in the stability of committed actions meant to realize the dream potential and embody the dream in waking manifestations. As we all dream this dream of our future earth differently, the convergence is not simply imitation or a recursive reduction. Each visionary has the opportunity to contribute to the dreaming processes, adding the quantum of his or her own visionary perceptions to the actualization of the whole. We may hear the music of the spheres, the vibrant melodies of Earth awakening as we, the dreamers awaken with Her. Our own awakenings to this visionary call are crucial in determining the form and contents of the shared reality, the conscious enactment of the dance, the partnered relationships that can hold the necessary energies of a full realization of that potential. No one person can hold this energy because it is not meant for one, but for many, if not all - thus, many or all must hold the energies together. This holding arises through our willing consent to shared global awakening, to be responsible creators whose ethical and spiritual concerns rise above pragmatism, party affiliations, and individual desires. The burden of this awakening is the "energy of openness" - a capacity to resist closure and subcollective identity that might result in only partial realization of depth.

To hold this openness requires discipline and not simply "letting go" that only seeks to attain an individual realization. In the shared tasks of psychonoetic dreaming, we can each offer the unique gifts of our individual understanding but those gifts are contributory to the greater gift of world integration. The dreaming earth is now is a stage of profound pregnancy, she is bursting with the life potential of a stimulated consciousness whose climactic birth-giving ecstasy will be the simultaneous awakening (or rebirth) of all her embodied children. The vision is one of lucid, shared psychonoetic awakening, where the field is no longer a subconscious influence but a conscious matrix of shared mentalities. It is a time for a redefinition of the sacred human, a reconstitution of what the human mentality can fully become, as an awakened illumination on a global scale. We have to imagine that Earth Dreaming is in a fore stage, a time of ferment, in which dreams collide, intersect, counter influence, transmogrify, and splinter into a thousand diversities only to be gathered in the dreams of others.

In this vital, alchemical process, the Earth Consciousness is dawning through the intersected mentalities of all living beings - human, animal, plant or mineral - in order to reach a new stage of planetary evolution. And we are the dreamers of the dream, the mediums through which the realization of the imaginal becomes actual. If we cannot imagine it, cannot accept it, cannot embody it, then resistance will become the wall against which the ocean of consciousness crashes. Do we embrace the change and take on the necessary responsibility to form the conduits for the change or do we resist and block the possible inflow? Every person is a potential medium for this change and the Earth Dream is active in the psyche of each person to the degree by which they embrace the potential for the sacred human. This for me is the crux of the matter, how we each embody the sacred human as a medium for spiritual transformation on a global scale. In this sense, we are tasked with the challenge of formulating the sacred human as a viable image of our deepest capacities. And this image is archetypal for each person, as a formative aspiration whose power is also reflection of the Awakened Earth.

What then, is the sacred human? This

> It is a time for a redefinition of the sacred human, a reconstitution of what the human mentality can fully become, through an awakened illumination on a global scale.

question is a spiritual challenge to each individual; it is not simply a summary of ideas or beliefs. Thus more precisely, what is the sacred human for you? How might you live your life as emblematic of the ideal that best expresses what we as human beings might become? In the dreaming of the earth consciousness, our individual answers to this question, are best expressed in how we live and act. Our ideas, as abstract notions, may be lucid and valuable but how we live within the Earth Dream is what will produce the fruit of our beliefs. Do we live with love and heart-centered concern for the well-being of others? Can we make sacrifices to improve the quality of life for all? Can we give up attachments in order to provide abundance for others? Can we accept the limitations of shared life and not lose our individual value? Can we dream the creative dream and make it real while honoring the dreams of others? Can we hold the creative energy necessary for the transformation or will we be only dreamers who never awaken? These are only a few of the questions that are integral to any concept of the sacred human. The sacred human, as I see it, is a dreaming being, a creative, imaginative, visionary individual whose practical skills are well developed and whose moral sense of concern for others is a leading aspect of that creativity. The sacred human is "sacred" because there is a heart-centered perception that is fully awakened to the lunar-solar consciousness that pervades and stimulates our growth.

As we reflect on the sacred human, we have models of spirituality across a multitude of traditions to help inform our ideals. However, we are not constrained to that which has been and that which is becoming may well surpass what tradition has held as irrefutable. I do not see the sacred human as a fixed image in the eye of God; instead I see the evolutionary potential of both God and the sacred human as a part of a process of a rich, shared, co-evolution whose goals will no longer be determined by traditional beliefs or exclusivity in conception. The future before us is rich beyond imagining, it cannot be constrained to what has been - but it can honor what is valuable and good in the formation of the sacred human over a thousand or ten thousand generations. The roots of the sacred human are in the past; the tree and branch is in the present; and the fruit in is the future - what is blossoming now is the flower, nourished by the root and branch. The sap of this Tree is the vital force and energy that permeated the Earth Consciousness, seeking to nourish the sacred in all possible forms so that it might live and be fruitful. Our role as dreamers is to access the vision and make it real, to embody the perfume of the flower, to create an atmosphere of joy, love, and shared health for the good of all.

In the processes of co-evolution, there is emergence, recapitulation, and refinement. This is a non-lineal process, one consisting of cycles that overlap and contribute to a deepening maturation. What is realized is reincorporated; what is limited is refined and given new possible expressions; what once failed, might succeed in a more benevolent context. What was destructive, violent, and atrocious must be abandoned. What denied and repressed the rights of others reflects the shadow of the dream, when conquest was the medium of a mentality that no longer serves the possibility of shared awakening. War is not part of the dream, but it is part of our history and collective action. An Awakened Earth mentality cannot thrive on war or violence because these are forces of repression and denial; fear, hostility, and suspicion are the storms we brew for the purpose of domination. The dream of world peace is inseparable from the Earth Awakening, and the enactment of that dream requires more than tolerance. Each dreamer is an ambassador of the ideal, to promote peace by living in peace means embodying the dream in real life relations with others. The stranger and the "other" are all part of the dream; in awakening, repression cannot be the means for the realization of the shared vision. Forgiveness balanced with honest reconciliation, a genuine realization of wrong-doing overcome by dialogue and deep regret for the harm done to others, is a basis for this awakened transformation.

There is a deep cry in the Earth Dreaming, a cry for honesty and shame at violations committed in thoughtless greed or in trampling the fruitfulness of earth or the rights of others. Indifference and excuses are not part of the dream, those only create resistance. To embrace the Earth Dream is to honor the diversity of every natural and cultural ecology that is fruitful and generative and to strive to maintain each unique diversity as a way of honoring the rich potential of what is already part of the Earth Awakened. Every loss diminished us all, every healthy ecology saved enriches us. The sacred human in the context of the living Earth is one whose wisdom is guided by a celebration of plurality, who nurtures life in all its diversity and beauty. The Awakened Earth is a bounty whose nature is full to overflowing with all creatures honored, all life protected, all beings balanced, with a recognition of limits and actions based in compassion. The dream is the ideal, the actuality will be earned through conscientious relations whose co-evolutionary potential will form and reform according to circumstances. As agents, we are only partially aware, far from the realization of our full spiritual capacities whose impact on the whole has yet to be fully imagined.

It is not only the current problems and challenges we face, but also the profound discovery of our potential as creators in a universe of mystery not yet grasped or comprehended. We do not know the full scope of our deep spiritual capacities in the Earth Awakened; it is not a rationalized extension of what-is but a leap to a new being-with whose capacity is greater than the imaginal. In the visionary depths of the Abyss lies the unformed potential for knowledge and expression far exceeding our current abilities or awareness. In science, art, literature, in psychology and philosophy, in spiritual teachings and revelations, lies the red gold, the dawning aurora of the psychonoetic field extending through and beyond Earth Awakened into the living cosmos. The ur-forms of the sacred human, now unfolding, have only begun to express the variety and diversity of our possible spiritual accomplishments. Our psychonoetic capacities, like the mind's ability to facilitate healing or to receive subtle psychic impressions, to commune across distances or to create geometries of artistic and mathematical brilliance, are only tentative signs of the Earth Dream awakening. As the dream unfolds, many abilities now dormant will become active and expressive.

What might the conscious collective mentality, a shared global consciousness, inspire in all areas of creative expression? Will human psychic ability expand into commonplace interactions through paranormal perceptions, such that the "normal" becomes what is only now "supernatural"? Will our expansive development reach other mentalities still hidden from our current knowledge? Will the domains of earth ecology, their multiple inhabitants, have speech and teach us what is now known only in monologue? Will we ground our visions in the fluid energies of embodied living or will we only create fantasies that never give birth? The unknown potential is stirred in the dreams of a water filled world, luminous with life and vitality, not stained or impure by human indifference but reconstituted through a shared vision in which health and well-being take precedence over aggression, lazy indifference, and rational denials. Together, we can recreate and refine what we have allowed to evolve chaotically because there was no guiding dream and old dreams cannot hold the energies for the reconstruction of the future. The dream itself, of the Awakened Earth, is based in a multitude of psychic influences that merge into a dynamic interconnectedness forming the tentative structures for new emergence. Can we find the courage and humility necessary to hold the dream for its full enactment?

Another aspect of the Dreaming Earth is the ways in which our future envisioning challenges us to grow beyond the habitual limitations we set on our own actions and thoughts. In dreaming potential into form, the dreamer must hold openness and also a still point of depth that remains undefined. The Abyssal ground, as the ontological source of our inspirations, does not seek closure in form but expressiveness through an abundance of manifestations. The dreamer's task is thus to remain a center of elaborations, with continuity, but also, with a self-transcending acceptance that allows for the birth of novelty and discovery. We are not seeking "the answer" - such seeking reflects an older and less fluid mentality - but the possibilities that will allow for integration on a global scale across multiple time and cultures. There is no "one answer" just as there is no "one way" to this integration. The still point that remains undefined is a "god-point" or a touch of "infinity" in the heart of every creature. Out of this mystery, comes a realization that what is created or formed or discovered and amplified, is not the answer but only a possibility for development. We can build on our discoveries, we can merge our disciplinary insights into paradigms of wholeness that will then be transformed and surpassed.

In the dynamics of cosmic creation, both in the long term evolutions of stellar matter and energy as well as in the lesser evolutions of measurable temporal, cultural understanding, the process is self-surpassing. And dreaming is the medium through which what is coming-to-be manifests in the minds of those embodied in temporal order. As dreamers engage the deep dreaming, the "big" dreams, the revelatory intuitions of what may become, the prophetic self is stimulated to construct forms and structures that will hold the dream contents for possible enactment. Sometimes, that holding is an act of mental clarity - that is, what we see in the revelatory dream, vision, or intuition, must be held in mind, nurtured, sustained as a possible template for actions, remembered and not forgotten. Every forgotten big dream is a lost possibility; every remembered big dream, held with positive regard, is a source of possible growth. And we grow beyond our dreams, as we embody the possible, thereby creating in the process a new ground for revelation. The cycles of revelation, informing the prophetic self, take us through the labyrinth of our collective life as well as into intersections with the dreams of others. As we embrace the dream and actualize it, we surpass our own limits and we meet our co-dreamers, those seeking a similarity in prophetic insight.

The prophetic self is an emergent identity. Where the core of self awareness is shaped by the psychonoetic history of each individual, the prophetic self accesses the emergent horizon of the possible. Every individual can carry the dream of Earth Awakening through the development of the prophetic self. And this is a moral development because at the very root of the process is a profound concern for the propagation of life and an honoring of its diversity, value, and contribution to the health of the whole. The moral concern is expressed through the protection and fostering of life. Such a prophetic self is not aligned with exclusivity or a denial of alternative prophetic visions; the emergent prophetic self is not a "prophet" of religious dogma, but a visionary self working in concert with others to sustain creative dialogues that will foster cooperation and a just way of life for every creature. The prophetic self is an awakening consciousness within each person able to dream the possible as a source for creative actualization.

This does not mean that all prophetic dreams are positive or ideal - in fact, many prophetic dreams are negative, frightening, and carry disturbing collective energies. The deep prophetic self accesses what must be transformed; it is confronted by the turbulence

> What the prophetic self seeks is… not a dominant worldview but a shared vision of diverse, cooperative communities whose ethical perspective promotes life and creativity without resort to threat or violence. The prophetic dreamer is the one who can envision how this transformation can be attained.

and trauma of old dreams of power, domination, and control. The dream of the Awakened Earth requires courage and inner determination to seek new resolution of the contested dreams of the past that will not accept compromise nor deny the value of alternative visions that do not claim sovereignty or mandate conformity. The collapse of visionary authority as an exclusive domain for a global worldview is the very terrain of recreation for the prophetic self. What we seek is not a dominant worldview but a shared vision of diverse, cooperative communities whose ethical perspective promotes life and creativity without resort to threat or violence. The prophetic dreamer is the one who can envision how this transformation can be attained; what must be given up, renounced, or reconstructed are attitudes of denial or dismissal of the healing dreams of others. If we want to embrace the Earth Awakened, then we need new dreams and visions to show us the way.

Finally, we need to think about the consequences of a failed dream. This is why I emphasize action over interpretation. We can envision two aspects of the dream that are interactive and provide perspective on how the dream can be enacted. One aspect is what I would call "participatory knowing" - that is the dream itself is a kind of knowing based on the dreamer's ability to recognize her or him self as the agent that holds the dream (whatever its "sources" may be). This kind of knowing requires memory and lucidity in dream recall, an ability to hold the emergent insight. A dream or vision to be enacted must be remembered, with detail and clarity; memory must be cultivated to reproduce the psychic content as exactly as possible, sustaining the dream event. The self as "participatory" in the dream is a self awakened to the dream, able to hold the dream, and to represent it for conscious reflection. The "I" of the dreamer is not always the "I" of the dream, but the awakened dreamer can hold the distinctiveness of the dream as a source of reflection for exploring the difference between the "I" that dreams and the "I" that remembers and reflects.

In turn, this leads to the second aspect, which I call "reflective knowing" - that is, an ability to regard the dream, its psychonoetic contents, as a source of insight for possible action. I do not regard "reflection" as necessarily a form of interpretation. The dream is more than a text, more than an account for analysis, and much more than a medium to be shaped by an ideology or psychological theory. The dream is a living expression of the psychonoetic field, far more than a text. Reflections on the dream, holding it within the mind's "I" allows the richness of its contents to act psychically on the

> The challenge is to live with the dream and, though reflection, to find strategies for enactment.

dreamer in ways that are often unpredictable and not necessarily rational or pragmatic. Carrying the dream means remembering and allow the dream to inform our reflections upon it; it means allowing the dream to be remembered in a waking context other than in therapy or in writing thoughts in a dream journal. Participatory knowing is a knowing of the dream in the waking context of everyday life - as I drive to work or walk in the city or talk with a friend, the dream comes back to me, it impinges into a context that also invokes the dream content. Participatory knowing is to take note of this dream presence, of a dream or visionary image or of a feeling or mood, that can then be a source of reflection. Thus the two aspects work together through participation in the dream in waking states and in using that participatory knowing as a source for reflection and insights.

From this synthesis of participatory reflection, comes action. If the dreamer stops with only knowing, the dream remains as potential unrealized. By "action" I do not mean any specific type of action, but refer to the creative challenge of discovering a method for action. Perhaps the action is more mental or emotional than physical; perhaps it is a smile rather than a frown, a state of receptivity rather than defensive closure, a condition of inner reflection rather than a habitual response to stimulation from others. Perhaps it is a drawing, a song, a walk by the sea or a discussion long held at bay. What does the dream suggest? What does reflection on the dream, in participatory knowing, indicate as a possible strategy for action? In Earth Dreaming, our participatory knowing, arising out of visionary intuitions, comes home to each person as what he or she carries of that dream. The challenge is to live with the dream and, though reflection, to find strategies for enactment. The dream of Earth Awakening is not a passive dream but a creative context for embodiment through celebratory action, through meaningful intentions, to give form and birth to a cooperative building of a visionary future.

The failure of the dream, its lack of embodiment in practice, the inability to create a context that supports emergence, means a failed possibility. This does not mean all dreams need to be enacted, but rather that we must choose wisely the dream we do seek to enact. Dreaming is a vast process, impinging on all aspects of human life. Among this plethora of dreaming activity, it is the "big dreams" that call to us, stir us, even frighten us, that require enactment. The big dream of Earth Awakening, is a shared dream, an event of cosmological proportion, whose enactment covers an extensive panorama of embodied practices. The basis for that action is love, respect, creative and critical reflection, and a willingness to adapt in concert with positive and compassionate values. Our evolution as a species depends on our dreaming capacities; our failed dreams are what will mark us in terms of our limitations. To succeed as dreamers and as participants in a creative Earth Dreaming and Earth Awakening, will require enduring commitment to enactment, reflection, and participatory knowing. Not only through dreams and visions, but also through a lucid clarity of mind and purpose in carrying out the shaping of the world. Our success then, depends on our cooperation in the dreaming and waking context. Our challenge is to wake up and not deny the role of dreams and visions in the process.

References

Barušs, I. & J. Mossbrige (2017). *The Transcendent Mind: Rethinking the Science of Consciousness.* Washington, D. C.: American Psychological Association.

Bogzaran, F. & D. Deslauriers. (2012). *Integral Dreaming: A Holistic Approach to Dreams.* Albany: State University of New York Press.

Bulkeley, K. (2016). *Big Dreams: The Science of Dreaming and the Origins of Religion.* New York: Oxford University Press.

Carr, B. (2015). Hyperspatial Models of Matter and Mind. In E. F. Kelly et al (Eds.), *Beyond Physicalism: Toward Reconciliation of Science and Spirituality* (pp. 227-274). Lanham: Rowman & Littlefield.

Cattoi, T. & D. Odorisio. (2018). *Depth Psychology and Mysticism.* New York: Palgrave Macmillan.

Ferrer, J. (2017). *Participation and the Mystery: Transpersonal Essays in Psychology, Education, and Religion.* Albany: State University of New York Press.

Hall, Z. (2016). Whose Dream is it anyway? Dream Telepathy (or Non-Local Memory). In M. Schroll (Ed.), *Transpersonal Ecosophy, Vol. 1 Theory, Methods, and Clinical Assessments* (pp. 289-300). Llanrhaeadr-ym-Mochnant, U. K.: Psychoid Books.

Irwin, Lee. (1996). *Visionary Worlds: The Making and Unmaking of Reality.* Albany: State University of New York Press.

Irwin, Lee. (2014). On Lucid Dreaming: Memory, Meaning, and Imagination. In R. Hurd & K. Bulkeley (Eds.), *Lucid Dreaming: New Perspectives on Consciousness in Sleep* (Vol 1, pp. 103-126). Two Volumes. Berkeley: Praeger, 2014.

Irwin, Lee. (2019). Religion and the Paranormal: Redefining the Sacred Human. In J. George (Ed.), *De Natura Fidei: Rethinking Religion across Disciplinary Boundaries.* New York: Macmillan Interdisciplinary Handbook. Forthcoming.

Krippner, S., F. Bogzaran, & P. Carvalho. (2002). *Extraordinary Dreams and How to Work with Them.* Albany: State University of New York Press.

Laszlo, I. (2006). *Science and the Reenchanment of the Cosmos: The Rise of the Integral Vision of Reality.* Rochester: Inner Traditions.

Penrose, R., S. Hameroff, & S. Kak. (2011) *Consciousness and the Universe: Quantum Physics, Evolution, Brain & Mind.* Cambridge: Cosmology Science Publishers.

Schroll, M. (2016). Understanding Bohm's Holoflux: Clearing up a Conceptual Misunderstanding of the Holographic Paradigm and Clarifying its Significance to Transpersonal Studies of Consciousness. In M. Schroll (Ed.), *Transpersonal Ecosophy, Vol. 1 Theory, Methods, and Clinical Assessments* (pp. 45-90). Llanrhaeadr-ym-Mochnant, U. K.: Psychoid Books.

Weiss, E. (2015). Mind Beyond Body: Transphysical Process Metaphysics. In E. F. Kelly et al. (Eds.), *Beyond Physicalism: Toward Reconciliation of Science and Spirituality* (pp. 455-492). Lanham: Rowman & Littlefield.

Subscription Renewals

Renew your personal or institutional Revision subscription **online:**

www.revisionpublishing.org

Click on **Subscriptions** in the left hand column

For renewal by **mail:**

ReVision
P.O. Box 1855
Sebastopol, CA 95473

Redwood grove (Photo by Gary Newman)

Daughter of mine, hold my hand.

Show me my way in this vast land. I lost sight of worlds within. My heart has bled … and bled … within.

I, who have no voice, ask that you speak in my voice … of all my tears, my fears, my heartache … I ask you – give voice … to all my pain.

Pain that I drank, and ate, and swallowed … fearing its measure of intensity.

I … who am mother … to All. I, who am the Spirit of all. I, who know not my own power.

I, who forget the passing hour … Daughter of mine, pray … give me your voice, give me the courage to own this voice, a voice I lost so long ago, a voice unheard … unfelt … unseen. A voice that asks to speak … and speak and … speak …. my voice, daughter is what I seek.

Give me your courage, give me your strengths, for the time has come, my time is spent.

For all those moments my heart was full, the unshed, the unsung, the moment … spent.

My sorrows I take with me to rest, my joys I share with all I bless. My heart grieves … and grieves – my child, my daughter … I am spent.

Gather me in your gentle arms lay me to rest in my mother's breast … forever silenced – to speak no more.

Daughter of life, this I ask – stand tall … speak loud and, do me proud.

Stay quiet no longer, stand firm, stand proud, for you are the one who saw … my Soul.

I am the One, the One who speaks of love … of life … of dignity! Stand tall … stand firm … speak with your Soul.

Let no man ever beat your bone … sing loud … sing clear … that ALL may hear.

I am woman … shed not a tear. I am one with the She of who I am made.

I am one with the Earth – forever … more.

~ Arti Punj Singh, May 29th '09.

from Vajra Publications

249 pages

Available from
Vajra Publications, Nepal
https://vajrabookshop.com/

Available from
Amazon

$17.00

Transformation of Consciousness is an exploration of various approaches to impact our consciousness. The book points to potentials we as a species may need for our future survival.

Shamanic approaches are frequently viewed as premodern and thus mere historical remnants. The implication is that they are fascinating to help explain our past evolutionary history, but have little relevance for our future. When we disregard the significance of these ancient shamanic and Eastern paradigms, we disregard possible avenues to shift our thinking and our cultural practices for the benefit of our future survival.

Each author in this anthology discusses exit strategies out of the hall of mirrors that our contemporary world has created. Each contribution validates the importance of ancient traditions today, and the need for a more appropriate epistemology to describe consciousness processes.

Transformations of consciousness are needed not only to serve individual needs, but also to serve our general human need to know, understand, and make meaning. These transformations also support socio-cultural practices that are holistic, integrative, and balancing for individuals and communities.

Shamans, Sacred Places, and the Healing Earth

Stanley Krippner, Ph.D.

For tribal shamans, nature was sacred; Earth was alive and special spots were engulfed with "power," filled with "energy;' or inhabited by "spirits." Although soil, water, and air all partook of the divine, some spots were especially numinous and these sacred places were visited by shamans for renewal, communication with the "other world," or entry into altered states of consciousness.[1] Shamans, both past and present, were socially designated practitioners who voluntarily altered their consciousness to enter the "other world," bringing back knowledge that they used to serve the needs of their community. Shamans were exceptionally sensitive to what biologist Rene DuBos referred to as "the spirit of place."[2]

Many shamans regarded the Earth as their mother. There were hills that looked

Wilderness lake. (Photo by Gary Newman)

Stanley Krippner, Ph.D., is professor of psychology at Saybrook University in Oakland, CA. He holds faculty appointments at the Universidade Holistica Internacional (Brasilia) and the Instituto de Medicina y Tecnologia Avanzada de la Conducta (Ciudad Juarez, Mexico). In 2002 he received the Award for Distinguished Contributions to Professional Hypnosis from Division 30, and APA's Award for Distinguished Contributions to the International Advancement of Psychology. He is a Fellow in the Association for Psychological Science, the Society for the Scientific Study of Religion and the Society for the Scientific Study of Sexuality.

like breasts, crags that looked like faces, rivers that could have been life-giving milk. But the concept of Mother Earth was not universal; each indigenous culture worked out its pantheon of deities in its own way, albeit with frequent interactions with other cultures.[3] Mother Earth was given visibility in North America by the Wanapum prophet Smohalla and the Shawnee cultural leader Tecumseh, although it had much earlier roots in the Pocahontas myth. However, many Native American tribes do not have a maternal Earth deity even though they have long traditions of respect for nature and care for the land.

In Ancient Egypt, Geb was the Earth Father. All the world's vegetation sprouted from Geb's back as he was lying on his stomach, prone. The Algonquin Indians worshipped Nokomis, the Earth Mother, and believed that all living things fed from her bosom. Balkan peasants considered Earth each person's parent and spouse, dressing the corpse for a wedding before burying it. Indeed, the first people who developed skills in the healing arts held a special reverence for Earth deities, whether they were male, female, or both.

Animism was a perspective that saw nature as alive and sacred; it was associated with hunting and gathering tribes, especially those in the Old and Middle Stone Ages (i.e., Paleolithic and Mesolithic Ages). Totemism, an evolved strand of animism, conceptualized various animal species as related to particular clans. For the mythologist Joseph Campbell, the bear skull sanctuaries of Paleolithic times provide the earliest evidence of the veneration of a divine being.[4] Shamanism was associated with both animism and totemism and has been called "applied animism."[5] Many contemporary writers refer to the living planet Earth as "Gaia," pointing out that active feedback processes operate to keep Earth temperature, oxidation state, and acidity constant while solar energy sustains comfortable conditions for life.[6] The Gaia concept is the most recent in a long tradition of perspectives that views Earth as a living organism whose capabilities include the ability to bear, sustain, and heal human beings.

This is a far different world view than that held by the Europeans who conquered the Americas. Despite the evidence of long-established, city-based civilizations like those of the Inca, the Aztec, and the Maya, European settlers regarded Native Americans as people with no real homes. This provided justification for "civilizing" the Indians "for their own good" into ordered communities."[7] No other approach could save as many souls; and no other approach could further the territorial and economic interests of the conquerors. The invaders overlooked the architectural accomplishments of Native Americans, such as building their homes in concert with nature rather than in opposition to nature, placing doorways towards the east where the sun rose, and devising floor plans so that when people awoke they would feel as though they had been reborn.

The Healing Earth and Treatment Practices

Pablo Amaringo is a contemporary shaman who has made a considerable effort to preserve the Amazonian ecosystem. Over the years, Amaringo has utilized a powerful mind-altering brew, *ayahuasca*, in his work, and painted several of his ayahuasca visions. A book containing forty-nine of these paintings presents hundreds of animals, plants, spirits, and mythological beings.[8] Journeys to various underwater, subterranean, and outer-space worlds are graphically detailed in these paintings. After retiring as a healer, Amaringo organized an art school in Pucallpa, Peru, dedicated to documenting the ways of Amazonian life. The school's philosophy is the education of local youths in the care and preservation of the Amazonian ecosystem.

The concept of the healing Earth has entered into treatment procedures used by indigenous shamans and other magi-

> The Gaia concept is the most recent in a long tradition of perspectives that views Earth as a living organism whose capabilities include the ability to bear, sustain and heal human beings.

co-religious practitioners since prehistoric times. For example, the central element in the Navajo healing ceremony is sand painting. This painting represents, simultaneously, the spiritual and physical landscape in which the patients and their transgressions exist as well as the etiology of the disease and the mythic

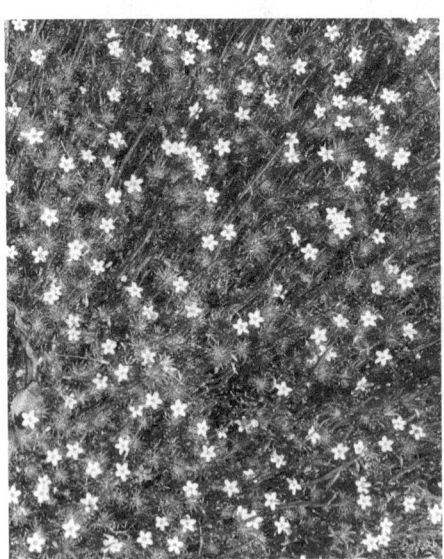
Tiny flowers. (Photo by Gary Newman)

meaning of the procedure that has been chosen for its cure. Stones, plants, and sacred objects often are placed inside the painting. Mythological relationships among the elements are represented in colored sand. The sand figures may be clouds or snakes or whatever is needed to portray the path of the disease as it proceeds through time and space.

Dangers and diseases have their place in the matrix as well; if they have been the cause of illness or misfortune, they alone can correct it. Chanting, drumming, and a vigil bring the elements together. Patients become aware of the pattern of their sickness and their life, and how both are joined in the cosmos. Usually patients are surrounded by their friends, neighbors, and relatives who sing and pray to that purpose.[9, 10]

A variation of the sand painting is the ground painting constructed by the Southern California Diegueno Indians during the puberty ritual of young tribesmen. They convey the design of their world by representing the horizon as a circle. Also included are the world's edge, various heavenly bodies, power animals (especially the crow, coyote, snake, and wolf), and the mortar and pestle used to grind up the mind-altering plants used in these ceremonies.[11]

Some psychohistorians believe that the placenta is represented in these Indian medicine wheels-both in the temporary sand and ground paintings and in the longer-lasting constructions, of which about fifty still exist in the western parts of the United States and Canada. These structures are composed of stones placed on the ground to form a small central circle, with lines of stones radiating outward; sometimes there is an outer circle around the circumference.[12] Used for ceremonies involving renewal and rebirth, some of the medicine wheels are said to "look more like placenta than any other religious symbols derived from intra-uterine life, including the tree of life, the pagan cross, and the sacred pole."[13] Medicine lodges are built each summer by the Plains Indians for sacred ceremonies; these lodges feature a central tree or pole-often with as many rafters as the medicine wheels have lines of stones. Although these designs could also emulate the sun, anthropologist R. B. McFarland says that he favors

> ... the placenta as the origin of the sacred circle, everyone starts life dependent on their placenta for nourishment and life's blood, long before we see the sun, and the sun doesn't have a central pole. The circle and the tree of life are both symbols of the placenta, the umbilical cord, and the network of blood

vessels resembling the roots and branches of a tree.[14]

I found a similar concern in the songs of Maria Sabina, the Mazatec Indian shaman I interviewed in 1980 and whose sacred mushroom *veladas* were recorded and transcribed before her death. Many of her verses reveal her close association with nature:

> Living Mother ...
> Mother of sap, Mother of the dew ...
> Mother who gave birth to us ...
> Green Mother, budding Mother ...
> These are my children ...
> These are my babies ...
>
> These are my offshoots ...
> My buds ...
> I am only asking, examining ...
> About his business as well ...
> I begin in the depth of the water ...
> I begin where the primordial sounds forth ...
> When the sacred sounds forth ...
> I am a little woman who goes through the water ...
> I am a little woman who goes through the stream ...
> I bring my light ...
> Ah, Jesus Christ ...
> Medicinal herbs and sacred herbs of Christ ...
> I'm going to thunder ...
> I'm going to play music ...
> I'm going to shout ...
> I'm going to whistle ...
> It is a matter of tenderness, a matter of clarity ...
> There is no resentment ...
> There is no rancor ...
> There is no argument ...
> There is no anger ...
> It is life and well-being ...
> It is a matter of sap ...
> It is a matter of dew ...[15]

These excerpts from several of Maria Sabina's songs reveal a woman who reveres the Mother who gives birth to us, a woman who has entered the primordial waters of oceanic consciousness but who does not stay there. The true nature of her consciousness is oriented toward service, toward healing, toward her community, and toward the children and babies to whom she strives to bring life and well-being. For her, the human being is a part of the natural world and must join its quest for life and well-being.

In general, North American Indians felt that nature-in-movement had magical power, hence the importance given the Deer Dance by the Huichols, the Buffalo Dance by the Hopis, and the Sun Dance by the Plains Indians. The Naniamo shamanic apprentices of Vancouver Island believed that their tutelaries were mythical monsters rather than the animal spirits who assisted other members of their tribe. When I visited the Cuna Indians of Panama in 1985, I observed a dance in which each tribal member moved to the spirit of his or her power animals, bringing the energy and knowledge from the "other world" into communal activity.

The Nature of Sacred Places

Some locations in what shamans call Middle Earth are held to be more sacred than others. Shamans frequently locate "power spots" and use them in their healing ceremonies. These are the areas that are said to contain more "energy" and "vital force" than surrounding geographic locations. Taking the position that "ancient peoples are still offering us their wisdom through their sacred sites and landscapes," mythologist Paul Devereux has found that they differentiated between the physical landscape as constituted by consensual agreements, i.e., the ordinary reality of the world, and the visionary landscape of the human mind.

For example, the Balinese language contains a well-developed sensibility of dual worlds (*niskala* and *sekala*). But English can only call the alternative visionary world "symbolic," at best. By whatever name it is called, Devereux suggests that a rediscovery of the human capacity to "see" as the ancients could "see," would assist residents of industrialized societies to understand that the existence of these other landscapes rests essentially on one's willingness to believe in them. Devereux does not simply dismiss the phenomenon of the symbolic reality as existing only in the imagination; he also documents the presence of naturally magnetic stones at a variety of recognized sacred spots, and presents reasonable explanations for the verified presence of strange bright lights at some "power spots." The nearby magnetic stones could have been employed both for healing work and for altering people's consciousness.

The well-preserved Neolithic landscape of Avebury in southern England is undeniably recognized as having been a ceremonial landscape for its ancient inhabitants. It follows from Devereux's argument that it was also a landscape of the mind. This is only one example of the legacy that Devereux believes native people left the world in their sacred sites and landscapes.

A contemporary example of such a site is given by Alfonso Ortiz, who as a child in his Pueblo village had a vision that was directed to the mountaintop, the place where the paths of the living and the dead were said to converge. Ortiz recalled:

> A wise elder among my people, the Tewa, frequently ... smiled and said, "Whatever life's challenges you may face, remember always to look to the mountaintop; in doing so you look to greatness. Remember this, and let no problem, however great it may seem, discourage you ... "Although he knew I was too young to understand, he also knew there was not much time left to impart this message to me and, perhaps, to others like me. In

accordance with our beliefs, the ancestors were waiting for him at the edge of the village the day he died, waiting to take him on a final four-day journey to the four sacred mountains of the Tewa world. A Tewa must either be a medicine man in a state of purity or he must be dead before he can safely ascend the sacred mountain.[16]

Ortiz's statement implies that the shaman can utilize sacred geographical spots such as the mountaintop. These spots are also the places where tribal "ancestors" can be found by the shaman and consulted in time of need. James Swan has reviewed more than one hundred case histories of people having unusual experiences at power spots, and he observes that the most common experiences reported were feelings of ecstasy, unification with nature, interspecies communication, waking visions, profound dreams, the ability to seemingly influence the weather, feeling unusual "energies," and hearing words, voices, music, and songs.[17]

One explanation of the nature of sacred places can be found in the creation myth of the Hopi Indian tribe. In the beginning, it is told, Tiowa, the Creator, saw a need to assign a guardian for Earth and he gave the position to a wise old woman named Spider Grandmother. Descending to Earth, Spider Grandmother saw that she would need help with her task as a steward. She reached down, picked up two handfuls of soil and spit into each of them. From each hand sprang a handsome young man. The three sat quietly in meditation for a time, attuning their minds to that of Tiowa. Then Spider Grandmother sent one young man clothed in shimmering silver, Poqanghoya, to the North Pole to work his magic of giving structure and form to Earth, holding the planet together. The other, Palongwhoya, wearing an equally spectacular costume of fiery red, carried a drum with him as he was sent to the South Pole. When Palongwhoya reached the South Pole, he sat in meditation for a time, reaching his heart-mind out into the universe. When he heard the heart beat of Tiowa, he began to imitate that rhythm on his drum, creating a harmony. Whenever two or more things come into harmony, energy is exchanged, and so Palongwhoya's drum directed energy from the heart of the Creator into the Earth through the drum beat. This stream of life-force energy coursed downward to the very center of the Earth. Striking the center, they radiated outward again, like the seeds of a dandelion. As they emerged from the Earth's crust, they were more concentrated at some places than at others. These places are the strongest sacred places, known to the Hopis as the

Rocks in a stream. (Photo by Gary Newman)

"spots on the fawn; places of light as on the back of a young deer.[18]

The Exploitation of the Living Earth

Some contemporary humans claim that their needs permit them to ravish nature. As former U.S. Secretary of the Interior, Manuel Lujan, Jr., stated, "I think that God gave us dominion over these creatures." Lujan also remained unconvinced that every species needs to be preserved, saying "Nobody's told me

> Earth meets the biological definition of a loving organism, as a self-producing and self-renewing system.

the difference between a red squirrel, a black one, or a brown one."[19]

In a San Francisco interview with several social scientists on May 8, 1992, former Soviet leader Mikhail Gorbachev took a different position, when he said:

> We must continue to move ahead on this issue in the spirit of innovative thinking. The destruction of the environment is a dramatic problem. We need to work toward a single global vision. For example, the Siberian taiga and the Amazonian rainforest are the twin lungs of the planet. In our new Foundation, we have a Center for Global Problems devoted to these issues. This is a global problem and it must be solved with global approaches.[20]

This vision of the living Earth is also implicit in the work of Nobel laureate Barbara McClintock. In studying genetic transportation, she focused on corn (a sacred food to many Native American tribes), working with nature to determine how genetic structures respond to the needs of the organism. In commenting on her work, biographer E. F. Keller states that nature is on the side of scientists like McClintock—although her underlying philosophy alarmed her peers (especially the male geneticists) and regulated her to the periphery of genetic research for many decades.[21]

Mythologist Elizabeth Sahtouris observed how Earth's relatively constant temperature and chemical balance is favorable to life. For her, Earth meets the biological definition of a loving organism, as a self-producing and self-renewing system.[22] Earth is the only planet in its solar system that had the right size, density, composition, fluidity of elements, and "the right distancing and balancing of energy with its sun star and satellite moon to come alive and stay so."[23] Mythologist Charlene Spretnak adds that on the smaller celestial bodies, the electromagnetic interaction overpowered gravity's pull; on the larger ones, the opposite relationship developed. Only on Earth were the two in balance.[24]

Western scientists and philosophers who agree with the shamanic conception of Earth as a living being are in a minority. But they, in consort with indigenous people, call for awareness and sensitivity on the part of human beings in regard to the balance that must be maintained. The ancient Greeks believed that in the beginning there was darkness, personified by the god Chaos. Then appeared Gaia, the Earth goddess. Western cultures have used their technology to insulate themselves from any limitations imposed by nature. Spretnak contends that the Western stance has been that if societies let down their guard, they would again be engulfed by chaos. But this is a misreading of nature and a dysfunctional mythology; humankind's destruction is more likely if the living, healing Earth is ignored.

Notes

1. Paul Devereux, *Shamanism and the Mystery Lines: Ley Lines, Spirit Paths, Shape-Shifting and Out-of-Body Travel* (St. Paul, Minn.: Llewellyn, 1993).

2. Rene Dubos, "The Spirit of Place." *Parabola* (Winter 1993, originally published 1972), 66-68.

3. S. D. Gill, *Mother Earth: An American Story* (Chicago: University of Illinois Press, 1987).

4. Joseph Campbell, *The Way of the Animal Powers* (New York: Harper and Row, 1988).

5. Neville Drury, *The Shaman and the Magician: Journeys Between Worlds* (London: Routledge and Kegan Paul, 1982).

6. Elizabeth Sahtouris, *Gaia: The Human Journey from Chaos to Cosmos* (NewYork: Pocket Books, 1989).

7. J. Bruhac, "The Families Gathered Together," *Parabola* (Winter 1992), 36.

8. Luis E. Luna and Pablo Amaringo, *Ayahuasca Visions: The Religious Iconography of a Peruvian Shaman* (Berkeley, Calif.: North Atlantic Books, 1991)

9. Richard Grossinger, *Planet Medicine: From Stone Age Shamanism to Postindustrial Healing,* rev. ed. (Boulder, Colo.: Shambhala, 1982), 105-106.

10. Donald Sandner, *Navaho Symbols of Healing* (New York: Harvest/Harcourt Brace Jovanovich, 1979).

11. Joan Halifax, *Shaman: The Wounded Healer* (New York: Crossroads, 1982).

12. R. B. McFarland, "Indian Medicine Wheels and Placentas: How the Tree of Life and the Circle of Life Are Related," *Journal of Psychohistory* 20, 1993, 543-564.

13. McFarland, 1993, p. 456

14. McFarland, 1993, p. 462

15. Alanso Estrada, *Maria Sabina: Her Life and Chants* (Santa Barbara, Calif.: Ross-Erickson, 1981), 107, 136, 150-151, 165, 175-176.

16. Halifax, 30.

17. James A. Swan, *Sacred Places* (Santa Fe, N.M.: Bear and Co., 1990).

18. Swan, 1990."

19. T. Gup, "The Stealth Secretary," *Time*, May 25, 1992, 57-59.

20. Personal communication, May 8, 1992.

21. E. F. Keller, *Feeling The Organism: The Life and Work of Barbara McClintock* (New York: W.H. Freeman, 1983).

22. Elizabeth Sahtouris, "The Dance of Life," in *Gaia's Hidden Life: The Unseen Intelligence of Nature,* eds. Shirley Nicholson and Brenda Rosen (Wheaton, Ill.: Quest Books, 1992), 18.

23. Sahtouris, 1992, p. 23."

24. Charlene Spretnak, *States of Grace* (San Francisco: HarperSanFrancisco, 1991).

Leaves. (Photo by Gary Newman)

Dreaming with the Earth

by Karen Jaenke, Ph.D.

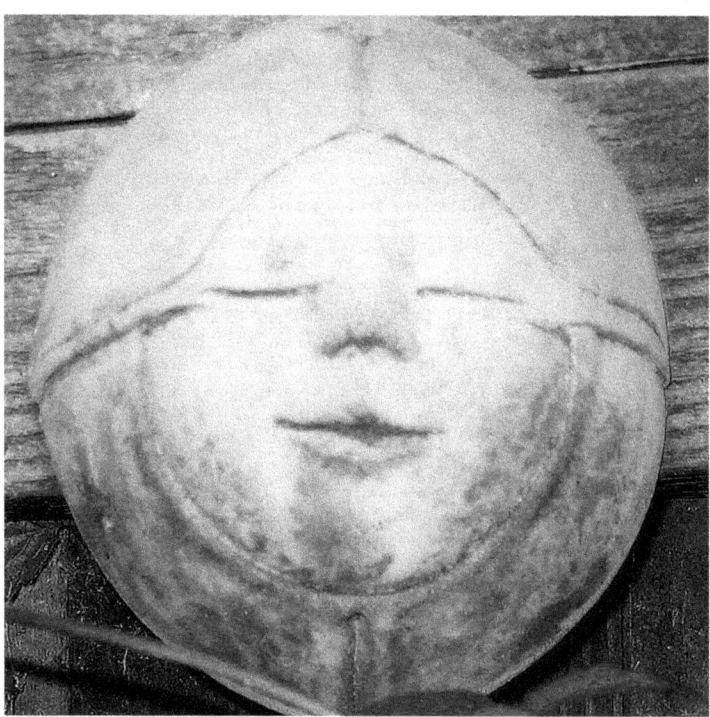
Dreaming face. (Photo by Karen Jaenke)

In the soft womb of the psyche lay the seeds of all creation. We enter that fertile darkness each night as we dream. Before anything enters into being, it must first enter imagination, and dreaming is the pure font of imagination. In the Australian Aboriginal creation story, everything in the universe comes into existence after first emerging in the dreamtime (Lawlor, 1991). If humans are to bring forth a new relationship to the Earth, its seeds will be in dreaming.

Karen Jaenke, M.Div., Ph.D., has taught qualitative research, dream studies, imaginal psychology, group process, and professional identity courses at Bay Area graduate schools since 1998. She currently serves as Chair of the Consciousness and Transformative Studies MA program at John F. Kennedy University in Pleasant Hill, CA. An executive editor of ReVision, she has edited issues on Imaginal Psychology and Shamanism, and contributed articles on dreams, participatory knowing, shamanism and evil. A graduate of Princeton Seminary and the California Institute of Integral Studies, her dissertation Personal Dreamscape as Ancestral Landscape explored the power of dreams to recover deep memory and indigenous ways of knowing. She founded Dreamhut Consulting, offering dissertation coaching, dream work, hypnotherapy consulting services in Marin, CA (www.dreamhut.org).

Our dreams express the leading edge of creation.

In addition to this indigenous perspective, evolutionary psychology recognizes dreaming as an ancient function, present in mammals for at least 220 million years. Dreaming sleep is a necessary evolutionary function that allows an animal to update its strategies for survival by integrating the total behavioral repertoire of the species encoded into the brain with the recent experience of the individual (Stevens, 1992). This "ancient mammalian process... evaluate[s] current experience against a store of encoded information... assembled over millions of years of evolution, [providing] a reliable template for guiding our actions" (Stevens and Price, 2000, p. 204). Because "our dreams nightly put us in touch with the wisdom of the two-million year old human being, who exists as a living potential within the collective unconscious of us all," ancient wisdom is available to us (Stevens, 1992, p. 36).

Throughout our human presence on the planet, dreams have served an adaptive survival function, transmitting vital guidance for individuals and communities in times of crisis. We should expect no less, and indeed, far more, amidst the current global ecological crisis, which threatens survival for untold species. The environmental dilemma marks an evolutionary call to unfold the next phase of species development, presenting an initiatory threshold for the human species. Likening the present day ecological revolution to three prior major human revolutions—the agricultural revolution, the industrial revolution and the technological revolution—Joanna Macy names our current global crisis the Great Turning (1998).

Global warming presents a crucible

for humanity, a heating up in which not only the planet but the human psyche is being cooked for alchemical transformation. Amidst this heating up, dreams offer sacred inklings and divine hints of a transformation both possible and necessary. Although dreams are only one pathway, they are our greatest source of inspiration and imagination, a perennial friend to the human soul in its trials, travails and triumphs upon the earth. As the global crisis heats to boiling point, earth dreams offer the first bubbles of awakening in the planetary imagination.

The universe addresses us personally in our dreams. Every night we are offered the opportunity to re-connect to our essential relatedness. Dispelling the illusion of separateness, our dreams pull back the veil, revealing the hidden energies into which our lives are woven. We are intimately part of the living splendor that spreads out on all sides before us, continuously in every direction; dreams transport us into this seamless fabric of being. Dreams are the experience of *All This*, entering the human psyche afresh at night, revealing interior depths and hidden threads that bind together the web of life.

Not only do dreams assist individuals to work through personal psychological issues, the dreaming soul carries and expresses a much larger agenda – as wide as the cosmos itself (Jaenke, 2000, 2004). Dreams labor to heal the fragmentations in our souls, in the nuclear family, in the wider community, with our ancestors, and with the entire web of earthly life. Dreams restore connection to the essential. Our immersion in this world – our dreams will help us remember that as well.

The most direct bridge from nature to the human being is through dreams. Jung recognized dreams as the language of Nature herself. "Nature speaks to us directly in dreams and myths" (Stevens, 1992, p. 30). Our dreams are voice of the natural mind, accessing an ancient database of images built up over the course of our evolutionary heritage, offering clues about how to restore the human-earth relationship. Even the chronicle of a single person's dreams can illustrate the process of a dissociated, postmodern person being woven back into the web of life.

The relationship between the individual and the culture, between microcosm and macrocosm, is an intricate one. Unresolved conflicts in the collective culture become deposited within the soul of individuals, where they are carried and suffered by the individual—often escalating towards unbearable acuteness, demanding attention. Through personal angst, individuals are prodded to wrestle with conflicts that are simultaneously personal and collective, so that their own lives can flourish. When tensions in an individual's life closely mirror unresolved tensions in the collective, the individual soul becomes a cauldron and laboratory for engaging such conflicts. By the deep work of inner wrestling, an individual participates in resolving discordant patterns found in the collective. While consciously bearing such conflicts, an individual's dreams may spew forth archetypal images that bring healing resolution for tensions simultaneously personal and collective. Thus tending to one's deepest wounds, fractures, and conflicts paradoxically carries medicine for the collective.

A growing chorus of voices today recognizes that collectively as a species, we have reached critical impasse. Here I contend that we must plummet the depths of our own psyches—to the point of resolving a pervasive human tendency towards psychological splitting—if we wish to heal the human-earth split, outwardly manifest as our ecological crisis. Our ecological crisis is the voice of the earth urgently beckoning humanity back into participatory kinship and balance.

Earth Communing Dreams

I have been blessed to receive many dreams of the earth. These extraordinarily beautiful and poignant dreams, among my most treasured ones, came over a period of approximately fifteen years at mid-life. Each time I come back into contact with them, I re-experience some of their power. Here are recounted some of my most significant earth dreams, along with the meanings I made from them.

Today I understand these earth dreams as addressing the pervasive effects of the bizarre circumstances that affected me at the beginning of my life. Although my parents loved me in their own way, as a young being I seemed to fall repeatedly through the cracks of their care, fated like Persephone to suddenly plunge into the clutches of the underworld. My early psychology was thus shaped by recurring episodes of being cast outside the networks of human protection, care and connection. These traumatic events left profound scars on my psyche that no human seemed able to perceive or touch. Thus I lived sealed within a strange prison of internal isolation, for which there were no words.

In mid-life, my dreams came to my rescue, giving me language for the hidden depths of being. The dreams coughed up images for all the unspoken things, furnishing pictures of the haunting monstrosities of childhood that secretly tormented me. Among the most remarkable dreams that I received were the dreams of the earth.

The first set of earth dreams to appear on the shores of my psyche seemed intent on mothering me. They provided mirroring for a psyche sealed in a void, cut off from humanity and the world. Counteracting my extreme psychological isolation, the earth dreams conveyed

> When tensions in an individual's life closely mirror unresolved tensions in the collective, the individual soul becomes a cauldron and laboratory for engaging such conflicts. By the deep work of inner wrestling, an individual participates in resolving discordant patterns found in the collective.

most dramatically that I was seen in the depths of my being by a larger-than-life presence, and that I belonged intimately to the earth.

Witnessing Rare Cosmic Events

When I first began attending to my dreams twenty years ago, one of the first striking and memorable earth dreams entailed witnessing the red-orange ball of sun falling into the ocean. If the story were captured in the newspaper, the headline would read: "The ocean swallows the sun!" It was not that the sun set behind the ocean, along some distant horizon, but rather that the ball of sunfire fell directly into the ocean, being swallowed alive. The orange-red disk became engulfed within the cool midnight blue waters of the ocean.

Even within the dreamworld, this scene registered as a cataclysm, a rare and unprecedented cosmic event, charged with shock and awe. A cosmic curtain opened, and I, an audience of one, witnessed an epochal event in the natural world, with that rare once-in-a-lifetime quality. Never mind the relative size differences of sun and ocean, as recognized by consensus reality. In the dream, these dimensions of scale were utterly reversed, with ocean, not sun, being the more all-encompassing reality, and with it, a clear sense of the absolute end of the sun's existence. The sun would not rise the next day, but had fallen into the ocean, consumed completely in the vast expanse of the sea.

Today it seems obvious that this dream signified, in the most radical manner, the end of the reign of solar consciousness in my psyche. Until then, I carried a strong identification with my father's world, and with a solar way of being. Fitting the classic description Sylvia Perera's 'daughter of the patriarchy,' my life was embedded in the values and strivings of the daylight world, focused on conventional achievements, as measured by the consensus standards of waking reality. The dream signified that something else was emerging on my developmental horizon: an internal shift of cosmic proportions, an emerging attunement to nighttime, lunar, watery consciousness. For this to happen, the sun, solar consciousness, needed to die. The death of the sun came not by outward explosion, nor inner exhaustion of its fuel, as predicted by contemporary physicists, but rather by engulfment in the cool waters of the ocean.

While this psychological explanation holds valid meaning, it fails to convey the numinosity bursting from the seams of the dream. Indeed, the most salient aspects of the dream were the *mysterium* (wholly otherness), *tremendum* (awe, overpoweringness, energy or urgency) and fascination (attraction and uncanniness) that Rudolph Otto associ-

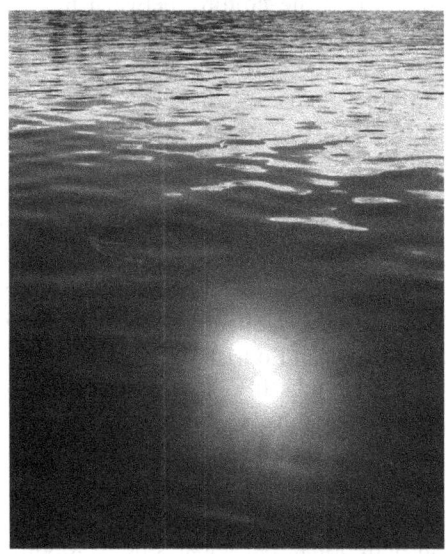

Sun reflection. (Photo by Gary Newman)

ates with experiences of the holy (1958). In fact, the impression of numinosity is what most remains with me today, nearly twenty years later.

It is noteworthy that I play no active role in the dream, except to witness. But witnessing entails receiving the cosmic event fully into myself, being affected by its stark potency, allowing the uncanny to enter me, forever altering my way of being. The act of witnessing implies radical receptivity. Receptivity, a capacity of the feminine, attends the lunar, dreamtime consciousness, into which I was being initiated.

Today we all are witnesses, witnesses to the global effects of a millennial reign of solar consciousness. The human species has set in motion massive changes in the atmosphere, the waters, and the land that may well be beyond our most heroic efforts to reverse. We are being called to see our one-sided identification with the fiery, daylight, active solar consciousness in all its guises – the fire of the combustion engine and of nuclear power, the fire of war and burning acquisitive greed that ravages our planet. Humanity is being beckoned toward the watery, nighttime, lunar, receptive consciousness of the feminine. The dream points toward dethroning the one-sided solar consciousness that has reigned with patriarchal culture, and cultivating a relationship with the dark, watery, receptive feminine. This dialectical solar-lunar way of being hints at the global shift in consciousness so urgently needed in our times.

Dream Travel to Place of Personal Destiny

Another dream journey transports me to the deepest place in the ocean, with a stark encounter between vast ocean and solitary human.

I float on the surface of the ocean, at the place of greatest depth. Floating alone in the expanse of the ocean, aware of an unfathomable abyss beneath me, trepidation and awe fill my awareness. In surrender to these greater forces lies my sole source of protection.

Never having travelled remotely near this spot in waking life, the dream inspires geographic curiosity. I imagine the depths of ocean floor to be located somewhere in the vast expanse of the far Pacific. Consultation with a world map confirms the location of the Mariana Trench, near the Mariana Islands, east of the Philippines. The lowest point on earth is Challenger Deep, at the bottom of the Mariana Trench, at a depth of 35,797 feet, nearly seven miles below sea level.

For Carl Jung, the ocean conveyed the depths, mystery, inexhaustibility and fluidity of the unconscious psyche. The ocean, the origins of all life, is suggestive of the emergence of consciousness from original unconsciousness. The radical otherness of sea life from life on land is an apt parallel for the disparity between the unconscious and conscious psyche. The fluidity of emotional life and the vast, opaque mystery of the human psyche are well-symbolized by the ocean.

For me, the ocean is saturated with

personal memories and meanings. As a child, my family made frequent weekend pilgrimages to the Atlantic Ocean, three hours drive away. I was never happier than during this family ritual to visit the ocean goddess. The ocean held a wonder that magically soothed my fractured psyche, though I did not yet have that story. As a child, the ocean simply was a great power and presence, to be revered and enjoyed. Failure to respect her majestic powers brought swift correction—in the form of crashing blows, with sand, surf and self tumbling in a murky mixture of threat and thrill. The ocean was also a generous giver of pleasure, offering full-bodied caresses in the waves. She granted endless wonder, along with visual delight—the endless play of shimmering sunlight dancing in motion across the dark surface of unfathomable depths. Many years later, at a major crossroads in my life as a young adult, when the psychic waters had all but dried up, I again sought refuge in proximity to the ocean, moving across the continent, far from family and friends, merging my life and destiny with the coastline of that other great ocean, the Pacific.

Yet lacking any actual connection to the place specified by the dream, the deepest place in the Pacific, I plunge into a search for the dream's subjective meanings. The place of greatest oceanic depth mirrors my central life purpose or destiny. It speaks of a central psychological necessity—to cultivate a relationship with the depths. The dream, acting as travel agent of the soul, arranges a journey to a place of soul significance, one that echoes my life-calling, as one who must learn to swim in the depths of the unconscious, then share this gift with others.

Destiny refers to one's core life purpose, the path that fulfills one's potential, the way that aligns with the requirements of the soul's unfolding. Destiny is not conferred by the human realm, but by a higher order of being—the spirit world or realm of ancestors. Personal destiny is revealed when the visionary dimension of being breaks through into consciousness, which occurs most typically during initiatory ordeals, near-death experiences, and destiny dreams. Destiny dreams bring epiphanies of the essential work of a lifetime.

Such destiny dreams weave us not only into connection with our higher purpose, but simultaneously into connection to the earth, tying the threads of biography to the threads of geography. The sacred place that marks one's destiny carries profound personal meaning, recasting one's life in a wider web of signification. By aligning with one's destiny, the haunting sense of alienation and meaninglessness that stalks modern persons at the edges of awareness is quelled. We find the single thread that connects us to the entire web of life.

Water lily. (Photo by Gary Newman)

Dream Travel to Heal Core Wounds

In another dream some years later,

I am transported to the North Pole. Upon arriving at this place, charged with great magnetic power, I lay face down, with my belly spot over the magnetic center of the North Pole. From this position of alignment with the planetary magnetic field, a mysterious transmission enters the navel center of my being.

The belly is the bodily site of my earliest and deepest wounds. At the formative moment of birth, my belly center became the site of a dual transmission—the birth-inducing drug pitocin applied by doctor and blood toxicity from my mother. Suddenly, the oceanic bliss of the womb erupted into a site of chemical warfare. Blasted by foreign chemicals, suddenly I am catapulted into a life and death struggle.

My middle adulthood years became dedicated to uncovering and healing this life-defining trauma. And then the dream deposits me at the North Pole, where a transmission more potent than the original trauma occurs. The dream acts as an energetic reset button at the somatic site of my core wound. Aligning my belly center with the magnetic center of the earth, the birth trauma vortex is overshadowed by the planetary magnetic vortex. My body center becomes energetically realigned according to the earth's central axis.

A short time later, *I am carried on the wings of a dream to the South Pole*. The dream experience of being at the South Pole almost defies description. A lifelong resident of the northern hemisphere, my basic orientation towards the north undergoes dizzying reversal, being turned upside down, inside out. Spatial disorientation and upheaval upend my familiar ways of organizing reality. As if to underscore the importance of the reversal effect, soon thereafter a second dream trip to the South Pole follows.

An analogy for the two dream journeys to the South Pole can be found in certain social rituals, in which an intentional reversal of the social norm is orchestrated. In such rituals, the norms of the status quo may be mocked and overturned, creating disruption of the usual social order. On "occasions of licensed reversal, or ritual inversion… the status quo is taken apart, relativized and often reconstituted in changed ways" (Bell, 1997, p. 120).

Being oriented to a Northern Hemisphere perspective, and having recently found healing at the North Pole, the visit to the South Pole invert reality. When taken together, the North and South Pole dreams suggest the insufficiency of healing personal wounds; one must also know the polar opposite of this reality. The polar opposite signifies a way of being defined neither by wounding nor healing. The visit to the South Pole neutralizes the dynamics of wounding-healing.

In a similar dream scenario, a friend dreams that the North and South Poles reverse their magnetic charge. The rivers began to flow in the opposite direction, upstream, towards their source. And so it may be that we are entering an era of planetary inversion, corresponding to the effects of global warming, with our dreams presaging reversals of planetary reality.

Earth Communing Dreams

Dreams of cosmic events and sacred places inspire and enliven, overflowing with numinous energy. Through the portal of a sacred site, one may be granted entrance into the secret interiority of special places upon the earth. Dreams journeys to sacred places impart a special sense of being chosen to receive a life-affirming or healing transmission. Such transmissions are simultaneously personal and transpersonal. Something objective and transcendent permeates these revelations, with the scale of forces so beyond the ordinary as to be transpersonal. The connection to macrocosmic forces both expands and humbles the self, bringing vulnerability and awe before the grandeur of creation.

Earth dreams may step in precisely where failures in parental and cultural transmission have left indelible scars on the soul. Such dreams compensate for the traumas and failures of family and culture that inevitably impinge on individuals. Earth-communing dreams touch places in the soul that have slipped through the safety nets of family and society, reclaiming us as children cared for by Mother Earth. Mothering, mirroring and mending the wounded soul, this initial body of earth dreams generated deep feelings of kinship between person and place.

Earth-communing dreams widen the horizons of the psyche. They bestow a sense of connection to the wider web of life; bring awareness of one's sacred purpose; offer healing balm for core wounds; neutralize polarized dynamics; and confer a sense of being embraced and loved as a sacred child of the earth.

Dreams of the Earth's Destruction

Once the process of mirroring and mending had rooted in the soil of my psyche, the focus of earth dreams seemed to shift, inviting me to enter into scenes of the earth's destruction. Being met by Mother Earth in the fractured places of my psyche, now I was being asked to witness our earth in her afflictions.

Bearing Witness to Manmade Disasters

In a memorable dream of this kind,

I watch in horror as my father waves his arms wildly in ecstasy while a forest fire rages out of control around him. He appears like an orchestra conductor, directing and encouraging the flames to burn onward. I am horrified to see my father conducting and enjoying the destruction, and am filled with unspeakable anguish for the trees. My father and the fire are at a distance from me across an impassable ravine. There is nothing I can do to stop the destruction. I can only witness it.

Dream tree eye. (Photo by Karen Jaenke)

In the dream it is unclear whether my father is the arsonist who started the fire, but he participates with full-blown excitement, deriving ecstatic pleasure from the fire's destructive fury. In actual fact, my father is a lover of trees, serving as a board member for a non-profit organization whose chief activity is planting trees. So the dream is not a literal depiction of my father's actual character, but rather presents a father figure possessed by a distorted relationship to fire and the energies of destruction. He represents a recognizable cultural male figure, one who achieves vitality through participation in violence and destruction.

Although we possess a god-given psychological need to enter into ecstatic states, neither apathy nor ecstasy is an appropriate response towards wide-scale destruction upon the earth.

Those who feed off mass destruction for their own ecstatic pleasure are possessed of a fundamentally problematic relationship to life. Being intoxicated by destructive forces, experiencing elation in the face of destruction, is a strange and horrifying aberration of human nature. To trade the life of countless other beings for one's own fleeting pleasure displays a degree of narcissistic rage painful to fathom. Yet the dream asks me to face precisely this human aberration.

Being separated from the fire and my father by an impassable ravine, the only response available to me is to witness. The dream asks me to bear witness to a distorted human relationship to fire, to take in the dying anguish of the trees, sacrificed and consumed by the fires of human rage, to hold the catastrophic destruction at the center of my awareness, to stand present and allow myself to be affected by the tragic horror of it all.

And so the dream implies that to bear witness to the destruction, with eyes wide open, to remain present, to allow oneself to be impacted by the devastation, is an act of immeasurable import. By the act of silent witnessing, a conscious observing presence is inserted into the equation of destruction. Images of destruction pass through awareness and enter one's being; they are preserved in the templates of consciousness for later recall.

The inclusion of a single conscious observing presence rescues a tragic event from meaningless oblivion. The presence of an observer confers on the event the dual possibilities of meaning and learning. Bearing witness to the violent wreckage is the only act of self-extension, of love, available to me, and the dream implies it is not in vain. My horror, grief, and empathy bestow silent honor on the trees, in their final vanishing from the face of the earth.

The witness, the one who surrenders to being affected by the dreadfulness of destruction, bears a noble though often unsung role, adding something vital to the total equation of destruction. In the midst of great desolation, the witness preserves respect for life and registers sensitivity to the tragic dimensions of loss. And not merely the loss, but the meaning of the loss is preserved through the witness. Through the witness, this meaning can enter the stream of human history, potentially altering its course.

The one who stays present amidst mass annihilation is forever changed—gifted with knowing something essential about the mysterious interplay between creation and destruction. The witness knows about the march of unleashed destruction and about the transitory precariousness of life. The witness knows the chilling horror of narcissistic rage, and the extreme aberrations that take residence within the human soul, wreaking havoc upon the world. The conscience of the witness becomes sensitized to life and death. For the great mistakes of humanity ultimately arise through our desensitization to the frailty of life and flailing of death. To those who bear witness, destructive events become initiatory encounters with the extremities of existence, where the fleeting breath of life meets the devouring jaws of death. Such encounters sear into consciousness the memory of life's fragile vulnerability, quivering beneath a thin veil of robust indestructibility. The act of witnessing, with an open, undefended presence, the dream seems to say, is the first step. Witnessing is the initial, essential step that makes right action possible.

Entering the Grief of the Earth Body

A few days after arriving in New Zealand for the first time,

> *I dream of the virgin land of New Zealand being bombed during World War II. As the bomb falls nearby, a small group of us scatter into the woods, in hopes of lessening its impact. I feel the bomb's assault enter the earth-body, which is simultaneously my body. My chest cavity, synonymous with the land, heaves with unspeakable grief and anguish.*

I awaken to the sensation of receiving the bomb's impact into the tissues of my flesh, with tightening across chest cavity and heart. Waves of profound grief roll through me in slow motion. The grief permeates my body, resetting my biorhythms to the heavy heave of heartache. Blanketed by grief, I lay still, breathing and absorbing unspeakable sorrow, for a long, long time. Ever so gradually the tightness and heaviness in my chest begins to lift. Then comes awareness of the pulsing of my heart, a surging in the midst of this weighty expanse of grief. Pain concentrates there. This is no ordinary human emotion, but a deep and enduring grief, wide as the landscape.

As my mind rises above the grief, I recall a recent conversation with a man whose pastime is playing internet war games, flying WW II virtual airplanes in a squadron with other New Zealand flyers. Intrigued and puzzled by his passion for flying virtual bombers, I became vaguely aware of a gender gap at the level of imagination. Now, in the wake of the dream, that shadowy vagueness coalesces into something more explicit. A vast gulf stands between his way of relating to WW II air bombings, via internet games, and my way, through dreaming, experiencing the grief of war in the cellular knowing of my body.

The dream presents a story at odds with the dominant cultural story of triumph that accompanies military victory. Beneath this heroic story lies another, hidden story that seems to reside in the recesses of bodily tissue. Wartime bombing brings a wound to the chest, a wound to the earth heart. Although the purported target of war is some human enemy, bombing involves a direct assault upon the earth.

Within the altered consciousness of the dream, a merging of human body and earth body takes place. My body, transformed into oneness with the earth body, absorbs the assault suffered by the earth into my own body consciousness. Within the gestalt of the dream, the human body becomes a conduit for the earth body. The interiority of the human body serves as a bridge to the interiority of the earth. My life feels strangely sacralized by the dream.

The dream descends into a topography where human body and earth body become joined in a holographic relationship. Similar patterns, arising across vast differences of scale, generate a single field of participatory knowing. The patterns of the larger reverberate within the smaller, the planetary within the personal. In these fluid intersections between microcosm and macrocosm, interchanges of knowing between human and earth and are mediated through the organ of the subtle body.

The dream also brings about a shift in identification—from the culture that drops bombs and plays war games, to the recipient of this action, the earth body. Under the spell of the dream, consciousness undergoes a radical shift from actor to receptor. Entering the standpoint of the earth receptively, we apprehend the speechless sufferings endured by the earth body.

The dream offers clues concerning successive shifts in consciousness necessary to restore psychic kinship with the earth. Implied as a first step is the releasing of our fantasy of violence as a game. A second step entails bending imagination to experience from a receptive place the impact of human violence on the earth, entering the other side of our aggression and violence, from the recipient's perspective, then allowing this awareness to sink into the caverns of cellular knowing. From these depths, a profound grief, locked within the human heart, opens. Surrendering to the

> *The one who stays present amidst mass annihilation is forever changed—gifted with knowing something essential about the mysterious interplay between creation and destruction. The witness knows about the march of unleashed destruction and about the transitory precariousness of life.*

waves of grief awakens buried kinship feelings for the earth. With this stirring of affective ties to the earth body, it is a small step to relinquish our species' role as enactors of violence upon the earth.

After the Destruction: Earth Healing Dreams

A third set of earth dreams, appearing more recently, move beyond the act of witnessing the earth's destruction, with intimations of healing energies that can follow cataclysmic disasters. These dreams couple destruction scenes with images of forces that effectively counterbalance destruction.

After Fire, Retreat to Mountain Snow

In 1996, I moved from San Francisco to the Point Reyes Peninsula, just a few months after the 1995 Mt. Vision fire ravaged the Inverness Ridge, backbone of the peninsula. Twelve years later, the fire instead burns in my soul. I dream of fire burning out of control on the Point Reyes Peninsula, my beloved home of the last dozen years.

> Facing the Inverness Ridge, I watch the fire climb the far side of the ridge, nearing the summit. Darkened sticks of timber along the crest of the ridge stand in contrast to the glowing bright orange background. Like a row of blackened pick-up sticks, each tree along the summit line drops backwards into the orange fiery mass, falling one after another, in a strange syncopated rhythm. It is horrifying to watch this beloved landscape undergo destruction. With all my being, I want to act, to do something, to halt the destruction.

Simultaneous to the dream, my body is undergoing the fiery ravages of menopause, my skin crawling with needling sensations, pricking indistinguishably from inside and out. My treasured job of seven years is in jeopardy, the entire work environment spinning into chaos and upheaval. My blood boils in protest, pounding fiercely against the vessels meant to contain it.

Ironically, synchronistically, two months after the dream, I move my residence to a cottage situated directly beneath Mt. Vision, the site where the sparks of the 1995 fire first ignited. During these same months, I visit an old lover, who re-sparks my affections, casting my choices and commitments of the last quarter century up in the air. My life situation is summed up by the dream's stark and piercing imagery: the entire landscape I have inhabited for the last twelve years is undergoing rapid-fire destruction. The dream signifies the major transition ahead: my identity, constructed over the last dozen years, will succumb to demolition.

The fire dream is followed one week later by a dream of *retreating to the mountains for ten days, in order to "listen to the sound of the snow."* In this pairing of dreams, extreme heat and rapid destruction are counterbalanced by the cool stillness and timelessness of the mountains, resting under a blanket of snow. Immersion in profound silence and contemplative solitude are shown as the means for restoring equilibrium following the ravages of fire. So the snow dream offers practical guidance about how to balance the dynamics of overheating and burning within a single human life, while also suggesting how these grand energies are balanced on vast scales within nature. In the pair of fire and snow dreams, the cool stillness and silence of the snowy mountains is revealed as the balancing agent capable of restoring equilibrium after the fire's destruction.

> In the pair of fire and snow dreams, the cool stillness and silence of the snowy mountains is revealed as the balancing agent capable of restoring equilibrium after the fire's destruction.

Counterbalancing Toxicity through Oneness

The motif of counterbalancing destructive forces appears in the next dream as well, although in this case, the destructive factor comes from toxic chemicals. We may well wonder how the increasing presence of toxins, released into the environment at unprecedented levels by our industrial way of life, can be counter-acted to support the continuation of life." A dream gives hints about restoring balance in a situation of chemical contamination.

> I work on the main floor of a large, warehouse-like building, while underground in the basement, toxic chemicals are being discharged into the workplace. The toxic chemicals, with the white stringy appearance of asbestos or angel hair, are already knee deep in the basement. Underground officials do not acknowledge the toxicity in their operations, and a strange atmosphere of danger and paranoia permeates the place.

In the next scene,

> it is the end of the work week, Friday afternoon, and I am meeting a former boyfriend from my youth—we are going away together for the weekend. Entering one another's presence in the hallway, after being separated by our work lives, mine in the warehouse and his in the office, instantly we are drawn into psychic communion. Without any exchange of words or touch, we are embraced by an all-encompassing field of oneness.

The dream strikingly juxtaposes a distrustful workplace infiltrated by toxins with the sweet bliss of communion between intimates. The two scenes stand side by side in sharp contrast. Indeed, the disparity between them suggests a rupture in the fabric of consciousness still in need of mending. The dream seems to offer a map for the soul work ahead, a guide for resolving conditions of toxicity through states of oneness.

Collective and personal meanings intersect in the dream. At the collective level, an industrial workplace operates blindly, producing and dispersing toxins with insufficient understanding or moral concern for the impact on human or environmental wellbeing. This attitude, commonplace in today's corporate world, is tragically exemplified by the Gulf of Mexico oil disaster.

The dream echoes with autobiographical references to the toxicity present at my birth, and the abrupt end of the symbiotic oneness of the womb. The origins, birth, contains the power to set in motion life patterns: oneness turns toxic. Yet the dream resolutely reverses this plot: toxicity is followed by oneness.

While still under the spell of the dream's altered state, I reach to translate the quality of oneness felt in the dream:

> In our togetherness, a containing vessel forms, the container from which our individual lives can unfold. There is no gap to cross in order to connect; together we coexist within a single harmonious field, a ready-made intimacy.

In the dream, we are two young souls, still emotionally permeable to one another, not yet having injured one another, sensing, though not yet knowing one another's deepest wounds. In waking life, we are two mature souls, having injured one another, a quarter century later finding our way back into connection, across the gap of years and injury. Our relationship now holds the full spectrum of possibilities: original oneness, injury and separation, reunion and restored oneness.

Although the specific image of oneness in the dream is highly personal, the field of oneness being depicted is universal. People experience merger states of oneness in at least three ways, according to Arthur Colman: through the religious experience of union with the divine, through couple love relationships, and through the dynamics of group life, when participation in a group becomes an engrossing experience and the individual is virtually lost in union with others (1995). Yet the original ground from which all three types of merger states arise is our primordial existence in the womb. "The concept of merger is a literal metaphor for one's origin; we start life as dependent beings fused with the physiology of another person. There is no 'I' at the beginning" (1995, p. 24).

Colman elaborates:

> Many philosophers and psychologists recognized that this early merged consciousness of infancy may hold the key to an entire range of ecstatic and mystical experiences and phenomenon… Many mystical and ecstatic traditions allude to fetal and infantile consciousness as the

Frosty thistle. (Photo by Karen Jaenke)

> prototypes of spiritual bliss…. In these ecstatic states we are likely to experience a sense of merger or union with something outside our personal boundaries: God, the cosmos, nirvana. This is the reunifying experience of the adult (1995, p. 24-25).

The loss of this original oneness is a shattering experience, inflicting a profound trauma on the human psyche. However it occurs, the initial rupture between human and environment brings a shocking blow and loss of innocence. This break has been named "the basic fault" by Michael Balint, suggesting a fault line running through the foundation of the self (1992).

Foundational to the shaping of Western consciousness, the loss of primordial oneness is depicted in the creation myth of Western culture, the expulsion of Adam and Eve from the garden of paradise. When ruptures with the caring environment impinge on the impressionable young human, the psychological phenomenon of primal splitting typically results. Primal splitting marks the beginning of the great divide in our psychological development when a division is made in consciousness between me and not-me. Primal splitting sets up a fundamental opposition in the human psyche. When not met with corrective experiences that restore a caring environment, this fundamental opposition becomes writ large, projected and splattered across the horizons of the world.

Today primal splitting is an almost ubiquitous cultural phenomenon; it is so commonplace as to appear normative. The penchant for war-making, seeing enemies in the other; the production and release of toxic, anti-life chemicals into the environment; and the splitting of the atom all appear as cultural manifestations of a primal split in the psyche of Western man. Fundamentalist religions, today on the rise, constructing the world in dualistic oppositions of good versus evil, saved versus damned, heaven versus hell, are also expressions of this fundamental splitting tendency. Given the ubiquity of primal splitting, one of the tragedies of our civilization is a loss of collective ability to differentiate between that which expresses harmony with the life force, and that which opposes life. Sadly, as a culture, the possibility of conducting life from a place liberated from primal splitting is not even on our radar.

Amidst this pervasive cultural phenomenon of splitting reality, the dream announces that primal splitting can be neutralized, healed, via a return to oneness. There is a healing balm for toxicity, and it is to be found in the recovery of merger states of consciousness. States of oneness effectively counteract the attack on life, and splitting dynamics, that toxicity represents.

The two contrasting scenes in the dream hint at a choice point, a fork in the road ahead. Either we suffer the consequences of a growing toxic wasteland, with increased fear and paranoia, or we take the path leading to merger states of oneness, which also means healing the primal splitting at the foundation of the

Western psyche. While resolving primal splitting is psychological work required of individuals, we can be supported or stymied in this most profound soul work by our communities and the surrounding culture.

Overcoming primal splitting entails a deep dive into the depths of the human soul, a descent into the core wound within each one of us. Perhaps as more individuals find the consequences of primal splitting intolerable, and are emboldened to descend into these primordial depths, a critical mass will be generated. The wake-up call of global warming may act as the igniting force for this alchemical transformation within the collective psyche, a call from our original Mother, the Earth, to come back into balance and oneness.

The Ecology of Earth Dreams

A Personal Story

In my twenty-year journey through the dream landscape, the earth dreams appearing along the path have led into the underground recesses of the human soul, and into psychic kinship with the earth. The path, which began in a fog of dissociation, opened in a clearing, with exquisite moments of being mirrored and met in the depths of my wounds by the Earth herself.

Then the path came upon horrific scenes of earth destruction—raging fires, bombings, toxic contamination—and asked that I return the gift of mirroring, by witnessing and feeling — in the cellular knowing of my body—the sufferings of the earth.

And finally, the path arrived at nature's secret: the amazing potential for reversal! The destruction of fire, the spewing of toxins inimical to life, are met by the Forces of Reversal—the soothing coolness, stillness and silence of mountain snow; the sweet bliss of communion between intimates.

It is our intimacy with nature, our oneness with the earth body, that can heal our planetary wounds. Oneness with the earth body is, however, reached through the humble doorway of the human body. Consciousness must marry, and make love to, the matter of the body.

As consciousness descends into the hidden recesses of the body, we may well find that at its core, the human body harbors a primal wound. The outer sign of the buried wound is the phenomenon of primal splitting, which, while remaining unconscious, becomes projected and enacted on the world at large. Yet as the phenomenon of primal splitting dissolves, as consciousness merges with the body, it transforms into psychic kinship with the earth. When consciousness meets, marries and makes love to the primal wound, the offspring is an earth-cherishing consciousness.

A Collective Story

In this extended series of earth dreams, some patterns appear. The earth dreams explored here coalesce into three major groupings: earth communion, earth destruction, and earth healing—which might suggest the archetypal patterns of earth dreams appearing in our time.

First, earth communion dreams overcome our culturally-inherited psychic distance or dissociation from the land, inviting the dreamer into a deep feeling connection, or subjective re-enchantment, with the earth. Second are dreams that invite the dreamer to engage with images of the earth's destruction. These dreams ask the dreamer to return the experience of being met by the earth, through the act of witnessing and feeling the earth's destruction. Third are earth-healing dreams, which point towards what is necessary to restore balance in the human-earth relationship.

Earth communing dreams ooze with numinous life force energy, evoking awe and fascination, thereby commanding our attention and respect. They also address gaps in the mirroring function of mothering, conferring experiences of being seen and met in one's depths by the Great Earth Mother herself! These dreams suggest that the initial step in recovering psychic kinship with the earth entails a subjective encounter with the earth's elemental life force. According to Brian Swimme and Thomas Berry,

> Without [the] entrancement... [that] comes from the immediate communion of the human with the natural world, a capacity to appreciate the ultimate subjectivity and spontaneities within every form of natural being,... it is unlikely that the human community will have the psychic energy needed for the renewal of the Earth (1992, p 268).

Earth communing dreams bathe the dreamer in the same bath of animating energy that washes over the planet. Experiences of this participatory field serve to reawaken psychic kinship between dreamer and earth.

Dreams that weave us back into a soulful connection with the earth may serve as preparation for engaging with a more difficult type of dream, those that confront us with destruction upon the earth. Such dreams feature cataclysmic events with massive destruction and

> **Earth communing dreams bathe the dreamer in the same bath of animating energy that washes over the planet. Experiences of this participatory field serve to reawaken psychic kinship between dreamer and earth.**

upheaval. Sometimes the destruction pictured originates in the natural world; other times, it is manmade.

We may wonder about the deeper purposes behind earth destruction dreams, so let us pause to consider this phenomenon. Natural catastrophe dreams can assist us in sorting out our relationship to the great powers of nature. As Swimme and Berry remind us:

> Violence and destruction are dimensions of the universe. They are present at every level of exis-

tence: the elemental, the geological, the organic, the human. Chaos and disruption characterized every era of the universe, whether we speak of the fireball, the galactic emergence, the later generations of stars, or the planet Earth (1992, p. 51-52).

Dreams of massive destruction can help us confront and accept this natural and inevitable part of the great drama of creation. The staggering emotions these dreams evoke speak to the reality of our interwoven relationship to the earth, that what happens to the earth happens to us. Being in the presence of unleashed elemental forces, whether in waking or dreaming, can awaken a profound sense of awe, aliveness and participation. Boundaries between self and world dissolve when such elemental potency is loosened in the world. Developing a felt relationship with these elemental powers ultimately allows one to feel more at home on the earth. Coming into a conscious, respectful relationship with the grand forces of the natural world is part of becoming a whole human being, capable of living authentically as a participant in the unfolding story of the earth.

Dreams of natural disasters often parallel cataclysmic changes happening in the dreamer's personal life, tending to appear during major life transitions, when our identity undergoes radical transformation. Drastic upheaval and change that disrupts our familiar identity structures are regularly depicted in dreams through tumultuous macrocosmic events that sweep through the landscape.

Still we should not assume that all natural disaster dreams are necessarily or only psychological in their import. Some natural disaster dreams may be premonitions or preparations for actual events, and others may ask the dreamer to become a psychic carrier of prior catastrophes, to bear some of the psychological weight of historical collective events.

Given that disruptive events in the natural world carry widespread impact, they require a collectively-shared effort to be metabolized psychologically.

Cultivating an attitude of respect and reverence towards the great powers revealed in dreams can aid our survival in the midst of actual catastrophes, rendering our judgments more appropriate to the necessities of the moment. Acting in grandiose ways, with an inflated sense of power, or in collapsed ways, with a too cowering sense of self, can increase our risk in extreme situations. Facing these grand forces with a proportionate sense of humility, we become psychically open to receiving vital guidance from beyond.

Witnessing cataclysmic events in nature often elicits terror in the dreamer. So earth destruction dreams ask the dreamer to come into relationship not only with overwhelming destructive energies, but also with our very human capacity to be overcome by fear and terror. To stay in conscious relationship with the energies of terror requires a capacity to metabolize the intense physiological and emotional states activated by the human terror response. Full-blown terror, associated with the responses of fight, flight, freeze and appease, has been estimated to be many times that of orgasm (Levine, 1997)!

The process of learning to metabolize fear entails remaining present and aware amidst the acute physiological arousal of terror that tends to scatter awareness. It requires progressively overcoming dissociative tendencies that eject awareness from the body—by cultivating a mindful still presence amidst the swirls of fear, something akin to the calm center at the eye of a hurricane.

A more problematic type of destruction dream concerns manmade disasters. Such dreams share many aspects of natural disaster dreams but include an additional complication: we often feel that manmade disasters could have been averted. Manmade disasters are the result of human mishap, human error, human misdeed, or worse yet, human malice. Hence there is a moral weight of responsibility that must land on someone's shoulders. Questions of human culpability and cover-up may cling insidiously to manmade disasters, hovering like a ghostly cloud. Not just human short-sightedness, but issues of deception and evil can enter the mix. The ills that attend manmade disasters can seem unbounded, with their effects elongating into future generations. Thus manmade disasters tend to collect psychic baggage that extends well beyond their immediate devastating physical impact.

Manmade disasters occurring within dreams invite us to engage with the psychic ramifications of such events, yet without having to contend with any physical effects. Hence these dreams offer a special opportunity to see what these events mean to us and how we can be in relation to them. Perhaps lessons learned on the psychic plane allow us to avert enacting disasters on the physical plane. For once destruction is unleashed into dense material reality, its consequences become more entrenched and weighty, far more difficult to disentangle.

When one faces the facts about the extinction of species, depletion of resources, destruction of habitats, and imminent global warming, the plight of planet earth may well seem doomed. Al Gore's book and film *An Inconvenient Truth* confront us cognitively with the growing data pointing towards impending environmental collapse. But I have noted that dreams of the earth, when taken altogether, do not yet pronounce this outcome. While they do confront us with shocking and terrifying scenes of destruction, acting as a wake-up call, they also provide clues about processes necessary for earth healing. Earth destruction dreams, along with our affective and somatic responses to them, may be followed by images that show what is necessary for healing our relationship to the earth.

And so a third grouping of earth dreams concerns healing the human-earth relationship. These dreams address questions such as: How can the tide of destructive energies—unleashed upon the earth by many generations of human beings, and now reaching a critical tipping point—be turned towards healing? What ingredients are necessary for earth healing, from the perspective of dreams?

Earth healing is frequently portrayed in dreams as a matter of balancing opposing forces that have become grossly imbalanced. This principle of balance appears in many of the dreams presented above. When the ocean swallows the sun, burning heat meets cooling balm, fire enters water, light passes into darkness, solar consciousness shifts to lunar consciousness, a balancing of forces is implied. The journey to the North Pole is soon followed by a journey to the South Pole, where the electromagnetic field reverses, and all sense of orientation inverts to its polar opposite. A dreamer floats on the surface of the ocean, directly above the depths, with an implicit expectation of bridging the two. These images affirm an ancient wisdom that opposing forces must be balanced in the creation and sustenance of life.

The principle of balance is profoundly understood and embraced by indigenous peoples. The dynamics of balance inform the ecological, cultural, and psycho-spiritual practices that enabled humans to flourish in harmony with the natural world for millennia. Apela Colorado of the Oneida tribe distills nine tenets of indigenous science, with the principle of balance as the centerpiece:

> The purpose of indigenous science is to maintain balance…. The end point of an indigenous scientific process is a known, a recognized place. This point of balance, referred to by my own tribe as the Great Peace, is both peaceful and electrifyingly alive. In the joy of exact balance, creativity occurs, which is why we can think of our way of knowing as a life science…. When we reach the moment/place of balance we do not believe that we have transcended – we say that we are normal. Always we remain embodied in the natural world (Colorado, 1994, 1-2).

Both the natural world and the individual human, macrocosm and microcosm, thrive according to the principle of balance. There are perhaps endless dream examples of a restoration of balance, following the dominance of one element whose hyper-manifestation becomes inimical to the balance of the whole. Sky and earth, air and land, spirit and matter, fire and earth, light and dark, solar and lunar, upper and lower, ascent and descent, masculine and feminine, north and south, hot and cold, surface and depths, form pairs of opposites forever being reconciled in our dreams. These same balancing principles figure prominently in dreams of the earth.

Ancient wisdom recognized balance as the deep and abiding principle that secretly permeates all of life, the organic dynamism behind the unfolding of the universe. Earth dreams return us to this ancient wisdom.

> Ancient wisdom recognized balance as the deep and abiding principle that secretly permeates all of life, the organic dynamism behind the unfolding of the universe. Earth dreams return us to this ancient wisdom.

[1] Freud and Jung both built their models of the psyche based upon keen observations of dreams, their own and others'. At the frontiers of consciousness, our dreams, and other altered states, may well be our most reliable informants, guides and teachers.

[2] Concerning daughters of the patriarchy, Perera states, "It is precisely the woman who has a poor relation to the mother, the one through whom the Self archetype first constellates, who tends to find her fulfillment through the father or the male beloved" (*Descent to the Goddess*, 1981, p. 11).

[3] Located in the Mariana Islands group, at the southern end of the Mariana Trench, Challenger Deep is a relatively small slot-shaped depression in the bottom of a considerably larger crescent-shaped trench, which itself is an unusually deep feature in the ocean floor. https://en.wikipedia.org/wiki/Extreme_points_of_Earth, accessed July 9, 2009.

[4] For more on the complex role of metabolizing destructive collective events, see Lisa Herman's recent *ReVision* article (Winter 2009) "Engaging Images of Evil: An Imaginal Approach to Historical Trauma."

[5] For more on accountability practices, see Anne Coelho's recent *ReVision* article (Winter 2009), "Erotics of Accountability: A Psychological Approach."

References

Coelho, A. (2009). The erotics of accountability: A psychological approach. *ReVision* 31(1), 36-43.

Colman, A. (1995). *Up from scapegoating: Awakening consciousness in groups.* Wilmette, IL: Chiron Publications.

Colorado, P. (1994). Indigenous science and western science – a healing convergence. Presentation at the World Sciences Dialog I, New York City, April 25-27.

Earth Structure. Retrieved from http://en.wikipedia.org/earth_structure.

Extreme Points of Earth. Retrieved from http://en.wikipedia.org/wiki/Extreme_points_of_Earth.

Gore, Al. (2006). *An Inconvenient Truth: The Planetary Emergency of Global Warming and What We Can Do About It.* New York, NY: Rodale Books.

Herman, L. (2009). Engaging images of evil: An imaginal approach to historical trauma. *ReVision* 31(1), 44-52.

Jaenke, K. (2000). *Personal dreamscape as ancestral landscape.* (Doctoral dissertation). Available from ProQuest Dissertations and Theses database. (UMI No. 9988406).

Jaenke, K. (2004). Ode to the intelligence of dreams. *ReVision*, 27(1), 2-9.

Lawlor, R. (1991). *Voices of the first day: Awakening in the Aboriginal dreamtime.* Rochester, VT: Inner Traditions International, Ltd.

Macy, J. (1998). *Coming back to life: Practices to reconnect our lives, our world.* Stony Creek, CT: New Society Publishers.

Otto, R. (1958). *The idea of the holy.* New York: Oxford University Press.

Perera, S. (1981). *Descent to the goddess: A way of initiation for women.* Toronto: Inner City Books.

Stevens, A. and Price, J. (2000). *Evolutionary psychiatry.* Clifton, NJ: Routledge.

Stevens, A. (1993). *The two million-year-old self.* College Station: Texas A&M University Press.

Swimme, B. & Berry T. (1992). *The universe story: From the primordial flaring forth to the ecozoic era.* San Francisco: HarperSanFrancisco.

Myth of the Earth

Lorraine Almeida

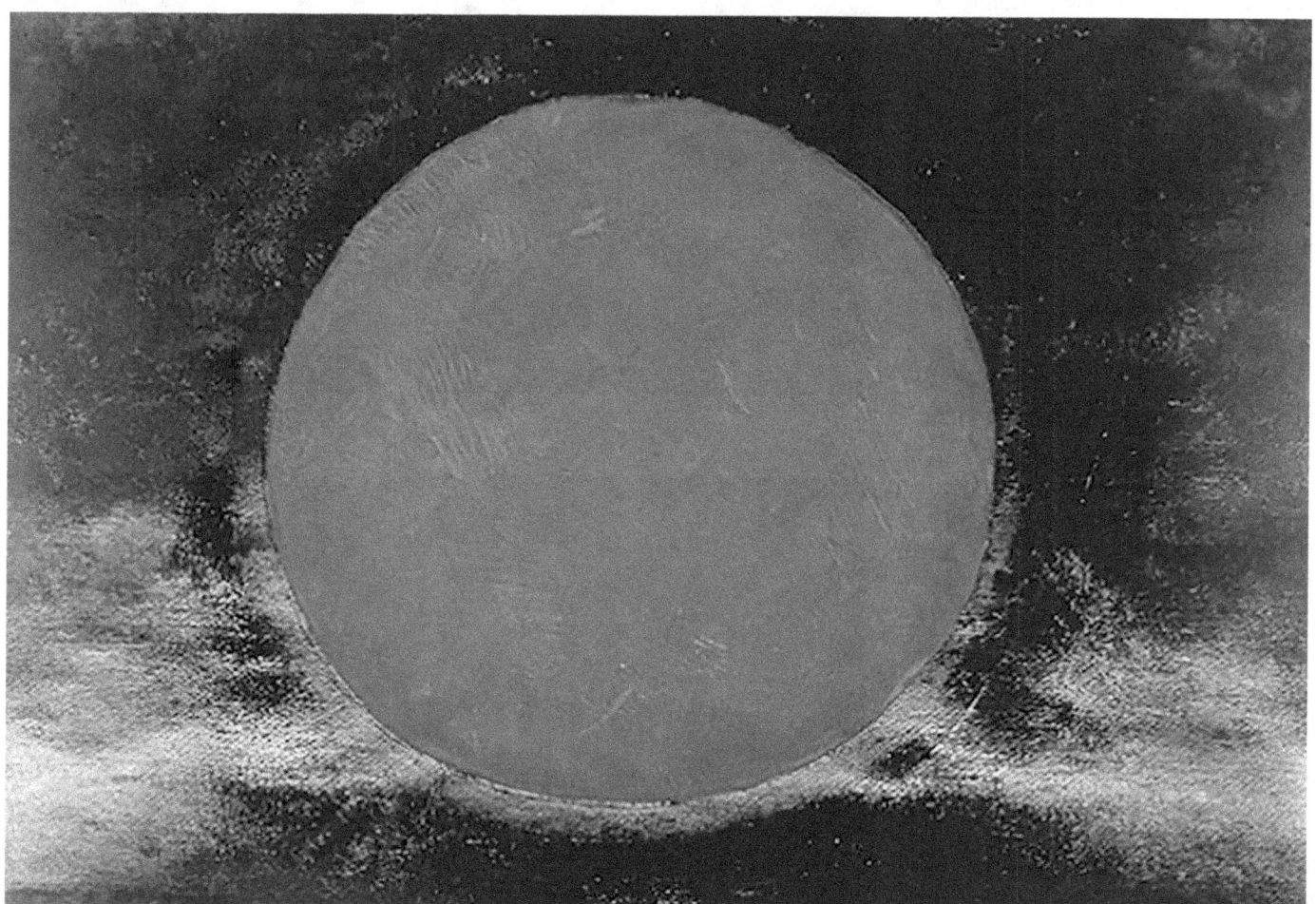

THE BLACK HOLE (21" x 29" / acrylics on paper)

Lorraine Almeida holds a BFA and MFA from San Francisco Art Institute with forty years of painting as a form of meditation. She has taught art to people of all ages and abilities, including disabled persons, seniors and college students. She now offers studio workshops as well as private classes. Her art has been exhibited at the Oakland Museum of California, Bolinas Museum, Gallery Route One, Richmond Art Center, and at galleries in the Bay Area, Arizona and Montana. In 2010 she published "Myth of the Earth." As long time meditator of 30 years, the last 6 years with Eknath Easwaran's method, she presently hosts a weekly satsang for local meditators.
www.lorrainealmeida.com

The mysterious dark matter, mother of the universe, was pregnant for eons, while she grew and nurtured the unseen future within her.

There once was a black hole in the universe that contained so much matter and energy, it had to explode. Dark matter gestated until its inner energy reached its capacity to explode, bringing forth new forms of itself.

The dark hole spewed out into the unknown with everything else that became part of our universe. The paradox is that the darkness contained all that we came to know and still try to understand.

That explosion was a big bang that spewed out a fiery mass, creating what Plato called "Ylem: the stuff of the universe."

Light and dark evolved from the one source. Light was scattered in the darkness and it was all one.

That fiery matter was dispersed throughout the darkness, where it became transformed.

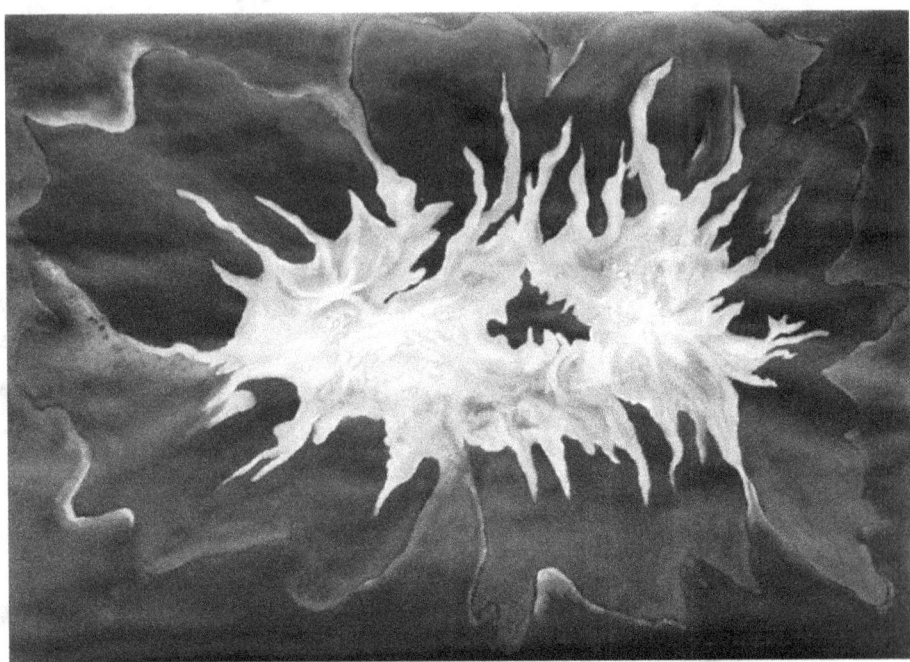

YLEM (21" x 29" / acrylic on paper)

Matter and energy continued to unite, explode and transform, giving birth to the sun and stars, meteors and planets. Lights were scattered throughout the darkness.

Out of the dense, compressed, dark hole of the Universe, our precious planet was born.

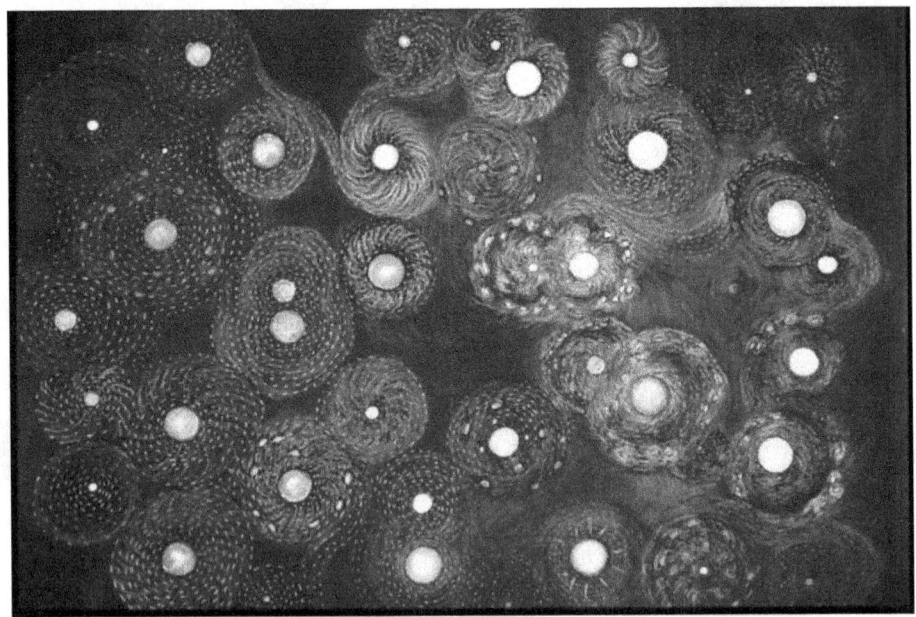

LUMINOUS OBJECTS (19" x 25" / watercolor pencils on black rag paper)

Earth had a cosmic birth. Earth was born in the explosive exit from the black hole and separation of the stuff of the universe.

BIRTH OF A PLANET (36" x 36" / oil on burlap)

The planet Earth was born as one of many, balls of fire. The Earth's surface was hot and fiery for a very long time. To this day, the belly of the Earth is still as hot as its crust was in the beginning. Sometimes the heat and pressure are so intense that red hot lava blows out of volcanoes in different parts of the world.

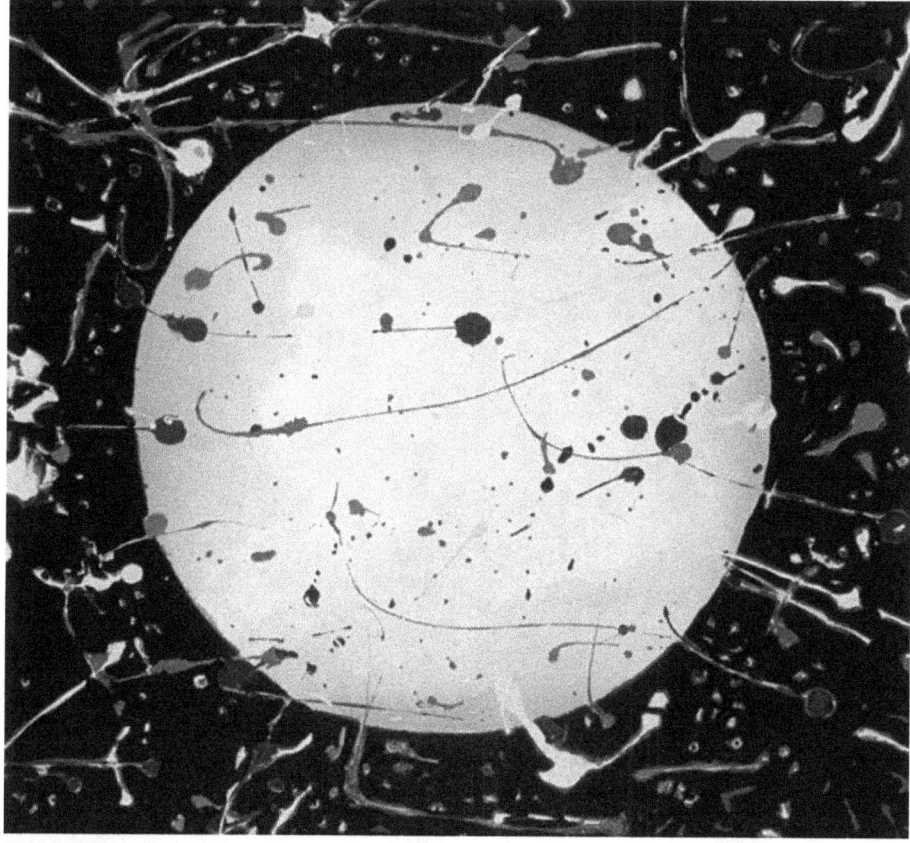

THE FIERY PLANET (22" x 29" / acrylic on paper)

It took a very long time for the earth to cool. The rotating core of the planet caused a magnetic field to form around the earth. The presence of the magnetic field trapped particles sent from the sun and created colored light forms near the poles that are called the Aurora Borealis.

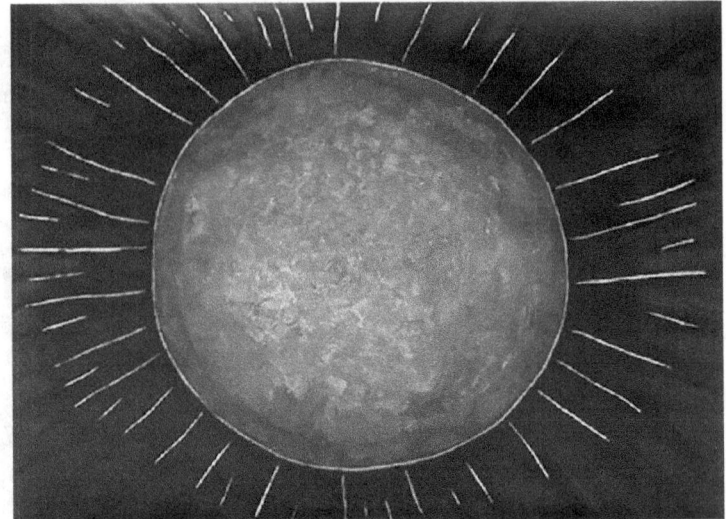

THE MAGNETOSPHERE (21" X 29" / acrylic on paper)

As the planet cooled, the magnetic field interacted with light, hydrogen and oxygen atoms. Water formed in the atmosphere that fell as rain and flooded the Earth. Many small life forms were born and evolved in the water.

Eventually, landforms arose through the water and adventurous life forms learned how to breathe air. Some grew legs to walk on the Earth as well as swim or float in the sea.

THE GREAT FLOOD (21" x 29" / acrylic on paper)

The planet Earth now had land and sun, water and carbon dioxide. As a result of the prehistoric fires and water, diverse, complex atoms allowed the formation and support of many kinds of plant forms. The growth created a green planet. A great diversity of plants covered the Earth. From tiny algae and ground covers, bushes and trees the planet was transformed again.

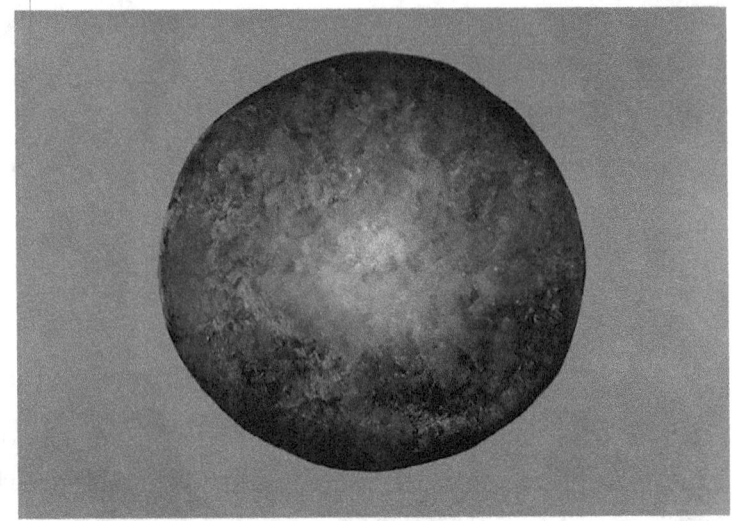

THE GREEN PLANET (21" x 29" / acrylic on paper)

BLOSSOMING EARTH (24" X 24" / collage & mixed media on paper)

When the Earth had reached its peak of maturity as a planet, it was full of diversity and blossomed with its many life forms.

Human civilizations that began as simple communities, grew to enormous numbers and complexity that caused them to collapse. Some cultures overcame problems that overwhelmed others. Eventually, there arose the question of whether or not the planet was now on the brink of collapse or at the edge of a transition to a new form, a new way of life.

The sun can continue to support life on Earth for about 2000 million years into the future. Though none of us can predict the future, each of us is free to choose our contribution to the circumstances out of which the future will arise.

EARTH'S EVOLVING JOURNEY (56" x 42" / mixed media on canvas)

Physicists theorize about a distant future period of entropy. This would be a time, long after the sun had enlarged, exploded and burned out. There would be no energy available for the planet. The Earth might become like our familiar moon.

INTO THE UNKNOWN (7" x 7" / acrylic on board)

Entropy might manifest itself on the planet Earth as a global sized luminous pearl. By living through its many stages, the planet may be ready to return to its source. Matter returning to Energy. Unity and oneness could be the fulfillment of all things past.

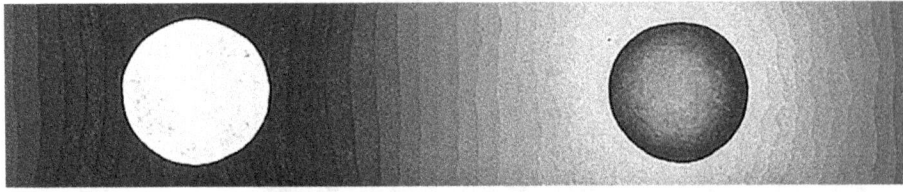

ALPHA AND OMEGA (30" x 120" / acrylics on board)

Be not afraid of death or the return to oneness. All that was created will have a new form. It is part of the creation cycle. It is destiny.

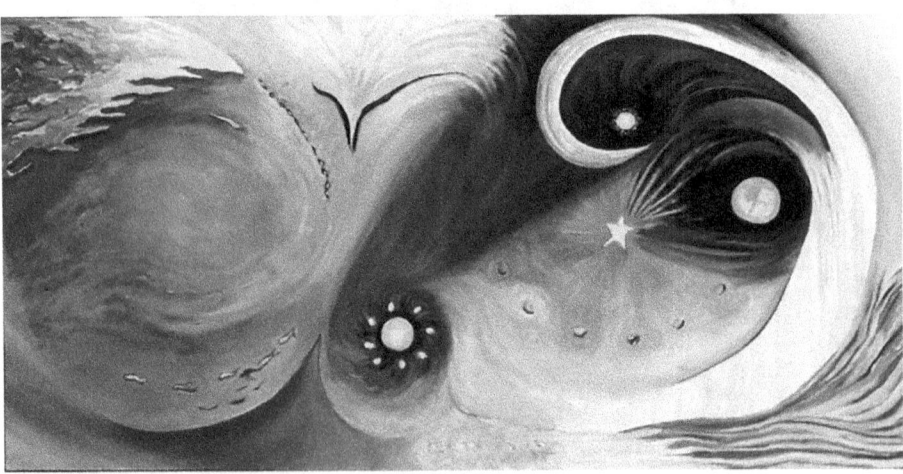

MICROCOSM – MACROCOSM (30" x 60" / acrylics on board)

Ecological Complexes:

Wounded Places, Wounded People

Craig Chalquist

I only went out for a walk, and finally concluded to stay out until sundown, for going out, I found, was really going in.

— John Muir
(Adams and Muir, 2002, p. 20)

To trace the history of a river, or a raindrop, as John Muir would have done, is also to trace the history of the soul, the history of the mind descending and arising in the body.

In both, we constantly seek and stumble on divinity, which, like the cornice feeding the lake and the spring becoming a waterfall, feeds, spills, falls, and feeds itself over and over again.

— Gretel Ehrlich
(Ehrlich, 1992, p. 29)

Craig Chalquist, PhD is a faculty member and former Chair of East-West Psychology at the California Institute of Integral Studies. He is co-editor with Linda Buzzell of the anthology Ecotherapy: Healing with Nature in Mind, founding editor of Immanence: The Journal of Applied Myth, Story, and Folklore, and author of several books studying the intersection of psyche, nature, place, and myth. He is a certified Master Gardener through the University of California Cooperative Extension. Visit his website at *Worldrede.com*.

Beach spiral. (Photo by Gary Newman)

Complexes haunt troubled people and cultures. Is it possible they also haunt the troubled land as well? How would we detect them? What could they want from us?

Although naturalists and deep ecologists often speak about restoring our inner ties to a world ensouled, a world alive out there beyond the clever solipsisms that derealize and depreciate it, the perspective I work from, which focuses on the animated presence or "soul" of places and things, assumes that these ties, now culturally unconscious, already bind us. They bind us more rigidly to the extent that we deny them and thereby fall into unconscious identification with them.

After offering a brief analysis of a common character syndrome that raises walls against our awareness of these ties, I will discuss what results from such a chronically dissociated relationship with place, namely an ecological complex:

a geographically localized syndrome of repeating historical motifs and radiating environmental injury. I will then touch on questions we are learning to ask about the psychology we share with the myth-drenched land. For what we do to the land, we do to ourselves as well.

Diagnoses being abbreviated stories, let's story the character syndrome Conquest Disorder.

A Prelude to Ecological Complexes: Conquest Disorder

Conquest is nothing new, of course. After succumbing to its ruddy lure, ancient Sumer crumbled into ruin as salt accumulated in the used-up soils. Much American religious and political symbolism derives from the Roman Empire, whose economy crashed after overused silver mines flooded. Heading the conquerors reaching out from Europe, Columbus wrote this in his journal shortly after arriving in the New World:

A couple of lombard shots off land the water is so deep around all these islands that it cannot be sounded. They are all very green and fertile and subject to gentle breezes. They may contain things of which I do not know because I did not care to land and explore them, being anxious to find gold; and since these lands show signs of it—for the natives wear it round their arms and legs, and it is certainly gold, because I showed them some pieces which I have—I cannot fail, with God's help, to find out where it comes from (Columbus and Cohen, 1992, p. 62).

Fed by this gold, the machineries of the Industrial Revolution clanked and hammered into the character traits of Conquest Disorder: group narcissism, inner deadness and necrophilia (Fromm, 1973), automaton conformity, an obsession with control, an unwarranted sense of specialness, an oral fixation on consuming, bingeing, and using things up (as Columbus succumbed to overt madness, he described Earth not as round, but mounded like a woman's breast), fear and hatred of what is wild and earthy, unbearable isolation, reductive cynicism about human nature, misuse of symbols degenerated into icons and emblems (i.e., flagolatry), chronic denial under a mask of manic optimism, and lack of social and ecological responsibility.

Unlike Conduct Disorder, Conquest Disorder has spread so widely that too many of us suffer from it for it to be considered abnormal. For that reason its introduction here is somewhat facetious rather than a bid for inclusion in any diagnostic manual. The reifications of diagnostic manuals are themselves forms of social and intellectual conquest.

> At bottom Conquest Disorder rises like a tattered banner over a tragic failure to belong and to relate.

At bottom Conquest Disorder rises like a tattered banner over a tragic failure to belong and to relate. As Jung pointed out in his paper on the Mother archetype, eros kept unconscious manifests instead as will to power (Jung, 1968). Whether military, financial, religious, or intellectual, conquest fights to overcome the pain of exclusion from the living world by dominating it, rearranging it, parceling it up, paving it down, and replacing it with abstractions, including materialist abstractions well-known to fascism and "factism" (Bortoft, 1996). As a result, centralized power accumulates as minds lift resolutely heavenward and the vivid sense of place inexorably gives way to the concept of space (Casey, 1993).

Armed with trade mandates, bulldozers, and the rhetoric of improvement, conquerors who feel at home nowhere pave a trail of broken treaties while inflicting their wounds of displacement wherever they rove. The conqueror's fencing away of aliens, for example, betrays projected alienation. Captain Ahab spoke for all of them by judging himself irrevocably damned in the midst of Paradise. "We ruin the lands that are already cleared," notes a letter written in 1779, "and either cut down more wood, if we have it or emigrate into the western country… A half, a third or even a fourth of what land we mangle, well wrought and properly dressed, would produce more than the whole under our system of management…." (Berry and Jackson, 1980, p. 40).

The author of this letter was George Washington, who feared that to the victor belonged despoliation. Lynda Sexson writes that "Europeans celebrated the continent as Paradise regained, although this time around they were going to have their way with it. Eden as terrarium" (in Olson and Cairns, 1999, p. 139). The ultimate results of this destructive mania include a worldwide mass extinction of plant and animal life.

Even as the aggressive mentality described by "Conquest Disorder" silences, ridicules, or assimilates stories and legends that connected the depth of people with the depths of earth and sky, it turns those depths upside down as the imported stories degenerate into self-fulfilling prophecies. Pluto may have been demoted in the heavens, but down here vast plutocracies convert Earth's surface into a literalized underworld of hellish internal combustion as nuclear families and nuclear nations fission from within. Is discounted Saturn yet above us, or has the fabled consumer of children reappeared in education under the nickname SAT (Scholastic Aptitude Test)? (Imagine what "No Child Left Behind" must mean from his point of view!) Is photographed Mars still to be found overhead, or has the most reckless and impulsive son of Zeus sat in the

> Is the growing pain of the suffering Earth trying to inform us about the psychic depths of our connection to it?

White House wearing a ten-gallon helmet and joking with his frightful companions Phobos and Deimos (Fear and Terror) and their wrathfully grinning sister Eris (Strife)? Left unchecked, conquest is a King Erysichthon, who for cutting down the sacred groves was doomed to devour his kingdom, his family, and finally himself: going in as going away.

Yet for many decades now, the collective psychic depths have been busy birthing two responses to Conquest Disorder: depth psychology and environmentalism, fields destined to be joined in our day. In a remarkable paper on individuation and colonialism, Mary Watkins and Helene Shulman point out that depth psychology was born as movements of national liberation rose and the colonial era came to an end (Shulman and Watkins, 2007). In fact, Eugen Bleuler coined the term "depth psychology" in 1910, a year of revolutions in Mexico, Portugal, and China. The NAACP (National Association for the Advancement of Colored People) was established, and Lucien Levy-Bruhl introduced the term "participation mystique." William James had been riding the leading edge of this liberatory wave from 1902 by protesting what he identified as "the spirit of corporate dominion" in religion, politics, and psychology (James, 1929, p. 337). Modern psychotherapy began in 1851 in Holland (Van der Hart and Van der Velden, 1987), the "nether land," with attempts to tend what "hysteria" was trying to announce one symptom at a time. The very word means "suffering in the womb," as in a birth so difficult that its pangs made unexpected movements at the periphery of the colonized body and the de-centered mind.

With these forces of political and psychological liberation rose up those of environmental liberation. Jacques Cousteau was born in 1910, the year the U.S. Bureau of Labor issued its first list of industrial poisons and the Public Health Service began to study industrial diseases. The First National Conference on this topic was held in Chicago that year, site of the nation's first skyscrapers, buildings named from the topsails converging on a once-brave New World. Slowly but inevitably, the inside story of deepening psychology and deepening environmentalism began to meet and merge.

Sufferings rather than psychology had taught Janet, James, Freud, and Jung about the shadowy depths of the psyche. Is the growing pain of the suffering Earth trying to inform us about the psychic depths of our connection to it?

Ecological Complexes: Sufferings We Share with Place

We know from a large and expanding body of research, much of it from environmental psychology and human ecology, that the integrity of our surroundings directly impacts our mental health (for examples see Buzzell and Chalquist, 2009). We know from common sense as well that living near a dump is liable to be depressing. What remains in the shadows is the strange persistence of a deeper kind of resonance: a resonance that reaches back and forth from place to self along bridges of symbol and metaphor and dream. A few examples of this will help explain the need for the concept of an ecological complex.

In Wyoming stands the Devil's Tower climbed by enthusiasts intent on close encounters of the juvenile kind, despite the courteous but frustrated requests of Native Americans for whom the place is sacred. A local Native tale shared by six tribes tells of six flower-gathering girls chased to the top by bears whose claw marks remain visible on the Tower's flanks. This would never occur to the climbers who ascend with claw hammers, pitons, and mountaineering boots, but is it possible that they stand in for the bears in a mountain-draping myth unconsciously repeated?

One of my graduate students, Sarah Rankin, was investigating cultural and geographical borders and splits in Petaluma, California, when she noticed herself struggling to unite two very different styles of writing in her master's thesis. Upon further reflection the place connection surfaced: one style was anecdotal and historical like the city's carefully preserved downtown, the other straight and structured and expansive like the subdivisions going up to the north. A river divides these parts of town (Rankin, 2007).

A brief glance at the history of Memphis, named after Egypt's capital, reveals a profusion of kings, including B. B. King, Martin Luther King Jr. (who died there), Elvis Presley, Royal Court of Carnival, Johnny Cash ("king of country"), King Curtis…

What these, a few examples of many, share in common is that they demonstrate the operation of an ecological complex: a geographically localized syndrome of recurring historical motifs and radiating environmental injuries that repeat themselves symbolically in the psychic life and relationships of local inhabitants and visitors.

Why a complex?

In the early 1900s, Jung observed that when he asked test participants to come up with a word in response to a word Jung gave them, they sometimes hesitated or uttered an atypical reply: for example, "crisis" in reply to the test word "marriage." Investigating further, Jung discovered that these unusual responses indicated partially uncon-

> In the core of the complex sits an unmetabolized memory waiting to be reexperienced and memorialized, and, permeating the complex, an archetypal image, often a myth, waiting to be consciously worked from the inside out. Until that work is carried through, the story held within the complex, a story part traumatic and part mythic, arranges troubling reenactments of itself in the outer world.

scious points of intensity in the psyche of the respondent. These "complexes" bend images, feelings, memories, and other psychic material around them like rocks on the bottom of a tumultuous stream or magnets pulling iron filings into unusual shapes. Many leave lasting psychic "dents" after arising from past or present trauma. This durability long after the original stimulus is gone can prove quite crippling psychologically unless healed.

Other indicators besides pauses or odd words can reveal an operating complex. For instance, each complex tends to exhibit a particular theme, and to organize perceived reality to conform to that theme, as when a patient suffering from a mother complex reacts emotionally to an analyst as though to a critical mother. The core issue in a complex carries a high emotional charge easily triggered by outer events, as when an abuse survivor panics at receiving a flirtatious wink. Triggering can also result in compulsive attempts to avoid the risk of re-injury by whatever inflicted the complex, as we see in much of the defensiveness surfacing between arguing romantic partners who both feel silenced (again). A triggered complex brings disorientation and dissociation of the ego, and often a rather obvious loss of control, especially of one's emotions. In the core of the complex sits an unmetabolized memory waiting to be reexperienced and memorialized, and, permeating the complex, an archetypal image, often a myth, waiting to be consciously worked from the inside out. Until that work is carried through, the story held within the complex, a story part traumatic and part mythic, arranges troubling reenactments of itself in the outer world.

Ecological complexes demonstrate all these characteristic features.

For my doctoral work in depth psychology I went looking for locally repeating motifs in coastal California, land of my birth and current residence. To detect them I read up extensively on the history, geography, ecology, and colonization of the fourteen counties and twenty-one cities I examined. I then asked: "If California were one of my therapy clients, what sort of recurring thematic material would I look for? What complexes could I identify?" From San Diegan borderline defensiveness to Sonoma County "bear-flagging" episodes of theft of land and law, I ran into one complex after another, some of them nested inside each other, as I monitored my dreams and moods and bodily states out on El Camino Real, the old Mission Trail running along our colonized coast.

A basic working assumption of Terrapsychological Inquiry (Chalquist, 2007), the methodology used to detect ecological complexes, is that the geographical site being explored can be interpreted much like a symptom, slip, myth, or dream. A dead hunk of matter would display no evidence of its being a psy-

> A basic working assumption of Terrapsychological Inquiry, the methodology used to detect ecological complexes, is that the geographical site being explored can be interpreted much like a symptom, slip, myth or dream.

chic entity: no patterns of recurrences in its history, no impulsion to reenact that history, no persistent feeling tones, no dissociation of the ego: none of the indicators of an operative complex. By contrast, the sites we investigate by taking a "place history" and screening their ecology, infrastructure, and other prominent features through what we know about complexes betray a psychic reactivity of such astonishing transgressive power and consistency that occupants and visitors alike come under its spell.

For example, Spring Street in Los Angeles used to be named Primavera: "First View." By itself, this fact means no more than a single nod or smile would. A closer look, however, reveals a long streak of firsts, making this a dominant motif. The uncanny repetitions of Southern Californian firsts along this "Wall Street of the West" include: first public school in LA, first multi-story building, first four-story hotel housing the first mechanical elevator, first brewery and beer garden, first swank café, first nightclub, first café to introduce an orchestra at Rathkeller, which was also the first place where motion picture contracts were signed, first ice skating rink on a stage at Fred Harlow's place, first terminus for transcontinental stage coach lines, first City Hall, first city jail house, first jukebox, first fire station… The street runs from Sunset Boulevard to the Cahuenga Pass where John Fremont entered the city as its first American conqueror, making Spring Street into the first primary artery to the outside world. Three noir films have been shot there, one with the title *The Postman Always Rings Twice.*

When an ecological complex is active, its dominant motif reveals itself in local human doings like a symbol repeating from dream to dream. When I mentioned these firsts to a new acquaintance who had just arrived from Los Angeles, he and his wife exchanged startled glances. They had first met on Spring Street! And this had come up in the first of my meetings with them. To substantiate this motif of firsts would require observing it across many domains of experience to verify it as a viable link between human minds and the psyche of the place and to study its relationship to other local motifs. The sum of these gives an indication of what in a human would constitute an enduring character structure: the active inner being of a place made visible through depth tools of observation and interpretation.

As the number of researchers doing this kind of verification slowly grew, we also noticed that the psychic intensity of these repetitions—their frequency, their persistence, the human pain and dissociation they bring—coincided with the depth of ecological devastation in the places where they originated. We also saw that they often infused us with heavy, ego-disturbing doses of "ecological (counter-)transference": disturbed feelings and fantasies that symbolically paralleled the feeling-toned disturbances thematically playing out around us: depressed and hair-trigger moods in paranoid San Diego, borderline city of the fortified border, for example, or ups and downs in hilly San Francisco. Matthew Cochran, a doctoral student at Pacifica Graduate Institute, was forced by ecotransference to make more than one trip out to a site near Trinity, where the first atomic bomb had been detonated, because the pain of that place radiated so severely into his dreams and his relationship. Centuries ago, Native people had inscribed petroglyphs shaped eerily like bombs and jets in the rocks of what was now a gunnery range. The mythic core of this place's complex resembles the Thunderbird inhabiting local lore, just as Hekate haunts San Diego, Coyote Marin, Hades Monterey, and Dionysus San Francisco, whose bridges reach outward from the peninsula like vines from the body of the bisexual god of ecstacy and drama.

Of course, mythological images are normally thought to have more to do with local culture than with local geography or ecology. Our impression is that certain myths favor certain terrains. For example, motifs out of Egyptian mythology pop up all over Bakersfield, California, including an Eye of Horus symbol looking back at the observer out of street configurations on maps, stylized pupils above the doors of local psychics, and even arcs of oil pipe twisted into the recognizable orb. How did Egyptian mythology get imported into the Great Central Valley of the Golden State? It didn't. The land in and around Bakersfield resembles desert in Egypt, with the agriculturally vital Kern River standing in for the Nile. If this idea of a land-myth connection is correct, then the original inhabitants of this region would have constructed a similar mythology. Instead of "Saint Barbara," a variant of Sophia, the Chumash, native inhabitants of Central California, tell stories about beautiful Hutash, the goddess who wove rainbows over the Channel. The place is the common factor.

The complex, then, lives "in between" the place and its inhabitants rather than being causally traceable to one or the other. When the two get along, the images and motifs that comprise the depth dimension of the relationship live harmoniously in the space between, as when native Hawaiians make ceremonial offerings to Pele, whose fiery energies shape and reshape the islands. When the relationship is disturbed from the human side, as when conquest and exploitation disfigure a landscape, the complex arises to similarly disfigure the souls of alienated occupiers. To say it figuratively, the land raises its voice until we realize we cannot separate ourselves psychically from where we live. Our dualism drives the dynamic forward until it hurts.

As Murray Stein points out, in the absence of healing, a complex tends to be stable over time, with the same patterns of emotional reaction and discharge, the same mistakes, the same unfortunate choices made over and over again (Stein, 1998, p. 49). It contains an archetypal core which can wear a mythic face like those mentioned above. Prometheus lives in Switzerland, land of alchemical innovation and home of repetitions of their central motifs for hundreds of years, forcing everyone in range to reenact the stories that wounded the restless land. During the Mexican War, General William Worth irrationally believed himself to be outnumbered by enemy forces dug in around Mexico City. He moved from residence to residence, staying first near the plaza where the Aztec nobility had once lived, then switching to the western entrance, and then to the east, retracing in reverse the march of outnumbered Cortés into town. General Winfield was caught by a different piece of the same story: he recreated the fall of the Aztec capital by attacking Mexico's interior with a relatively small and handy force independent of any fixed base of operations. Before his final victory, Cortés had been driven up a gangway by Aztec warriors at whom he fired, retreating in such haste that his men left behind their bags of pillaged gold; in the mid-1800s, Alonzo Horton, future developer of San Diego, found himself retreating up a gangway as a mob attacked the Panama hotel in which he left his gold behind. Firing his revolver to cover his band's retreat, he and his fellow passengers reached the safety of their cruise ship, which, curiously enough, happened to be named Cortez. In this case the repetition did not confine itself to the neighborhood, but radiated across an entire conquered region.

> When a place has been damaged—conquered, paved over, ground up, torn down—the damage leave a psychic imprint in the inhabitants: the point of intensity around which grows an ecological complex shared with the wounded land. For the complex lives in both, occupying the imaginal space between self and place, dweller and territory.

Jung, who as he aged believed the spirits of the land and the anima mundi to be less a matter of projection than of psychic realities abroad in the world.

Complexes of place, referred to as "placefield syndromes" in Terrapsychology (2007, p. 58), can inflict

Ecological complexes also demonstrate the reactivity of their human counterparts. Repressing them triggers them, as I learned when the militarized paranoia I tried to ignore in post-911 San Diego personified itself in dreams as an angry bronze-skinned woman who frowned at me until I acknowledged her to be the soul or spirit of my home town (Chalquist, 2007).

Where do such complexes originate? In the West, where self and nature are split from each other psychologically, we automatically assign psychic troubles a purely human origin. But if ecological complexes were primarily social, a psychic legacy handed down locally, why would they cleave so strongly to the environmental features that symbolically recur in them? At one time Manhattan Island was covered with forests and hills; they are gone, but skyscrapers continue to replace them.

My impression is that we speak and act in the style or "discourse" of place all the time, but when a place has been damaged—conquered, paved over, ground up, torn down—the damage leaves a psychic imprint in the inhabitants: the point of intensity around which grows an ecological complex shared with the wounded land. For the complex lives in both, occupying the imaginal space between self and place, dweller and territory. That is why studying this resonance must be less a matter of "proof" (which would require two separate entities joined by a causal relation) than of becoming sensitized to common patterns stirred into repetitive action. We do not hunt these patterns with a microscope, we read them as though place were a work of art or literature packed with recurring symbols.

Having studied these placefield effects all over California and traced their operation in a dozen capital cities around the world, I find myself inclined to accept Jung's late-life belief that everything is animate: objects, places, the world itself. Everything possesses a subjectivity, a "within," and through our own, which ultimately evolved from the ground below, locations without nervous systems participate in their own self-reflection…if we are willing.

As with cultural complexes, ecological complexes can interlock with personal ones, painfully. Yet personal sufferings can open a door to greater empathy for a conflicted place whose features and history symbolically recur in its sufferings, and therefore in ours. I grew up in the county of San Diego, named to commemorate an ancient border defense in Spain before a border split California from Mexico. A fortified border is not just a very tall fence: it also aches as a psychic division, a cleavage of the heart, a spiritual dam, a cultural barrier, a split within the self, a political regression, an ecological absurdity, and a demonstration of how the matter we would master enters into us at will through openings of metaphor and painful reenactment. The symbolic presence of an environmentally damaged or damaging feature like a border is what distinguishes an ecological complex from a cultural or personal one. The wounded terrain shows up as the feeling-toned motif that organizes and permeates this kind of complex.

And so it is wherever people live among places that act like magnets attracting mythologies, pathologies, stories, and lore. Whether the revolving hub motif in Moscow, warrior hierarchies in volcanic Rome, where excavated Bronze Age urns resemble soldiers' helmets, native jimson-weed visions and messages projected within and above the City of Angels, fallen fortifications in New York City, the drama god at large in mood-swinging San Francisco, singing the blues in emotionally and geologically depressed New Orleans, Left Bank-Right Bank cultural-intellectual separations in Cartesian Paris, or shifting fault lines in quaking Jerusalem, what the Greeks and Romans knew as the genius loci, the spirit or soul of a place, speaks in a persistent and intelligible voice. Features of the landscape cross through the frontiers of consciousness to image themselves as psychic beings without relinquishing their environmental qualities. What the conscious mind is trained to see as nonliving places and things, the unconscious reacts to as animated presences and symbols—and signals of Terra trying to get our attention in a language far more ancient than our own.

How do we know that we don't simply project our own complexes onto local landscapes? To some extent the very question implies a clean Cartesian division between self and world. As Richard Tarnas and others have pointed out, the accusation of anthropocentrism very often turns out to be a form of covert anthropomorphism directed by the modernist assumption that the world possesses only such animation as we bestow upon it (Tarnas, 2006).

Picking up on an ecological complex is similar to picking up on the operation of an archetype. How do we know whether an archetype is really being constellated, especially since the very act of looking changes the image it presents to us? The task becomes one of comparison combined with substantiation: the more that Trickster imagery surfaces urgently in dreams, fantasies, and synchronicities, the greater the likelihood that the fabled agent of chaos is knocking on our door. A former classmate of mine going through such a series of Trickster manifestations, from nightmares to symptoms to bizarre events, kept walking into local banks only to realize they had just been robbed. At one point do we admit to ourselves that something extra-human is addressing us? That we are target rather than source?

By contrast, an unhelpful dualism does come up when inner turmoil clouds our sense of a place. We can take steps to minimize our projections through self-inventory of the shadow, use of a peer group outside the field,

> As with cultural complexes, ecological complexes can interlock with personal ones, painfully. Yet personal sufferings can open a door to greater empathy for a conflicted place whose features and history symbolically recur in its sufferings, and therefore in ours.

careful study of the history of a place. A key indicator of a projection onto the site we investigate is that the relationship immediately goes dead. It lights up again when we are on the right track. Place personifications in dreams are generous with their feedback—as when Orange County corrected my misperceptions by appearing in a dream as a woman who handed me back a document I had typed awash in red corrections. I had entirely missed the presence of the local god: the blacksmith Hephaestus, whose constructions sprout as giant cathedrals and malls and whose metal hammers pound the ground for oil in Huntington Beach. Excavated Native artifacts of stone were once carved into shapes like cogwheels. It would be interesting to know what their version of the blacksmith of Olympus was like. Evidently he had been busy there.

Reconciling Ourselves with Place and World

As imperial pretensions crumble under the weight of their own shameless excesses, knowings we thought we left behind resurface as redemptive wisdom, whether lore dismissed as superstition, the "public homeplaces" of bell hooks and Mary Belenky (Belenky, Bond, and Weinstock, 1997, p. 164), ancient farming systems that feed the land, tribal forms of symbolic reparation restoring harmony to split communities. That we share psychology with Terra requires adding her voice to this list of percolating outcast knowings.

Fortunately, we need not reinvent what turns out to be a long, rich history of taking the psychic presence of Earth seriously. For example:

- Many indigenous cultures experience the world as the living abode of a deity like Changing Woman, the Diné (Navajo) personification of the Earth.
- For the Western Apache, locales are aware of the human activity that takes place on them and deserve great respect, which is reflected in their elaborately situational namings (Basso, 1996).

Beach shells. (Photo by Gary Newman)

- Aristotle believed things to be actuated by their own telos or inbuilt purpose. Steering a course between the atomistic materialism of Democritus and the otherworldliness of Plato, he thought of matter and even the universe itself as a vast unfolding from potentiality to actuality.
- The Greeks and Romans of old experienced each stream, grove, forest, mountain, and city as inhabited by its resident spirit, its genius loci. Every pre-industrial culture knows similar figures. A handful of examples from Europe include the Yarthings and Hyter Sprites out of Anglican folklore, the Doire well guardians of Celtic mythology, and the following pairings: dryads with trees, naiads with springs, oreads with hills and rocks, nereids, mermaids, sirens, and oceanids with the sea, and trolls and gnomes with caves.
- Neoplatonic writings mention an anima mundi or World Soul, an idea brought back to life by Jung and elaborated in the work of James Hillman and Robert Sardello.
- The alchemists who sweated to transmute base metals like lead into silver and gold were also reimagining and enlivening the human relationship to living matter.
- Johann Wolfgang von Goethe used "exact sensorial imagination," an observational discipline akin to what would eventually be called "phenomenology," to experience an "archetype" (his word) operating behind the plants he studied (Seamon and Zajonc, 1998, p. 133).
- The school of Naturphilosophie burgeoned with German Romanticism, Idealism, and the philosophical musings of Friedrich von Schelling mixed with those of Georg Hegel. One of its goals was the reweaving of natural-world roots in human thought and aspiration. Schelling in particular intuited what he saw as comparisons between the evolution of human thought and nature's continuing creativity. For him, the natural and the spiritual were different ways of observing the same unitary process ultimately inaccessible to reduction as an object of intellectual knowledge.
- Jesuit scientist and scholar Teilhard de Chardin proposed a "within" of things, arguing that everything--a hillside, a stone, a piece of paper--has an objective face and a subjective face, an outer side and an inner (Teilhard de Chardin, 2008, p. 53). The more complex the nervous system it possesses, the more conscious the subjectivity or interiority can be of itself.
- In some sects of Buddhism, things considered in the West to be inanimate, such as minerals,

are seen as endowed with a living "Buddha nature," an attitude that has worked its way into the field of deep ecology and its goal of Self-realization.
- Shinto offers imagistically elaborate descriptions of local kami (gods).
- Nineteenth-century proponents of panpsychism, the belief that qualities of mindfulness do not restrict themselves to human brains, include Gustav Fechner, William James, Wilhelm Wundt, Rudolf Hermann Lotze, William Clifford, Friedrich Paulsen, Morton Prince, Ferdinand Schiller, Josiah Royce, Ernst Häckel, who coined the term "ecology," and Eduard von Hartmann, among the first to write about the unconscious. Spinoza and Schopenhauer could be included as honorary father figures in this long tradition.
- Extending the findings of the Gestaltists (Wertheimer, Koffka, and Kohler) of the 1920s, social psychologist Kurt Lewin applied their field orientation to human relationships, demonstrating how features of the immediate environment acquire psychologically symbolic values that interact dynamically within the psychological field. This field, which Lewin called the "life space," organized inner and outer interactions into a unified psychological whole of the kind described by later psychoanalysts and Gestalt psychotherapists.
- The depth psychology tradition rooted in these ancient philosophies and inaugurated by Pierre Janet, Sigmund Freud, and C. G. Jung and further extended by James Hillman and Robert Sardello imagines consciousness as situated upon a primary process or substrate of fantasy, image, and myth that informs every realm of human experience. Irreducible to neurochemistry and resistant to literalization or centralized ego control, this polycentric language or layer of being can only be approached, like the presence of place, in terms of its own mythopoetic movements—movements which exist prior to thought and reflection, like a shimmer of myth already at work under everything we perceive and categorize.
- The practice of discerning the consistency and order structuring these symbolisms as they unfold in the animated world is as old as art, ritual, sacred dance, and dream interpretation. The intuitively felt "aha!" connection valued by all the deep psychologies—psychoanalytic, humanistic, existential, Jungian—represents a valid and highly reliable internal shift in understanding, not a calculable proof.
- More recently, Val Plumwood describes an "intentional panpsychism" that escapes the on-off, "it is or it isn't" mode of thinking about consciousness:
- The rich intentionality the reductive stance would deny to the world is the ground of the enchantment it retains in many indigenous cultures and in some of the past of our own, the butterfly wing-dust of wonder that modernity stole from us and replaced with the drive for power (Plumwood, 2002, p. 117).
- Along with adepts at geomancy and practitioners of the Chinese art of feng shui, examples of contemporary artists who take the presence of place seriously include landscape designer Lawrence Halprin and sculptor Andy Goldsworthy.

Jung wrote often about the psychic presence of matter. His view of the relationship between psyche and nature moved from a dualistic one in which humans project our aliveness onto the world to a recognition that things are enspirited and ensouled (see Jung and Sabini, 2002, for many examples of this). In Aion, where Jung describes vegetal and mineral aspects of the Self, he insists that matter and spirit partake of each other in an identity of inner and outer (Jung, 1969). The recently published Red Book (2009) contains many psychic images described in the language of natural processes, as does *Memories, Dreams, Reflections*, in which Jung writes of his identification with stone, of his work as an outpouring of crystallizing magma, and of alchemy as having awakened him to the nature and importance of archetypes (Jung, 1965).

Since Jung, work on understanding the deep ties between nature, place, and self has continued within analytical psychology as well as at its edges. Marie-Louise von Franz did a study on psyche and matter in which she stated, "A great part of what we recognize today as being psyche belonged, in the view of the old Greeks, to a superindividual, objective world soul" (von Franz, 1992, p. 6). James Hillman, not only a founder of Archetypal Psychology but also an early ecopsychologist, states unequivocally that "..I can no longer distinguish clearly between neurosis of self and neurosis of world, psychopathology of self and psychopathology of world," for pathology can no longer be framed as purely personal (Hillman, 1992, p. 93). The world is in a state of breakdown: ."...by drawing attention to itself by means of its symptoms, it is becoming aware of itself as a psychic reality" (Hillman, 1992, p. 97). Marco Heleno Barreto uses case material to illustrate an "eco-logical form of consciousness" in which destructive acting out of the paradigm of human domination of nature gives way to a strengthened sense of the human place in nature (Barreto, 2006, p. 257). Calling for language, modes of thinking, and an "ecological imagination" more consistent with the natural order and viable earth-human relationships, art therapist Laura Mitchell also believes that "the articulation of deep-seated primary place relationships is essential

> The world is in a state of breakdown: "…by drawing attention to itself by means of its symptoms, it is becoming aware of itself as a psychic reality."—James Hillman

to the practice of community resiliency and advocacy" (Mitchell, 2006, p. 112). One form of such a practice, suggests Meredith Sabini, is a cultural dreaming practice in which dreamers listen in on what "big dreams," a natural resource, have to say about Earth and our troubled relationship with it (Sabini, 2009, p. 212).

For a terrapsychological perspective attuned to the voice of place, continuing to extend depth psychology's exploratory focus outward—from the intrapsychic to the intrafamilial to the intergenerational, cultural (Singer and Kimbles, 2004), and political (Samuels, 1993)—eventually must hone in on the psychic presence of disturbed places we try to feel at home in.

One way to sharpen this focus is to become more aware of the stories and symbols we share with the land. Story is the weave that holds together not only inner with outer and theory with practice, but mind and body and people and place. Radiant and gifted, Saint Barbara was locked up in a tower to prevent her from mingling with the villagers below. She received the finest of private educations, but such was her yearning to work as a teacher and healer in the world that she ordered a window cut in the tower so she could gaze down at the people she finally succeeded in joining one day after freeing herself of confinement. Is it possible that the people of Santa Barbara partake of these local motifs, perhaps even to playing out old roles on local stages? An attractive friend I helped move to Santa Barbara cut a hole in her fence so she could gaze down at the Channel from the Riviera. She had come there to enter a school of psychological healing. Does something of the place's spirit shine through the ancient tale? In Santa Barbara, where the Santa Ynez Mountains look down on the people below, those who live on high refer to their abodes as "castles." Yet its heights also look far into the depths of the south from here at continent's edge. The site was named by padres who entered the area on the saint's feast day and thereby walked fable into locale.

John Steinbeck suspected that places participate somehow in their own namings. Their inhabitants can participate in post-Conquest Disorder healing by getting to know the storied places where they live and bringing their earthy motifs and plots to fuller consciousness. Complexes then mutate into contexts and contacts.

Tending the presence of place on

> Tending the presence of place on its own terms includes holding, hearing, and making room for its untold histories.

its own terms includes holding, hearing, and making room for its untold histories, much as a psychotherapist provides a living receptacle for taking in the client's intolerable emotional states, digesting them, and giving them back in manageable portions. Such ongoing dialogs could inform the social and ecological structuring of sustainable human communities in which people learn how to experience themselves not merely as autonomous egos, but as indigenous openings or nodes of deep communication with each other and the environment. This

> How much of what we interpret as personal or archetypal material also bears an ecological face?

would be heartsteading rather than homesteading, with personal stories transparently embedded in those of community, region, continent, Earth.

Questions Raised by Terrapsychology

Questions raised by a terrapsychological depth perspective include:

Under what conditions does repression of the sense of place or commodification of a landscape by turning it into an ideology lead to projections of darkness or earthiness onto people regarded as Other: those seen as animalistic, bestial, "children of nature," primitive, savage, or otherwise subhuman?

How do certain myths and legends—Prometheus, for example—come to prefer certain landscapes (Switzerland)? Near Verona, the setting of Shakespeare's "Romeo and Juliet," two 5,000-year-old skeletons were recently unearthed. They were locked in a timeless and apparently passionate embrace of love doomed to end prematurely, for both had died before their time. Or think about ritualistic London, home of so many altars—such that the land itself is a kind of altar—and where the Public Cleansing Department occupies the site of an old public privy, a sauna on Endell Street recalls an ancient bath, and a Small Pox and Vaccination Hospital, now Whittington Hospital, was built over the healing wells at Barnet. "At All Hallows, Barking," notes Peter Ackroyd about the London Underground, "a buried undercroft and arch of a Christian church were constructed with Roman materials; a cross of sandstone was also found, with the inscription WERHERE of Saxon date; it is somehow strangely evocative of WE ARE HERE" (2000, p. 40).

How much of what we interpret as personal or archetypal material also bears an ecological face? According to E. A. Bennett, the famous house with a Roman cellar and underlying cave of bones which Jung dreamed about in 1909 corresponded to his uncle's house in Basel, an old structure that included a cave-like lower cellar built on Roman remains. House and cave as psyche, as collective unconscious, yes; but what does the tangible house announce about itself? Was it trying to get Jung's attention? Who better to mentor him about the value of tracking the archaic than an old family home built on ancient foundations?

Do our personal stories always interlock with those of the places we occupy? When I moved to Sebastopol in Sonoma County, I did not know what to make of a dream figure named Evie calling me Cain instead of Craig. It made no sense until I grasped the local Garden of Eden motif, from uninterrupted highways crossing like flowing rivers, to unknowingly renting a cottage from the local butcher, to winged sculptures at the town's southern entrance, one bearing a plaque identifying it as the Guardian of the Gate. Overlooked by a clock whose constant inaccuracy evokes a sense of timelessness, the sculptures were recently replaced with two pole-shaped works of art, one with grasping hands entwined upon it like branches, the other with small figures holding disks the color of apples: a Tree of Knowledge and a Tree of Life witnessed and recorded by a terrapsychologist whose right forearm bears a large circular birthmark.

What if we reimagined personality disorders as ecocultural disorders: narcissism as a mirroring of elitism, borders protested against by borderline permeability, perfectionism as personalized imperialism, avoidant disorder as collective fear writ large?

Do animals too express the sentient power of place? From the standpoint of a consciously applied animism, animal behavior seems alarmingly symbolic, from skunks in their black-and-white coats invading a black tie party in San Francisco, to monkeys making off with the cameras of tourist-spectators, to tricksterish Coyote patrolling the suburbs at night. The fire that recently burned, pruned and locked up Montecito roared out of control on Coyote Lane. Seen from without, these are random occurrences causally explained. Seen from within, they look more like gestures, bids for our attention, even symptoms troubling Terra's psychology.

Do events like storms and earthquakes seem to gesture at us, parody us, or react metaphorically—like Katrina invading one oil-rich gulf while American troops attempted to seize another? Is it just an accident that the name of Wilma, given to the record-breaking storm whose immense eye looked down at the rain-washed path formerly taken by incoming conquistadors, means "Determined Protector"? Can we hold this idea of symbolic signaling without splitting Terra into good mommy and bad, or falling into the punishment paradigm of divine vengeance?

What can we do toward fashioning imaginative and holistic research that takes place seriously before climate change and other perils destroy civilization and perhaps the human species? "When a large tree hits the ground, the earth trembles," notes farmer Gene Logsdon.

I can feel it in my bones and my soul trembles in response, like a tuning fork....In a few more generations, no one in this place will know the sounds that a two-hundred-year-old tree makes when it falls. Should a philosopher ask in those days whether a tree falling in the forest makes a noise if there is no one to hear, the answer will be: "Not anymore" (Logsdon, 1993, p. 200).

Five decades ago writer and reporter Sterling North wrote, "Every time you see a dust cloud, or a muddy stream, a field scarred by erosion or a channel choked with silt, you are witnessing the passing of American democracy" (Berry and Jackson, 1980, p. 47). But with Earth we comprise one psychic system of immense adaptability. Psyche's natural polycentricity reasserts itself over and over, washing like the tide against the monolithic structures of conquest. A core observation of terrapsychological work that offers some hope builds on an insight of Jung's about the unconscious: Nature turns toward us the face that we turn

> Nature turns toward us the face that we turn toward it.

toward it. The natural forces that surround and sustain or maim and kill us seem to reflect the collective attitude we take up toward them.

Encounters with places felt to be sacred offer polychromatic glimpses of possible futures whose numinous outlines breach the borders of religion, ideology, and Time itself, showing us not only how it could be here on Earth, but how it already is for some. They also suggest that where we practice our craft is at least as important as what we practice. Here is Thomas Berry, philosopher and priest:

The field was covered with lilies rising above the thick grass...This early experience, it seems, has become normative for me throughout the entire range of my thinking. Whatever preserves and enhances this meadow in the natural cycles of its transformation is good, what is opposed to this meadow or negates it is not good. My life orientation is that simple. It is also that pervasive. It applies in economics and political orientation as well as in education and religion....(McLuhan, 1996, p. 221).

George William Russell, poet and theosophist:

This world of Tir-na-nogue, the heaven of the ancient Celt, lay all about them. It lies about us still. Ah, dear land, where the divine ever glimmers brotherly upon us, where the heavens droop nearer in tenderness, and the stones of the field seem more at league with us... (McLuhan, 1996, p. 189).

Sufi philosopher Lex Hixon suggests in one beautiful image that the prayers of Muslims facing the Ka'aba in Mecca transform the entire planet into a sacred mosque. Carmelite nun Tessa Bielecki says about Mount Carmel, where John of the Cross ascended:

Carmelites are mountain climbers, who go by way of the straight path. Thus Mount Carmel is the homeland of the heart for every Carmelite.... We are called to meditate day and night on the law of the Lord, unless engaged in some other just occupation. 'Law' in this case does not merely mean the Ten Commandments, but also the law that is written in the universe: the law in our hearts, the natural law, the cosmic law (McLuhan, 1996, p. 205-6).

Lama Anagarika Govinda of Tibet speaks of "the soul of the landscape" into which we are woven, and "in which the rhythm of the universe is condensed into a melody of irresistible charm. Imagination here becomes an adequate expression of reality on the plane of human consciousness..." (McLuhan, 1996, p. 218).

From Nobel laureate George Seferis:

I know a pine tree that leans over near a sea. At mid-day it bestows upon the tired body a shade measured like our life, and in the evening the wind blowing through its needles begins a curious song as though of souls that made an end of death, just at the moment when they begin to become skin and lips again. Once I stayed awake all night under this tree. At dawn I was new, as though I had been freshly quarried (McLuhan, 1996, p. 33).

And to bring us back home, this last from scientist Gustav Fechner, a founder of physiological psychology:

One spring morning I went out early: the fields were greening, the birds were singing, the dew glistening; smoke was rising here and there, and here and there appeared a man; there fell upon everything a transfiguring light; it was only a tiny fraction of the earth, only a tiny moment of its existence, and yet, as I comprised more and more in the range of my vision, it seemed to me not only so beautiful but so true and evident that it is an angel, so rich and fresh and blooming, and at the same time so stable and unified, moving in the heavens, turning wholly towards heaven its animated face, and bearing me with it to that same heaven—so beautiful and true that I wondered how men's notions could be so perverted as to see in the earth only a dry clod, and to seek for angels apart from earth and stars or above them in the vacant heaven, only to find them nowhere…. (Fechner and Lowrie, 1946, p. 153).

References

Ackroyd, P. (2000). London: The biography. New York: Nan A. Talese, Doubleday.

Adams, A., and Muir, J., eds. (2002). America's wilderness: The photographs of Ansel Adams. Philadelphia: Courage.

Barreto, M. (2006). On the death of nature: A psychological reflection. Spring Journal, Vol. 75(1), Fall 2006: 257-273.

Basso, K. (1996). Wisdom sits in places: Landscape and language among the western Apache. Albuquerque: University of New Mexico Press.

Belenky, M., Bond, L., and Weinstock, J. (1997). A tradition that has no name: Nurturing the development of people, families, and communities. New York: Basic Books.

Bennett, E.A. (1985). Meetings with Jung. Zurich: Daimon.

Berry, W., and Jackson, W. (1980). New roots for agriculture. San Francisco: Friends of the Earth and the Land Institute.

Bortoft, H. (1996). The wholeness of nature: Goethe's way toward a science of conscious participation. New York: Lindisfarne Press.

Buzzell, L., and Chalquist, C. (2009). Ecotherapy: Healing with nature in mind. San Francisco: Sierra Club Books.

Casey, E. (1993). Getting back into place: Toward a renewed understanding of the place-world. Bloomington and Indianapolis: Indiana University Press.

Chalquist, C. (2007). Terrapsychology: Re-engaging the soul of place. New Orleans: Spring Journal Books.

Columbus, C., and Cohen, J. H., trans. (1992). The four voyages: Being his own log-book, letters, and dispatches with connecting narratives. New York: Penguin.

Ehrlich, G. (1992). Islands, the universe, home. New York: Penguin.

Fechner, G., and Lowrie, W., ed. and trans. (1946). Religion of a Scientist: Selections from Gustav Th. Fechner. New York: Pantheon.

Fromm, Erich (1973). The anatomy of human destructiveness. New York: Holt.

Hillman, J. (1992). The thought of the heart & the soul of the world. Dallas: Spring.

James, W. (1929). The varieties of religious experience: A study in human nature. New York: The Modern Library.

Jung, C.G. (1969). Aion: Researches into the phenomenology of the self. CW 9 ii.

Jung, C.G. (1965). Memories, dreams, reflections. New York: Vintage.

Jung, C.G. (1968). Psychological aspects of the mother archetype. CW 9 i.

Logsdon, G. (1993). The contrary farmer. White River Junction: Chelsea Green.

McLuhan, T. C., ed. (1996). Cathedrals of the spirit: The message of sacred places. New York: Harper Perennial.

Mitchell, L. (2006). Charting the ecological imagination: Between leaf and hand. Spring Journal, Vol. 75(2), Fall 2006: 111-127.

Olson, W., and Cairns, S., eds. (1999). The sacred place: Witnessing the holy in the physical world. Salt Lake City: University of Utah Press.

Plumwood, V. (2002). Environmental culture: The ecological crisis of reason. London and New York: Routledge.

Rankin, S. (2007). A terrapsychological study of the psyche of Petaluma as found in the stories of the land and as mirrored by my own psyche. Unpublished master's thesis, Sonoma State University.

Jung, C.G., and Sabini, M., ed. (2002). Earth has a soul: The nature writings of C.G. Jung. Berkeley: North Atlantic Books.

Sabini, M. (2009). Dreaming a new paradigm. In Buzzell, L., and Chalquist, C., eds. Ecotherapy: Healing with nature in mind. San Francisco: Sierra Club/Counterpoint, 211-218.

Samuels, A. (1993). The political psyche. New York: Routledge.

Seamon, D., and Zajonc, A. (1998). Goethe's way of science: A phenomenology of nature. New York: State University of New York Press.

Shulman, H., and Watkins, M. (2007). Individuation, seeing-through, and liberation: Depth psychology and colonialism, from Myth*ng Links, http://www.mythinglinks.org/LorenzWatkins.html (retrieved March 1, 2007).

Singer, T., and Kimbles, S. (2004). The cultural complex: Contemporary Jungian perspectives on culture and society. New York: Routledge.

Stein, M. (1998). Jung's map of the soul: An introduction. La Salle: Open Court.

Tarnas, R. (2006). Cosmos and psyche: Intimations of a new world view. New York: Viking.

Teilhard de Chardin, P. (2008). The phenomenon of man. New York: HarperPerennial.

Van der Hart, O., and Van der Velden, K. (1987). The hypnotherapy of Andries Hoek: Uncovering Hypnotherapy before Janet, Brueur, and Freud. American Journal of Clinical Hypnosis, Vol. 4, April 29: 264-271.

Von Franz, M. (1992). Psyche and matter. Boston: Shambhala.

TerraPlaces:
Enlivening Relationship with Place

Katrina Martin Davenport

Introduction

The TerraPlaces project was birthed on a June evening a few weeks before the summer Solstice. Craig Chalquist, Renee Levi, and I pondered how to make terrapsychological inquiry applicable to those outside academia. Terrapsychology "studies how the patterns and shapes and features of the human and nonhuman world sculpt our ideas, our habits, our relationships, and even culture and sense of self" (Chalquist, 2009). We wondered if helping people connect with a specific place in nature, coupled with a curriculum in terrapsychology, would develop a deeper relationship with place. Out of this meeting came the TerraPlaces project, designed to allow people to choose a place in nature to sit with (or walk through or observe in other ways) for an amount of time they chose. (The seed for the project was sown in a graduate school class activity at John F. Kennedy University. Kimmy Johnson asked students to find time to be outside, even just for five minutes, in order to reconnect with nature, their dreams, and the ancestors. Katrina found this activity to be highly beneficial and wanted to share its benefits through this project.)

The goal of the project was twofold: to teach participants how to conduct terrapsychological inquiry, and to determine the effects of sitting with a place in nature for a set period of time. Craig and Katrina wrote curriculum to share with participants. The first curriculum was a crash course in terrapsychology, laying the foundation for group members to engage deeply with the place in nature they chose to sit with. The second curriculum took participants deeper by examining the relationship between place and dreams.

The project began August 2010 and continued through December, with phase

Sierra rainbow. (Photo by Gary Newman)

Katrina Martin Davenport, MA is a dreamer. Her work involves illuminating the soul and reconnecting with nature, and she brings her love for dreams, deep connection, beauty, myth, archetypes, and ancestry to her work. She has a master's in Consciousness and Transformative Studies from JFK University and is a board member of the Earth Medicine Alliance. She is also a member of the International Association for the Study of Dreams, the Depth Psychology Alliance, and the Powers of Place Initiative.

one running from August 1 to September 20, and phase two from the fall equinox on September 21 through the last day of fall, December 20. Thirty-three participants signed on to the summer phase and 31 joined the fall phase.

Each week, participants shared their experiences online through a group forum. This stimulated dialogue among the members and helped create a sense of community. We held several conference calls as well. People joined the group at any time during the project and members participated for anywhere from one to four months. The length of participation did not necessarily translate into deeper or shallower interaction with place; some members who only participated for a few weeks experienced deep shifts.

Several outcomes were expected as a result of people's participation in the group. We looked for obvious shifts in consciousness, actions taken on behalf of place, feelings of stewardship toward place, and increased intimacy with place. Specific examples of hoped-for outcomes include:

- Feeling calmer, less stressed, and greater connection
- Creating closer ties with neighbors, family, friends
- A growing sense of protectiveness toward place
- Increase in community-level activity
- More interest in learning about local flora and fauna
- Interest in where resources, food come from
- Increase in resource conservation
- More regular and deeper spiritual practice

The results we saw included participants spending more time outside, becoming more intimate with their spot, gaining more awareness of their surroundings, and enjoying contact with others who were interested in the power of connecting with place.

Purpose

The structure of the project created a container for participants to enter into what Chalquist calls the "preparation phase" of terrapsychological inquiry. During this phase, researchers might

> All I could do was just stand there and feel the beautiful drops of rain all over me. I felt as if Mother Earth was putting up a show just for us. The rainbow got incredibly close and it truly felt like we were being blessed.

participate in several activities Chalquist delineates in *Terrapsychology* (2007):

- Holding an awareness of place that investigates both its exterior and interior as well as the exterior and interior of the researcher
- Giving questions higher priority than answers
- Allowing preconceptions to fall away, creating space for the spirit of place to emerge
- Watching for synchronicities and imaginal musings that arise
- "Employing a *nomadic awareness*" that moves from seeing the land as something owned into an awareness that allows the land agency and a voice

Process

During phase one, project members got basic lessons in the background of terrapsychology as well as introductory techniques for studying the land, such as learning the biome and bioregion of their place. With the start of phase two, we added elements that helped participants deepen their study, including how to incubate dreams of place and utilize various dreamwork techniques in order to communicate with place.

Participants eagerly put what they learned into practice and experienced several of the outcomes we hoped to see. Some had dramatic experiences within a short period of time. Others witnessed a deepening over the entire span of the project. Some felt an increase in community, while others experienced growing intimacy with their place. Many reported significant internal shifts and a greater respect for their place.

Questionnaires were used to track the changes participants experienced. An initial questionnaire was given at the beginning of each phase, and a final questionnaire given at the end of each phase. Results were also ascertained from participants' responses in the online forum. In the initial questionnaire, participants were asked to share how often they spent time outside and explain their relationship with place. We also asked them what they hoped to gain from the project. In the final questionnaire, participants relayed what had changed as a result of the project.

Outcomes

Rapid Shifts.

Two participants in particular experienced dramatic results from participating in the project. (Note: all participants will remain anonymous and be referred to as "Participant," followed by a number.) Participant One joined the project in the summer phase. She chose to visit a local beach and found herself enjoying the time she spent there. One afternoon, about a month into the project, she experienced a phenomenon that she felt changed her life:

> I often just watched the beach goers, kite surfers, swimmers and people just walking by... I listened to the wind and the water but that was it... Suddenly one day I started to become more aware about what was really happening... the wind was talking to me, the ocean sounds were singing for me... the more aware I became the more I felt it, being present in the moment allowed me to really experience the beauty of what I was witnessing... I was no longer just sitting there... I was part of it.
>
> One day, [the beach] was packed with people; I guess the wind brought in lots of kite surfers and there were a lot of onlookers. Suddenly the clouds in the sky got incredibly dark even though it

was still very sunny. It was clear there was rain coming in from offshore. As it started approaching I could see a rainbow forming. As the storm got closer and closer the rainbow seem to get closer as well. Suddenly there was a full rainbow in the sky. We all could see where it began and where it ended and the colors were so incredibly intense! It seemed for a moment as if all stopped; everyone was just standing there in awe. A few minutes later it started raining.

We didn't run for cover. All I could do was just stand there and feel the beautiful drops of rain all over me. I felt as if Mother Earth was putting up a show just for us. The rainbow got incredibly close and it truly felt like we were being blessed.

At that moment I felt life couldn't be more beautiful. I felt complete, fulfilled, and at one with the Earth. When the rain passed people started expressing what they felt. I think we all realized the interconnectedness amongst us all. It was just absolutely amazing! I can tell you it will live with me forever.

Since I started this project with you, I have taken to meditation, and my meditation practice has become much better. I am also writing a journal which I now find incredibly insightful.

Participant One clearly experienced some of the intended outcomes of the project, most notably increased connection with nature, as well as the beginning of a spiritual practice (meditation) and a deepening of that practice. Furthermore, she experienced a greater sense of community. When she witnessed the rainbow on the beach, she was not alone. She was not only with her significant other, but she was also with other beachgoers who all stopped to see and pay attention to the rainbow and the rain. What is especially poignant here is the fact that people shared with each other how they felt about seeing the rainbow, all realizing "the interconnectedness amongst us."

Participant Two also witnessed the power of storms, but in a completely different way. She chose to sit in a ravine downhill from her house. She would bring her lunch down to the ravine and open herself to the land and the trees. She shared that it took several weeks for her to get motivated to be part of the project. She fully intended to choose a spot and sit with it, but she struggled to actually get outside. About three weeks into the project, she had a "very dramatic" experience.

One windy night in early October, right in my spot, a tree fell down, taking down two or three others with it. I had spent time the evening before in my spot, and when I went back the next day at lunchtime, an oak tree had literally fallen across my path on the way to my sitting place. During the following week, my landlady had several more dead trees in the immediate area taken out, along with those that had gone down initially. This dramatically changed the whole area, from being wooded and sheltered to being largely open, with only a few ground shrubs and bushes, and lots of dead tree trunks and wood. The area looked brown and dead; the rains had not yet come. The surrounding area has been badly hit by sudden oak death.

This experience was quite dramatic for me. I had to work with what death in this spot, and by extension death on the planet, means. I felt depressed when spending time in the spot after it first happened.

After a couple of weeks, I realized that nature was already beginning her rejuvenation process; that other species were already and would continue taking advantage of the void left by the oak trees. The relative proportion of various species in the area would change over time, with less oak trees, perhaps more bay and pine, more low growth shrubs, etc., yet nature's green presence would continue. This was an amazingly liberating realization for me.

After a few more weeks, I found I was not content to just sit in the area; I had a strong urge to clean up the brush, twigs, and dead branches. So I began to collect them for kindling for fires in my wood burning stove. There is still dead wood to clean up in the area, but it looks neater than it did. This made me aware of how strong the human impulse is to participate in the transformation and beautification of natural surroundings, especially after a catastrophic event.

My connection to this spot has strengthened. I feel that the place has dramatically changed in a short time, and this change has been present in my psyche. I was blessed to be part of a dramatic shift in the area that caused me to reflect on radical changes in nature, and how this process of change affects human moods and the human psyche, and how it can be engaged by humans. I have let the place be a teacher to

> I had to work with what death in this spot, and by extension death on the planet, means. I felt depressed when spending time in the spot after it first happened. After a couple of weeks, I realized that nature was already beginning her rejuvenation process; that other species were already and would continue taking advantage of the void left by the oak trees.

me about natural cycles of change.

She demonstrates one of the projected outcomes of the project: an increased feeling of protectiveness toward place. After the winds brought down the trees, she felt the urge to help nature's rejuvenation process by going to her spot chosen spot. I [feel] much more richly related to my world."

Participant Four, who sat with a lake in Maine, said that when she began tuning into the sounds and smells of the place, her attention became more nuanced.

What I'm finding for now is that

> The water is lapping around me, the wind tickles my skin and dances my hair around, and I can feel the sun moving in and out of the clouds even with my eyes closed. This movement, this vibration I sense is very powerful. It reminds me of how very alive this place is.

and clearing the dead wood. Although she did not comment on it specifically, one could guess that she also did some clearing in her psyche as she picked up the branches and twigs. The land reflected to her things she wanted to learn about "natural cycles of change." Additionally, she mentioned that she became especially attuned to watching how the spot shifts now that the trees are gone.

Increased intimacy.

Another possible outcome from the TerraPlaces project was increased intimacy with place. Participant Three demonstrated this when she described her experience of the second phase:

> I ended up bonding with and becoming quite attached to a place in the woods on campus of the university where I work part time. I missed it when I didn't have a chance to visit it for a few days....I found myself daydreaming about it. I took a few friends there too, like I was introducing them to another friend.

Changes in attention.

Many TerraPlaces participants shared that they noticed a change in the type of attention they had for place after starting the project. Participant Three mentioned, "I am more conscious and more aware of where I am, even if I am not in my chosen spot. I [feel] much more richly related to my world."

it's the wind and the sounds of the place as much as it is the spectacular visuals. The water is lapping around me, the wind tickles my skin and dances my hair around, and I can feel the sun moving in and out of the clouds even with my eyes closed. This movement, this vibration I sense is very powerful. It reminds me of how very alive this place is. Although I believe that every place is alive, I think that the sensory stimulation available here, in a place so deeply embedded in nature, makes me just so much more aware of what the earth is saying.

This more complex awareness led her to deepen her practice of coming into a more balanced relationship with place. As she describes it, she began relating—

> to a place simply as a place... simply observing what is there—a mountain, water, a few ducks or loons gliding by—and not trying to interpret it as a message for my life. When I can hold Others (nature, people, my work, etc.) simply as Other, perhaps I can be in true reciprocal and reverent relationship. For me it's the I-Thou type of relationship Martin Buber speaks of, not the I-It, where Other is there to be of some kind of service to me. It hasn't been easy doing this, but I'm practicing.

Participant Five noted a similar shift between phase one and phase two: "What changed was the quality of my observation, listening, and inspiration," as did Participant Six: "There has been a tremendous change. I am much more observant and cherishing the tiniest of things I see. I also experience where I am in a much larger context, like layers of meaning awaiting my reception."

Increased community.

One outcome not necessarily on our radar was how participants felt an increase in community with each other. Many of the participants noted that they felt grateful to be in communication with other people who were putting their attention toward the land. As the weeks went on, a deeper sense of connection and friendship developed among the group, an experience enhanced by conference calls we began hosting during the fall phase. Participants shared the ups and downs of their time in the project as well as their concerns and difficulties. While we had anticipated that participants would feel greater community in the actual place they chose, what happened instead was the growth of community online.

Participant Seven described this phenomenon well:

> You ask how I am different since beginning the project. Well, I took in the loss of a heart-made altar, and of someone's friend, the miracle of mountains, lakeside sanctuary, cityscapes, the ever-shifting, but ever-present sky, the light shining through golden-orange autumn leaves, a goldfish in blue water turning my world upside down, a tiled image of a possible new world, a woman finding the one needed moment of clarity of presence and vision in a busy life, gentle, insightful sharing of information relevant to soul growth, heartful and generous encouragement, new and diverse perspectives and a vista view that broadened out into an ever-expanding sphere of connectivity through the online community.
>
> How am I different? I have experiential knowing, however limited in online or other contact, of a

group of really inspiring people and of the places they are in conscious relationship with. Through their experience of place, I took in something of the person that lives in the place and something of the place that lives in the person. I am enlivened and transformed by this kind of encounter with people and places.

External Shifts.

Participant Five had a unique experience during phase two. She walked through a neighborhood in Oakland each day and noticed one spot in particular, a paved area with a structure that seemed to be someone's abandoned garage. It was apparent to her that homeless people were using the area as a bathroom and trash receptacle. For some reason, she felt drawn to this spot and wanted to bring it healing. She asked her friend to create a wooden altar that she could place there and shared her thoughts about the project on the forum.

> I had a vision of creating a shrine in this inlet—a place where humans could stop to pray, be silent, give thanks, make an offering, sing, chant, meditate, listen—a place where they could seek comfort.

Could such a place inspire attachment, love, care for this place? Or would humans tear it down and continue to deface it? I am curious. I feel cautiously hopeful.

On the autumn equinox, she placed the altar there with the help of her daughter. She told the group about her experience placing the altar:

> I first picked up trash and broken glass before retrieving the altar from my car. I quickly placed it towards the back of the inlet and then smudged the entire space with a rosemary stick I made last year with rosemary from my garden
>
> I tied some Tibetan prayer flags on the top… and placed an empty round balsa wood box with a granola bar, a pack of Kleenex, and a box of Slippery Elm throat lozenges inside. I also placed a picture of an adult bird feeding a baby bird on top, along with some feathers, and some shells from a beach on Kauai, a dried rose, and a rock from Sunol Wilderness Park—all things that I have collected. On the bottom I placed a red journal and a writing pen in a Ziploc bag, along with a small card with the word 'strength' printed on it. I also placed a note introducing the altar in a Ziploc and tacked it to the inside of the altar. I acknowledge that this altar could be stolen or defaced, and know that I cannot be attached to it and must release it to the universe.

What happened next was quite interesting. Participant Five returned to the altar the next morning, and already people had written in the journal she'd placed with the altar. Comments in the journal included, "Autumn is the beginning of the dreaming season," and "I am glad this is still here." Clearly, others who cared for the place wanted to express themselves. One man wrote: "My daughter, Matriya, and I often come here to walk and breathe beneath the trees. Thank you for this sacred place and moment created by your intention. Let's care for this place, and world, together."

Over the next few days, the altar grew, enhanced by objects left by others and several more entries in the journal. Participant Five wrote about the objects: "Many items have been added to the altar including leaves, acorn tops, tree bark, a tree branch, and a bead." It seemed she had created a healing space, a spot where people could come together and share their love for the area and build community.

But she could not anticipate what happened next. She wrote:

> It has been difficult for me to write this entry today, but I know I must tell. Today I took my usual walk along my route. The altar was still there and new entries had been added. I placed a new flower on the altar and continued on my walk. On my way back about 50 minutes later, I glanced at the altar as I was passing it and noticed that the note I had written explaining the intention of the altar was gone—taken during the short time I had last left it.
>
> Upon closer inspection, I noticed that bits of the plastic bag I had placed it in to protect it were lying on the floor of the altar. I had hammered it in so that it would not be easy to remove, but someone had torn it off. I decided to return to my place, print out another one, and come back and hammer it in place. This was very upsetting.
>
> I quickly returned by car to post the new one. As I was leaving the space, a woman with a dog across the street began calling out to me to come and see her. She said, 'I would like to speak with you.' I crossed the street and was sternly confronted by a very unhappy woman. This space where I had placed the altar was, according to her, at one time her garage. There was no roof anymore and she did not have the money to replace it.
>
> "She claimed that she was a 'Christian too,' but that she could not understand why I would just set up my business in her space without knowing who it belonged to. She clearly had been checking it out and visiting it. She also commented that certain people were regularly coming to visit it. I got the sense that she felt left out, but also violated.
>
> "I apologized to her several times and told her that I meant her no harm. I told her that it was for a research study that I was participating in and

that I had chosen this space after observing it for two years. I told her that I had no idea that it was someone's garage and that in two years time I had never seen a vehicle parked in it, but that I had noticed lots of trash and evidence that the homeless use it often to do their business. I told her that I was drawn to the space and felt protective of it and that is why I had chosen it.

None of this mattered to her. I told her that I would remove it right away if that is what she wanted, and

Internal shifts.

Many participants reported sensing internal shifts as a result of this project. Participant Eight is one example. She joined because she wanted to "stop working and pay attention to the natural world." This goal proved elusive for her throughout the project as she entered the time of year when her job demands the most attention from her. She often added "sit in my place" to her "To Do" list, but never ended up checking it off. Then she had a revelation.

hoped-for outcomes of this project was a decrease in stress for participants, and Participant Eight shows one way that result manifested.

Participant Nine chose a surprising place to study: the sky. He combined the practice of observing place with the exercise called subject/object reversal, which he describes as "contemplating something, then imagining that object contemplating me." It was the marriage of these two practices that created internal shifts for him.

> I stop when I'm walking the pedestrian overpass between hotels and notice the great blue heron standing perfectly still in the shallow pool below me. I hold the moment with that same stillness, breathing in the patience and expansiveness.

she said, 'Please do.' She watched me the entire time from across the street and I felt so bad. I felt bad for her, mostly because I sensed that she was a lonely, unhappy woman. I sensed that she was challenged by this altar and needed to know where it came from and why. I felt bad also because I knew that this altar was transforming the energy of this place and people, bringing beauty to this place, but this did not matter to her. I thought it was interesting that she assumed I was Christian. I never mentioned the word God or religion in the note.

What had caused this woman to act this way, to feel threatened by the altar? Why did she assume that what Participant Five was doing was a business? Why did she confront Participant Five in this way? How are these women's reactions an extension of the place? Did it react against the creation of the altar as well? Were the shifts occurring as a result of the altar and the community it created too much for the woman to handle? We can't know for sure, but we can say that Participant Five's altar had a definite effect on the spot.

I have decided I will not worry myself, berate myself, stress out over yet another thing to do. Instead, I will befriend my strength, thanking it for what it brings me, and then find small ways to refresh myself within the context of 'my place.' So my place travels with me now. I take tiny breaks now, wherever I am, allowing myself to refresh in an undisturbed moment, no matter how short or how long, and rest with the natural world, whether I'm in it or looking out on it.

I stop when I'm walking the pedestrian overpass between hotels and notice the great blue heron standing perfectly still in the shallow pool below me. I hold the moment with that same stillness, breathing in the patience and expansiveness.

Participant Eight's ability to internalize her place in this way represents a significant shift in her psyche, for now she can tap into her place's gifts throughout the day. Additionally, her place is not just one spot…it is the many faces of nature she encounters on her extensive travels across the country. One of the

When doing this with clouds, I found that I often experienced a shift in consciousness when imagining myself a cloud contemplating me. It was as if my consciousness became more cloud-like, with shades of difference depending on the type of cloud. These images of cloud consciousness have begun showing up in my meditation. Overall I often have an expanded sense of space, as if discovering a new sense organ.

I became much more attentive to the sky, clouds, and by extension more aware of the space above and around me. And I have become at least somewhat more observant of the external world.

Participant Nine felt greater connection and saw a deepening of his meditation practice as a result of his participation in the project, and he also gained an expanded awareness of place.

Finally, Participant Ten expressed that she felt several internal shifts, saying the project "left an indelible print in only a matter of mere weeks." For her, the project helped her better tune into the city she's studying for her doctoral research.

I listen more intently to hear what Los Angeles has to say from the ground up. I am more mindfully aware of the face I turn to the City. I look at Her landscapes far more differently, thanks in large part to this amazing group and work.

I am discovering how varying parts of me (psyche and soma) intersect and interact with the place of Los Angeles and her many facets— from Beverly Hills to 'L.A. proper.' One most notable change is the connection between how the seasons of the City, the climate, the elements, affect my body and soul. Another change is finding more sacred moments among the places that are often deemed ugly and profane.

Implications

The TerraPlaces project has been renewed for another season, and it is my hope that it will continue at least for an entire year so we can track changes among participants over the course of 12 months. It is already apparent from what has been shared here that shifts happen as a result of sitting with place and such shifts will likely be more profound and lasting over a longer period of time.

Why is it important to think about the impact of sitting with a place? We have lost our connection to the natural world. We have forgotten that we are part of this world and that our actions cause immediate reactions in the natural world. Were humans to remember this, it seems, especially in light of the shifts that occurred during this project, that it is possible major shifts in how we treat plants, the land, and animals would occur. We would understand our surroundings, and ourselves better. We could reduce our stress to a great degree and perhaps even discover that many of the things that stress us out are things we can let go.

Furthermore, the communal implications of the impact of sitting with nature could be huge. For instance, if each person in a town chose a spot and sat with it for an extended period of time, say six months, thus developing a deep relationship with that piece of land, it is likely they would experience shifts. These shifts in awareness and the increased feeling of community they would develop might lead them to band together to protect the land in the town. If we expanded this phenomenon out to counties, states, regions, countries… we could create a global movement. We could create a world of people committed to having deep relationships with place that would lead to conservation, protection, and just treatment of the land and its inhabitants.

References

Chalquist, C. (2009). *What is Terrapsychology?* Retrieved December 27, 2010, from http://terrapsych.com/whatisTP.html

Chalquist, C. (2007). *Terrapsychology: re-engaging the soul of place.* New Orleans: Spring Journal Books.

From Pet to Planet:

Our Attachment to Companion Animals as a Portal into Grief and Loss

Lesley A. Osman

My 17-year-old cat is dying and what is startling, surprising about this, is how painful her death process is to me. I've asked myself repeatedly why I thought this would be any different? As a psychotherapist, I understand how significant a relationship with a pet can be. But while I have experienced the pain of an animal dying before, I have never had to be present with a prolonged terminal illness in a pet, watching the steady decline, loss of weight and agility, messes to clean up almost constantly. My cat BB is clinging to life, eating constantly without absorbing any nutrition. Her system is slowly shutting down.

Sleeping cat. (Photo by Gary Newman)

From an eco-psychological viewpoint, the following points and questions are of particular interest to me: Why do we feel the need to have our *domesticated* animal friends around us in the first place? How does my process with BB mirror the *grief and loss* of connection to all things natural? Why is feeling deeply for a pet considered somehow inferior and therefore not socially acceptable? And, finally, how do we need animal friends in order to maintain the tenuous *attachment* we have to the rest of life and to our own wild natures?

Let me explain why it felt so compelling to wrestle with these issues in writing. While it's not necessarily talked about openly, if the subject is broached, everyone, it seems, regardless of background, has a painful memory to share around the loss of a beloved pet. One woman told me recently that the death of her beloved German Shepherd-wolf mix was far harder for her than the deaths of her parents. Shocking to some, I'm sure, but she said the unconditional love and loyalty she consistently received from her pet far surpassed the love she felt from her parents. Her attachment to her dog was greater and more highly regarded than the closeness she was able to develop in her family system.

Others shared that they had run up thousands of dollars in vet bills but felt foolish sharing the information. A colleague told me she'd moved her mattress to the floor to allow her ailing cat access to a favorite sleeping area. These stories aren't unusual, and they started me thinking about why these losses aren't shared more openly, which led me further to wonder about the value we place on animals, our attachments to the other-than-human, and acceptance of our need for connection and relationship to the more-than-human.

Lesley Osman, MA, MFT, graduated in Transpersonal Psychology from John F. Kennedy University's Graduate School of Holistic Studies, and specializes in Ecotherapy. She is a certified Applied Ecopsychologist and Earth-based healer. Concerned about vanishing species, pollution, depletion of natural resources, deforestation and genetically modified organisms, Lesley acts as a guide to agencies, companies and individuals concerned about these issues. As an Ecotherapist, educator and writer, she has a private psychotherapy practice in Mendocino, where she regularly takes clients outdoors. Lesley offers trainings to other professionals who have an interest in "greening" their group or individual practice.

Because I myself grew up with the cultural imperative that animals are lesser beings, it never occurred to me that during my cat's decline I would be making some of the choices I have made—fluids to re-hydrate injected under the skin every other day, x-rays, oral doses of prednisone. I can hear in the background the voices: "She's probably suffering. Why don't you let her go?" "She's an animal; it's okay to put her to sleep." While there are those who judge me, I have to be okay with my choices, hoping that I will know instinctively, as this cat's "mother," when she is ready to go.... waiting for a sign. It's not like these questions and statements haven't occurred to me, and yet, I'm still hanging in with her, waiting for that sign.

This is important to look at more closely, because not only am I a licensed psychotherapist who guides clients through their own grief and loss issues, but also, as an eco-therapist who's interested in our relationships and connections to the more-than-human world, my cat's soul seems to me no less important, no less integral to the larger planetary system. I want to thank her for her contribution to the thoughts, feelings and ideas contained within this essay.

The Human-Animal Relationship

The question has to be asked – why did we, as humans, feel the need to domesticate animals in the first place? Apart from the obvious, breeding for food, was it somehow an unconscious attempt to bring wildness, or "all our relations" closer to us? In *The Earth has a Soul: The Nature Writings of C.J. Jung* edited by Meredith Sabini (2002), Jung conjectured that the lower layers of the human psyche have an animal character, recapitulating our evolutionary heritage. I understand this to mean that evolution hasn't eradicated our animalistic psychological characteristics but rather incorporated them. Jung goes on to say that because this is so, there is a probability that animals and humans have the same archetypes or images imbedded in their psyches, and therefore have instinctual drives to be in symbiotic relationships with plants and other animals (Sabini, 2002, p.83-84).

Perhaps because humans have an inherited relationship with animals, the gods are symbolized as animals—even the Holy Ghost is symbolized as a bird. Indigenous peoples have not lost their sense of awe, fascination and respect for the wisdom of wildness. In some cultures, the wisest of all animals, the most powerful and divine of all beings, is the elephant, and then comes the python or the lion, and only then comes the human. As Paul Shepard discusses in *Nature and Madness* (1982), before civilization animals were seen as belonging to their own nation and as bearers of messages and gifts of meat from a sacred domain. But in the settled village, they became subdued into human possessions. He also suggests that pet keeping is both a covert and unconscious use of animals in service of human psychological need.

We look around us and anthropomorphize all manner of things we see. We are constantly caught up in our own narcissism, attempting to fashion things in our own image. I have certainly endowed my ailing kitty with many human-like qualities that may have no basis in the true nature of her life: "she's sneaky, deliberately naughty, cute, loving, needy...." The list goes on. Does this tendency to anthropomorphize occur simply because we look through human lenses and therefore can relate only through human perceptual frameworks in our interface with the world? Perhaps the purely instinctual nature of our animal friends keeps us somehow grounded in our own instinctual natures.

This tendency to attribute human qualities to animals and the nonhuman world is a projective process, and a well known psychological mechanism, but Jung's approach to this phenomenon gives us a new perspective, which points to the interconnectedness of all life. He considered the capacity to identify with animals an innate instinct arising from our shared evolutionary heritage. To disavow this capacity, he believed, may point to the immaturity of our species and our modern effort to create artificially firm boundaries between ourselves and other life. This boundary making, he thought, was an attempt to protect our own fragile consciousness, a boundary which among tribal people is not considered important. And why are we so fragile? Jung suggests "that if consciousness could be viewed as the head of a gigantic, million-year-old creature-..., this creature also has a body and tail that includes the evolutionary history of all life" (Sabini, 2002, p.13).

In taking the perspective of the fragility of human consciousness, is it any wonder that our desperate need to survive and thrive led us into the activities of domestication--to develop safe shelters, raise and store crops for food, organize ourselves into structured communities and domesticate animals to act as help-mates and companions?

Attachment and the Ecological Self

Attachment theory, currently in vogue in psychological circles, emphasizes that an internalized sense of safety and security is achieved through the presence of a consistent and caregiving other.

John Bowlby proposed that attachment bonds involve two behavioral systems—an attachment system and a caregiving system. First, individuals come into the world equipped with an attachment behavioral system that is prone to activation and serves a major evolutionary function of protection and survival (Bowlby, 1969; Bretherton, 1987).... Adults as well as children benefit from having someone look-

> Jung conjectured that the lower layers of the human psyche have an animal character, recapitulating our evolutionary heritage.... evolution hasn't eradicated our animalistic psychological characteristics but rather incorporated them.

ing out for them—someone who is deeply invested in their welfare, who monitors their whereabouts, and who is reliably available to help if needed. (Collins & Feeney, n.d.)

A second tenet of attachment theory stipulates that the caregiving system is another normative, safety-regulating system that is intended to reduce the risk of a close other coming to harm. Caregiving refers to a broad array of behaviors that complement the attachment behavior of the young, and may include help or assistance, comfort and reassurance, and support of autonomous activities and personal growth (Collins & Feeney, 2000; Kunce & Shaver 1994) (Collins & Feeney, n.d.)

To expand on this theory of attachment and take it to the global scale, the biophilia hypothesis, developed by Kellert and Wilson (1993), much like Bowlby's attachment theory, asserts that humans have an innate and instinctual need to have close contact with the natural world. More than likely, these instincts are remnants of our ancestral need for protection and survival; we are attracted to those things in nature that serve us in some way, and on the contrary, repelled by those things that may harm us, known as biophobia. We also have an inherent and essential attachment to the more than human world. Our food, our medicines, the air we breathe, the water we drink are gifts from the natural processes of this planet that provide for us, as would any good caregiver.

So what happens when we deny these natural bonds and behave in ways that dismiss the natural world? In modern times, we humans have begun to view everything not human as nothing more than a useful resource: the river becomes merely a source of water for human consumption; a mountain a mine, a source of mineral or stone for our roadways or construction for our suburbs; forests a vast resource for construction and paper products; other species of animals meat for our bellies—until these things become to us dead, soulless things. The western worldview, and psychotherapy along with it, separates self from body, soul, and land. The more we are disconnected and removed from the natural world, the more we inhabit the artificial construction of man, and the more it becomes okay to destroy, because the attachment, the psychic kinship, is no longer there. In an attempt to evolve, we are depleting the living system that we are attached to and dependent upon in essential ways. We are cutting ourselves off from our intimate relationship with the rest of life, and consequently making ourselves ill. According to Uchino, Cacioppo and Kiecolt-Glasser (1996), intimate relationships play a critical role in promoting health and well-being in adulthood, while relationship disruption in adulthood is associated with a wide range of adverse health outcomes (Collins and Feeney, n.d.).

Due to our embeddedness in our western constructs of reality, it's no wonder that when we choose to welcome an animal into our home, it's hard to confess that we become profoundly attached. Because in the wider culture animals are typically regarded as soulless things, as objects, there is a shaming and silencing of the depth of our experiences of attachment to these animals. And yet, in their very non-human ways, our pets continue to provide us with constancy, unconditional love and comfort, all behaviors associated with a good caregiver.

This cultural shaming and silencing can lead us to do ourselves as well as our pets a disservice if we don't experience the grief at the passing of a beloved pet. Often euthanasia is used all too readily as a remedy for our uncertainty and pain when an animal friend is sick and dying. We avoid a prolonged death process that we both don't understand and can't trust. We stop listening to the inner knowing and intuitive, nonverbal communication. Reynolds and Kowalski in *Blessing the Bridge*, which focuses on what animals teach us about death and dying, suggest that euthanasia, while a merciful option, requires not doing what is convenient, economical, or practical at the moment, but rather what is called for on a very high level of consideration for another living, sentient being (2010).

What if cat and self are more than skin and bones? If soul or essence transcends, and acts as an ethereal connection or bridge, then our attachment to companion animals may form the beginnings of an identification with the ecological self. The ecological self, a term introduced by Arnae Ness, refers to the process of self-actualization, through which one transcends the individuated "egoic" self and arrives at the "eco-self," which results in environmentally responsible behavior as a form of self-interest ("Ecological Self," n.d.).

When we dismiss our attachment to our pets, and deny our grief at their loss, then we contribute to our own soul loss. When we identify with the more than human world, so that the boundaries between cat self and human self become amorphous, but then deny our feelings of attachment, we lose an essential part of ourselves. This loss of self and soul feeds our deepening hunger, which can turn into addiction—consumer addiction, substance addiction, or a host of other substitutes to fill the hole.

We are surrounded everyday by losses in the form of a myriad of failing natural systems, which translate into soul loss, and are deeply painful for those who recognize the indisputable physical need and emotional and spiritual attachment our species has to the natural world. We are a part of and not apart from the rest of the living planet whose biosphere is alive and adapting to more heat, less available water, and other changes. However, if

> The western worldview, and psychotherapy along with it, separates self from body, soul, and land. The more we are disconnected and removed from the natural world, the more we inhabit the artificial construction of man, and the more it becomes okay to destroy, because the attachment, the psychic kinship, is no longer there.

we can allow ourselves to deeply grieve and release the maniacal grip we have on our perceived independence from the animals, minerals and plants of this planet, the tremendous gift we receive is love, interdependence and living in harmony with the natural world around us. Furthermore, we realize we are no longer alone. And where there is life, there is also death and regeneration, and the benefits gained in being fully present with death and separation, including a strange, haunting beauty, does something to mitigate the agony. Suzuki Roshi, the founder of the San Francisco Zen Center, once said, "You learn best from things that are dying." And I wonder how we are learning from the dying of the trees, the tigers and the bears?

The Grief and Loss Cycle

While in the process of drafting this essay, BB passed. Although terribly painful, her passing also brought relief, and a sense of sad calm has become my reality. As I had hoped, she let me know when she was resigned to her death. The day I made my decision to play "god" and "put her to sleep," her face had changed, she could no longer support her emaciated body weight, her spirit was already exiting its physical flesh.

Most of us at some point experience the excruciating pain caused by the loss of a loved and treasured other. Upon the loss of relationship, whether through physical death or some other type of ending, whether we're aware of it or not, we undergo a grief-process. We all grieve differently and at our own pace, and for some the journey is completed more slowly than for others, but we need to feel the pain before we can experience the healing.

The grief process is made up of a number of nearly universal subjective states, and the initial ones are often shock, disbelief or denial. At the onset of her decline, I certainly believed that BB's symptoms were due to her longstanding thyroid problem, thinking, "her medications need to be increased, perhaps her body had somehow been rejecting the medication, her medications had been given improperly by cat-sitters." There seemed to be an endless list of reasons for her symptoms. Not until after several visits to the veterinarian and several different tests could I no longer deny the realization and truth that I was going to lose her.

On a larger global scale, our denial can be debilitating. As Joanna Macy and Molly Young Brown state in *Coming Back to Life*, "When we deny or repress our pain for the world, or treat it as a private pathology, our power to take part in the healing of our world is diminished" (1998, p.59). When we learn of the numbers of species becoming extinct, the acres of virgin forests being cut, and millions of children of our own species dying of starvation, it's all too, too much! We feel overwhelmed, helpless, impotent, and often very hopeless. We just can't believe that it's actually happening, and so find distractions, ways or keeping our anxieties and grief at bay. Our defenses are endless, but the defense of denial creates a strong barrier against feeling anything. Yet without the psychic energy generated by feeling and experiencing these losses, there will be no creative action.

Ecotherapists consistently observe an array of predictable symptoms presented by clients around the denial of loss and grief over the decline of the natural world. Our burgeoning psychic angst manifests symptomatically as depression, eating disorders, substance abuse, panic, phobias and anxiety. A cadre of physical complaints also overwhelms medical doctors: insomnia, lethargy, breathlessness, high blood pressure, ulcers, headaches, constipation and on and on. None of us are immune from somatic complaints because our nervous systems daily absorb the impact of stress and angst that often goes unprocessed due to our busy and demanding lifestyles.

When it's no longer possible to deny the loss, a sense of awareness slowly trickles in. "It is true! I do really hurt!" When I moved out of denial, my response to the plain truth that my cat was dying was to face her imminent death and move into action around her comfort and care. This of course was also a response to my own anxiety, and anxiety channeled into creative action brings relief on two levels, internal and external. It was important for me to feel that I'd done everything possible to allow for her passing in her own time, and with as much integrity as possible. The pain, of course, sometimes seems more than one can endure, and in these moments, we can slip once more into distraction and denial. Without social recognition and acceptance around the pain associated with a pet's death, we also face shame and confusion about our actions.

With access to feeling comes a torrent of emotion, which the armor of denial formerly kept at bay. Anger, guilt, shame, confusion, wishful thinking, and profound love are among some of the feelings I recall from this intense time. All of these may be present simultaneously and in an ever-shifting and unpredictable mixture. I felt guilty that I'd left my beloved cat with a sitter who had never stayed with her before and had confessed that she'd never been fond of felines. Although BB had always seemed to thrive after her sitter experiences, I blamed myself for having been gone, my partner and myself for not noticing her decline, and a lifetime of seeming neglectfulness, none of which, of course, had any basis in fact. I also loved her more deeply, felt joy at any displays of affection, and utter disbelief and confusion at the prospect of not having her physical presence. Her dying process created a profound opening to the soul.

Globally, we're coming into a greater state of awareness around the current planetary situation of great loss. When the front page of *Time* (April 3, 2006) features a photo of a polar bear sitting on a small isolated icepack, with a caption reading "BE WORRIED. BE VERY WORRIED," it's rather hard to deny that global warming or "climate change" is happening, that environmental degradation is having a noticeable and frightening impact. The front page of this issue also read: "Climate change isn't some vague future problem—

> The benefits gained in being fully present with death and separation, including a strange, haunting beauty, does something to mitigate the agony.

it's already damaging the planet at an alarming pace. Here's how it affects you, your kids and their kids as well…" If we're awake to the world around us, we can't help but experience some of the emotions mentioned, so what to do with them?

To languish in a state of perpetual denial is to be complicit in disconnection and inaction. Denial perpetuates the secret - that we're on a sinking ship! The sinking of the Titanic offers an apt metaphor for our collective situation in the late 20th and 21st century.

> To somehow contain the flood of feelings that want to carry us away, to come to a place of acceptance, and to take healing steps are the emotional challenges we face, whether we're grieving the loss of a pet or the planet.

This disconnection makes me feel like I'm a therapist on the Titanic. We do some great work restoring our relationship with ourselves and other humans, of reconnection with our personal origins, all of which can be truly liberating in many ways - but how often do we mention that the ship is in crisis? (Rust, 2005, p.1).

To somehow contain the flood of feelings that want to carry us away, to come to a place of acceptance, and to take healing steps are the emotional challenges we face, whether we're grieving the loss of a pet or the planet. This emotional work is really not about technique or particular tools. It's about a quality of presence, an understanding that psyche, like the rest of nature, has a self-organizing principle. Healing happens through tending to the beauty and love of all life, through creativity, through listening to the inner voice of intuition, and through expressing through story, myth, poetry, and art. In truth, there is no simple fix, there are no pat words. Much as our animal friends find different ways of communicating, we have to watch for signs, trusting that we'll know what to do in moments of aching loss and shattering soul pain. Ritualizing our grief can help provide a container for the chaotic rush of emotions that spillover.

The last day of BB's life, I lay with her soaking up the sight of her, the hair of her, the smell of her. I wept a thousand tears with her. I allowed myself to be fully present with her and in some ways entered a ritual space with her. I told her the story of her life: How as an almost newborn feral kitten, I had found her being tossed around by children in Balboa Stadium in San Francisco. Hence she became known as Baby Balboa or BB. I told her how I took her home and fed her formula in a syringe for at least two weeks, how she had almost died as a newborn, and had near misses on several other occasions. I shared how she moved with me several times, and how on one move, she had jumped out of a friend's arm and disappeared. How it wasn't until the middle of the night that I heard her distinctive meow, and had gone looking for her. I told her how on finding her under a poison oak bush, I realized that she had been too far away for me to have actually heard her, and how I knew without doubt that we had an unexplainable connection. I told her that Josephine, her cat companion, who had died a few years earlier, was waiting for her, to curl-up together. More than all of this, I told her how much I loved her and how much I would desperately miss her. I gave her my day. I followed my instincts. We created healing together.

After we buried her in her carefully crafted casket, made by the hands of my loving partner from a recycled bee box, we created a simple ceremony, placing flowers and catnip on her grave. I read a poem I created for her. This essay is also in honor of a small animal that had such an important presence in my life for seventeen years. BB gave me the profound gift of living with death in a conscious and present way.

We can learn to meet such terrible grief. By being a kind and loving guide in the face of grief and loss, creating ritual, accepting all and any emotion, dancing, singing, screaming, crying, laughing. By being open to healing through the intuitive process.

Whether or not it was human folly to domesticate animals in the first place, our pets give us the opportunity to connect to the more-than-human world. Animal-facilitated therapies are becoming commonplace as practitioners have begun to understand that a relational bond with an animal maybe less threatening, with less risk of abandonment, with more chance to receive and give unconditional positive regard, and with fewer negative projections. The instinctual nature of pets somehow makes it okay to be instinctual creatures ourselves. Likewise, ecotherapy, the application of eco-psychology (soul's home story), brings the natural world, with its well-documented healing capacity, into the therapeutic process. Our animal companions may be a part of the journey to reconnection with the planet.

And, finally, a poem:

Oh BB, cat of great repose
From near and far, we suppose
Your hair claims distant galaxies

We love the way you fuss and meow
When breakfast is being prepared
Your sweetness has claimed many hearts

Always you fling yourself over
On the sofa for your daily massage
Pampered by those who travel to be with you

BB, you find the best places to lie
Stretched out for at least a mile
On the table in the sun

We love you and your ginger and tabby spots
Munchy, little B, you're always here to greet
And we know your presence with be greatly missed

Rest your tiny bones in peace.

And a dream:

I see my pet cat Josephine, who had passed on a couple of years prior to BB's passing. After a long journey, Josephine is there welcoming me to the "other side." I am standing on a shore by a vast ocean, and Josephine is able to communicate with me in a language I can understand. She, along with my grandmother, want to take me to see all those I'd loved and lost.

In this dream, Josephine becomes a dear and trusted guide, no longer simply a pet but a being of great value and esteem, responsible for my wellbeing. She, along with my grandmother, become my guides to another life. It seems it would be a happy, secure one of ease, freed of a sense of separateness, loneliness, isolation or fear. There is a welcoming sense of familiarity with everything and everyone around me. Josephine is clearly more sophisticated and wise than I had ever imagined while in this life.

References

Bowlby, J. (1969/1982). *Attachment and Loss,* Vol. 1: *Attachment.* New York: Basic Books.

Bowlby, J. (1973). *Attachment and Loss,* Vol. 2: *Separation.* New York: Basic Books.

Bowlby, J. (1979). *The Making and Breaking of Affectional Bonds.* London: Tavistock.Bowlby, J. (1980). *Attachment and Loss,* Vol. 3. *Loss.* New York: Basic Books.Bowlby, J. (1988). *A Secure Base.* New York: Basic Books.

Bretherton, I. (1987). "New Perspectives on Attachment Relations: Security, Communication, and Internal Working Models." In *Handbook of Infant Development,* 2nd edition, ed. J. Osofsky. New York: Wiley.

Collins, N. L., and Feeney, B. C. (2000). "A Safe Haven: An Attachment Theory Perspective on Support Seeking and Caregiving in Intimate Relationships." *Journal of Personality and Social Psychology* 78: 1053–1073. Collins, N.L. and Feeney, B.C. (n.d). "Attachment - Couple Relationships." Retrieved from: http://family.jrank.org/pages/118/Attachment.html" Attachment - Couple Relationships, Parent-child Relationships. Ecological Self. (n.d.). Retrieved from: http:/en.wikipedia.org/wiki/Ecological_Self.

Kluger, J. (March 26, 2006). "Earth at the tipping point: Global warming heats up." *Time.* 0,16641,20060403.00, cover page.

Kellert, S. R. and Wilson, E. O. (1993). *The biophilia hypothesis.* Washington, D.C.: Island Press.

Kunce, L. J., and Shaver, P. R. (1994). "An Attachment- Theoretical Approach to Caregiving in Romantic Relationships." In *Advances in Personal Relationships,* Vol. 5, ed. K. Bartholomew and D. Perlman. London: Jessica Kingsley.

Macy, J. and Brown Young, M. (1998). *Coming back to life: Practices to reconnect our lives, our world.* Stony Creek, CT: New Society Publishers.

Reynolds, R. and Kowalski, G. (2010). *Blessing the bridge: What animals teach us about death, dying and beyond.* Troutdale, OR: NewSage Press.

Rust, M. J. (2005). "Ecolimia Nervosa? Eating Problems and Ecopsychology." *Therapy Today: British Association for Counseling and Psychotherapy Journal.* December 2005, 16: 10-11.

Sabini, M. (2002). *The Earth has a soul: The nature writings of C.G. Jung.* Berkeley, CA: North Atlantic Books.

Shepard, P. (1982). *Nature and Madness.* New York, NY: Random House.

Uchino, B. N.; Cacioppo, J. T.; and Kiecolt-Glaser, J. K. (1996). "The Relationship between Social Support and Physiological Processes: A Review with Emphasis on Underlying Mechanisms and Implications for Health." *Psychological Bulletin* 119: 488–531.

I dreamt the earth was dying

I dreamt the earth was dying
I watched but did not see

I dreamt the earth was dying
I heard but let it be

And on I slumbered in my blindness
Twisting in the pain

I failed to see my pain arose from
Ways that I'd gone numb

I dreamt my vision opened
And found a way to start

I dreamt my vision opened
And with it grew my heart

—Darlene Cimino-DeRose

Sustaining Wellness:

Drawing from the Roots of Horticultural Therapy

Jay Stone Rice

Redwood sentinels. (Photo by Gary Newman)

Master of the Universe,

Grant me the ability to be alone; may it be my custom to go outdoors each day among the trees and grass—among all living things—and enter into prayer, talking with the One to whom I belong.

May I express there everything in my heart, and may all the foliage of the field awake at my coming, to send the powers of their life into the words of my prayer so that my speech is made whole through the life and spirit of all growing things, which are made as One, by their transcendent Source.

—Rabbi Nachman of Bratslav
(1772-1810)

Jay Stone Rice, Ph.D., integrates training in psychology, community development and nature-based wisdom traditions. He teaches at the Horticultural Therapy Institute in Denver, CO and practices psychotherapy in San Rafael, CA. Dr. Rice studied San Francisco Sheriff Department's Garden Project. He co-edited The Healing Dimensions of People-Plant Relations, Center for Design Research, University of California, Davis. Dr. Rice consulted with the Center for Mental Health Services and the National Institute for Corrections on developing ecologically sensitive treatment programs. He has written about the social ecology of inner city family trauma, substance abuse and crime, and gardening as a treatment intervention.

Wellness Under Threat

When I consider the images currently shaping my feelings regarding nature, the future of our earth and the lives of our children, I feel more fear than hope. Each day we receive more information that confirms we are living on a dangerously warming planet. The loss of arctic ice and the imperiled polar bears, the increases in fires, hurricanes, and drought impact each of us consciously and unconsciously. In my psychotherapy practice, I observe the growing strains in the lives of those I work with. Rarely is the state of the earth seen as a contributing factor. This speaks to our alienation, confusion, and dissociation from our essential nature. Michael Pollan (2002), in his exquisite book *The Botany of Desire*, notes how strange it seems that humans have a "relationship to nature." His book eloquently makes the case that we are of nature, we are nature.

These thoughts of our current ecological/existential crisis came upon me unbidden, when recently I was invited to consider the applicability of horticultural therapy for sustaining wellness.[1] My writing flitted upon the surface of this question of human wellness, until I turned towards my own growing despair regarding the health of our earth. I felt my soul stir when the shape of this inquiry moved from a unidirectional focus on how nature and gardens can foster human well-being and health, to how horticultural therapy might foster healing in completing the circle of human/nature. In the absence of hope, I call upon a faith that turning towards these pressing concerns will deepen our inquiry into the heart of our work.

In attempting to understand our contemporary ecological situation from a wider perspective, I first turned to mythology. Michael Meade (2008), the psychologist, mythologist, and activist, suggests we are in the "end of days" time of our cycle. In his book *The World Behind The World*, Meade looks to the old world tales and myths to learn how to live one's life in troubled times. He tells a story of lions hunting in the savannah in Africa. The pride sends its oldest and weakest member to the far side of the hunted herd. What this elder lacks in vitality for the chase he amply makes up for in the strength and volume of his roar. As the lion begins to roar, the herd flees in the opposite direction where they meet the young hunters of the pride. Meade suggests the feeling that the world is going to end is represented by the roar of the elder lion. As the story portrays, sometimes the strategy for survival is counter-intuitive and we must go towards the roar. To go towards this roar, we must face our fears. Meade notes that the root word for fear is the same as for "fare," as in thoroughfare. Fear means "to go through," find our way through to a place of deeper understanding (p.6).

Turning to the root meanings of the concepts of sustaining health and wellness, I reexamine these terms in light of this new direction. Dunn (1959) defines wellness in the article "High-Level Wellness for Man and Society" as the balance of body, mind, and spirit that contributes to an overall feeling of well-being. Well-being is defined in *The American Heritage Dictionary of the English Language* (1981) as "the state of being happy, healthy, and prosperous" (p. 1454). Each of these terms harkens back to "well." One definition of well is "to rise and surge from an inner source" (p. 1454). The literal root meaning of sustain is to "hold up from below" (p. 1296). When we think of prospering, Americans often think of material success. Yet as we delve into the etymology of material, we find that its Latin root is "mater," meaning mother. In Greek this was "meter" and harkens back to Demeter, who is the goddess of produce and grains. The "De" in Demeter means earth (*www.etymonline.com*). This suggests that we are unable to truly prosper, archaic root meaning to "flourish and thrive" (American Heritage Dictionary, p. 1051), without also attending to the health of our mother earth.

Sarah Anne Edwards (2008) writes of eco-anxiety as an intelligent response to the very real threat that the world as we have known it may be coming to an end. Global warming, resource depletion, extinction of species and plants, changing habitats, increases in fire and other environmental crises are having far reaching affects. In fact, she observes, they are connected to our worsening economic and social pressures, such as rising cost of food staples, housing, utilities, and transportation and play a role in our loss of economic opportunities. It is our collective economic and ecological survival that is currently being challenged. Edwards notes that "we may face an extended series of minor and significant losses throughout our lifetime that will erode the constants that underlie our sense of security" (p. 2). How is it possible to look at this without fear?

Michael Meade (2008) characterizes fear as the great awakener. "Healthy fear wakens the soul and guides it to greater connections to the living Soul of the World" (p. 6). Meade further counters the whole premise of security. He suggests that "nature is itself ever-changing, always cooking something up and shape-shifting and starting things over again" (p.18). He recalls a poet's quip that false security is the only kind there is. Indeed he notes our current conditions are essential to "find our true selves and the dream threaded into our lives from before it began" (p. 6). *The conditions we find ourselves in are the necessary conditions we must go through in order to find our true selves.* What he is suggesting is that these global conditions have meaning, purpose, and intention.

He maintains there have always been troubles in the world, and the world has always seemed to be held together by a slender thread. Turning to the roar at times like these entails preserving the beauty and meaning in our individual lives and recognizing the preciousness of all of life. Meltzer and Williams (1988) suggest the ability to apprehend beauty is connected to the recognition of loss and the passage of time. To authentically respond to times such as these, we are called upon to draw deeply from our own roots and bring forth that which we have been born to bring to the world. In becoming wholly ourselves we are able to add to the healing of our world.

Seeds

To be wholly ourselves. To know who we are and what we bring to life that expresses our unique gifts and understandings. How many of us feel challenged by that task? There are many good reasons for this. Most of us have had to adapt to the misunderstandings of our culture and perhaps our families. For many of us, education has been a process of having to absorb the thoughts of others. We are taught how to think, be, and act, rather than supported in discovering who we are.

James Hillman (1996), archetypal psychologist and author, writes in *The Soul's Code* that we are much like the acorn that carries the design of a mature tree within it. Drawing upon Plato's Myth of Er, Hillman describes how each soul arrives at birth with an inner Daemon that carries one's inherent knowing. The conditions of the soil and quality of the nutrients help determine how much of each individual's unique shape is expressed.

A seed story that has brought me to my life's work comes to mind. During my 13th year I attended a summer long

Hebrew-speaking camp in Ontario. It was the practice at this camp to celebrate the Sabbath in a full and integrated way. The Jewish Sabbath begins on Friday evening because time is measured according to the moon. We began preparing for our Sabbath celebration on Friday morning after breakfast, when we cleaned up our cabins and the camp common areas. The campers in each cabin would take their weekly showers and dress in white clothes. Afterwards, we gathered in an outdoor forest chapel where we would have Kabbalat Shabbat, a welcoming the Sabbath service.

The Kabbalat Shabbat service traditionally includes the Lecha Dodi prayer. This prayer was written by a kabbalist, Rabbi Shlomo Halevi Alkabetz, in the 16th century in Safed. In Lecha Dodi, the Shechina, the feminine, immanent manifestation of the sacred, is welcomed. The kabbalists would don their finest white clothes and go out into the fields to greet the Sabbath bride as the sun was setting and bring her into their house of prayer. In current practice, when the last verse of this prayer is sung, the congregation turns to the door to sing and welcome the Sabbath Queen. It is important to note that much of what I am explaining about this prayer and its origins was unknown to me consciously the summer of my 13th year. As we sang this prayer one Friday evening, we turned at the last verse towards the cypress trees behind us. I looked about me and noticed all of the trees were shimmering with a golden light. Then I looked down at my body and noticed I was shimmering as well with this same light.

In Hebrew the word for wilderness is mid'bar – that which resonates. In this moment, I directly experienced the meaning of the mystical Kaballah creation myth, as interpreted by Isaac Luria (1534-1572): *In the beginning the Ein Sof – The One Without Limits – emanated creative sparks which became covered with matter creating all life forms. It is our task to recognize the Sacred Spark in all things thereby reconnecting with the Source of all life* (Vital, 2008). Knowing emerges through sensory perception and then moves to thoughts and ideas (Winkler, 2003). While understanding the illumination I experienced that Sabbath eve has been a life-long endeavor, I knew at a young age that everything was different than what I had previously thought or imagined.

Much later (about 27 years) I encountered horticultural therapy when studying the effect of the San Francisco Sheriff's Department's Garden Project on the lives of chemically dependent county jail inmates (Rice 1993, Rice &

Spring planting. (Photo by Christine Capra)

Remy, 1998). Horticultural therapy is a treatment modality that utilizes gardening to help clients adapt to the challenges life has brought them. It spans a continuum from occupational therapy in hospital settings, to community gardening for the homeless.

Our research showed that the inmates who participated in the garden project used fewer substances post-release and had a greater desire for help. The desire for help was viewed as containing an implicit hope for a better future. The hope generated through a direct, intimate encounter with nature and the cultivation of life enabled some students of the Garden Project to face the difficult challenges of recovery from chemical dependency.

When doing research for the literature review for my study on the Garden Project, I came across a reference to Edith Cobb's (1993) *The Ecology of Imagination in Childhood*. The title intrigued me and I tracked it down. In this book, Cobb looked at the biographies and autobiographies of 300 creative people. She discovered that each person described a period in their lives when they had an experience in nature that brought them synergistically to an understanding of their essential work in the world. In a sense we could say they experienced their seed potential expressing its essence under the right natural condition. A significant contribution that horticultural therapy can bring to the conversation regarding health and wellness is the recognition that we are seeds needing to express our true natures for our individual and collective well-being. When we enter the garden, we are also planting our selves.

Psyche and Soil

Carl Jung emphasized the role nature plays in supporting our psychological health. He observed that our psyche is best understood in relation to nature; we experience daily and seasonal variations and go through cycles of death and rebirth (1960). Jung maintained much of our current predicament (which he foresaw clearly by the end of his life in 1961) emerged from the modern prejudice of over valuing the conscious mind (1977)[2]. Jung notes that despite our attempts to control nature, we are still at her effect. He observed it was as if "our consciousness had somehow slipped from its natural foundations and no longer knew how to get along with nature's timing" (1969, PAR. 802). Jung's prescription was "that every human should have a plot of land so that their instincts could come to life again" (1977, p. 201). For Jung, these instincts represented connection and relationship to the non-human world and the depth of our unconscious archetypal psyche, which contains 3 million years of experience living in the natural world. Jung theorized that just as we inherit physical genetic material that has been honed over millennia to foster our survival, we too inherit archetypal knowledge that provides us with the psychological tools to survive. When this connection is made, Michael Meade movingly suggests a doorway opens that leads to the renewing capacity of the Old Mind – "the inner ancestor who carries our instincts for survival and our intuitions of creation" (2008, p. 9).

Yet the question remains, is there time to pull out of our growing ecological peril? In truth, I fear not. What then can horticultural therapy or nature offer to support us? Jung maintained, "the wheel of time could not be turned back. Things can, however, be destroyed and renewed" (1975 p. 209). In medicine wheel teachings, which are directly drawn from nature, death is not an ending (Star Blanket & Dream Weaver, 2009). As we note in each season, there is birth, life, death and rebirth into the next cycle.

In exploring this area of endings and beginnings, Michael Meade observes "when there is no time left at all, it is time for the eternal connections to be rediscovered" (2008, p. 13). Indeed he rekindles our understanding of apocalypse by explaining that it means "to lift the veil between one thing and another" (p. 24). "When things unravel before our very eyes, when people become lost and the world seems to have lost its bearings," Meade suggests, "it is lost ideas and ancient imaginations that seek to be found again" (p. 25). It is a time of returning to the garden to allow nature to affect us and bring forward our conscious participation in the great wheel of life.

Joni Mitchell's voice enters my mind and with a few short quick keystrokes, the words are in front of me on the screen and the internet radio is playing *Woodstock*, (1970)

I'm going to camp out on the land
I'm going to try an' get my soul free
We are stardust
We are golden
And we've got to get ourselves
Back to the garden

Nature helps us move beyond our limited human identification and provides us with intimations of the sacred. Gershon Winkler (2003), a rabbi who's research, writing, and teaching has focused on recovering and reclaiming the indigenous roots of Judaism, says this of the life crisis that brought him to his life's work:

> …it had to do with a deeper yearning that had been buried beneath layers and layers of living my life the way that it had been defined for me by everyone *but* me. This long unheeded longing had to do with retrieving my ancestral roots as a tribal, earth conscious people engaged in an intimate relationship with the land (p. xviii).

Winkler titled his book on Jewish indigenous wisdom *The Magic of the Ordinary*. He affirms it is in the direct experience of the "so-called ordinary, mundane, material existence" that we can discover the mystery we often attribute to more transcendent realms (p. xxii).

This observation is also found in the theology of Emanuel Swedenborg (1688-1772). Swedenborg was a Swedish scientist, philosopher, Christian mystic, and theologian. The Swedenborg Society has compiled a list of reknown artists and thinkers who have noted his influence including: William Blake, , Henry James, Sr., Ralph Waldo Emerson, William Butler Yeats, Walt Whitman, D.T. Suzuki and Carl Jung (Writers Influenced by Swedenborg, N.D).) He was a prolific thinker and writer whose careful empiricism brought him to an appreciation for the organic wisdom found in the study of nature, medicine and physiology (Frankiel, 2003). Swedenborg attempted to reintroduce to science the earlier understanding found in Egyptian and Greek thought, as well as in indigenous cultures, that there are direct correspondences between nature and the Divine Realm. Swedenborg was not merely speaking about symbolic or allegorical reflections. Rather he proposes through direct and conscious engagement with nature, we learn to live our lives with meaning and reverence and come to know the unseen heavenly realms (Toksvig, 1948).

Plant Ancestors

What of the plants the horticultural therapist work with? What part do they play teaching us about health and wellness?

"Who are you?" Star Blanket asked when I first met him just after completing my doctoral dissertation on the Garden Project. I felt compelled to tell him the story of my experience in the Cypress forest. Star Blanket drew a circle (medicine wheel) on a blank piece of paper and placed a few words at the cardinal points and within the center of the circle and described simply what the trees had in store for me.

In an instant, I recognized my dissertation was not an end point; rather it was an entry into a deeper passage. I wanted to know more about the wisdom available through our conscious engagement with the natural world. Star Blanket explained that the plants are our ancestors. Plants populated the earth before we arrived and in fact created the necessary conditions for our ability to live and survive here. He spoke of how the trees were the communicators of the natural world. When one receives a vision of their work or a new name from Great Spirit, a tobacco bag is tied to the tree and the tree lets all the worlds know of you. The trees were mirroring to me my true nature. I opened to the possibility of more conversations with the natural world.

Claire Cooper Marcus (1990) was able to observe the communication between plants and humans as an intern at Findhorn in Scotland. The Findhorn community began with a few people living on unemployment, who moved

> Nature helps us move beyond our limited human identification and provides us with intimations of the sacred.

to a trailer park on the Scottish coast. They started a garden by their trailer and struggled to grow anything in the sandy soil. These people were long-standing practitioners of Christian Insight Meditation. They began to hear the voices of plants in their meditations, which made suggestions for improving the growth of their garden. They felt they had nothing to lose and began to follow the directions of these plant devas or spirits. Miraculously they started to produce gigantic vegetables that caught the attention of others who believed something magical was happening in this garden. Many people were drawn to this area and a community was formed. Their meditations, gardening, and communal life were an abiding study of a co-creative relationship with nature and spirit. Cooper Marcus concluded that "gardens are places of reconnection with the intuitive, right brain functions, with holistic, ecological thinking" (p. 32).

Michael Pollan notes that plants have been evolving longer than we, particularly in the area of developing new co-evolutionary strategies for surviving. We sometimes fail to appreciate what plants accomplish because we humans place a value on mobility and miss the internal work plants are doing with their biochemistry in order to cultivate the partners they need to survive. In *Botany of Desire*, Pollan turns our usual human way of thinking on its ear, by confronting the assumption that intentionality is only a human property. Plants that successfully develop qualities that attract insects to help them reproduce have a better chance to survive. So too, plants that develop intimate partnerships with humans are showing evolutionary fitness that supports their continued existence. According to Pollan, plants, perhaps better than humans, understand that evolution favors interdependence.

Plants teach us the value of experimentation in adapting to changing environmental conditions. Each apple contains within its star pattern of seeds five new potential apple types. Not all of these experiments are successful; nature does not promise this or require it. How often as humans are we caught in patterns that do not support our own evolution? We can certainly learn to be freer in expressing the various seeds of our nature that we carry within us. We may face some failures, that is true, but the willingness to take this risk may bring about new growth in surprising ways.

Heather. (Photo by Jean Hutchinson)

Plants teach us that growth takes time and goes through many stages. In my work with Star Blanket, he taught me to plot new projects according to their moon co-creation cycles. There are 13 moon cycles in a year. Each can be linked to a stage in the cycle of creation. The stages of manifesting are (beginning in the east of the wheel): Seed, Union, Egg, Sprout, Root, Trunk, Budding, Flower, Fruit, Return, Compost, Silence, and Renewal (2009, pp. 124-130). When we birth new ideas, such as horticultural therapy programs to promote and sustain wellness, it can be helpful to think of the stages these ideas will go through in growing on this Earth. This awareness is medicine in a culture that values the instant at the expense of maturation.

Realm of Time

Herein lies a paradox. I find myself noting ever more clearly the passage of time, along with my growing anxiety over the slowness of our collective response to our environmental peril. Yet the growth of consciousness can not be rushed. Pollan notes that our greatest happiness arrives "in such moments, during which we feel as though we've sprung free from the tyranny of time -- clock time of course, but also historical, psychological time and sometimes even mortality" (2002, p. 164). Michael Meade proposes, "In the end or near it, the real issue isn't the future of humanity, but the presence of eternity" (2008, p. 24).

In his seminal book *The Sabbath*, Abraham Joshua Heschel speaks of the Sabbath as architecture in time (1951). He notes that we tend to think of time passing and passing ever more quickly. What we perceive is the passing of our human, material built world. When we are able to stop our doing, and enter a moment of quiet non-doing, we access the part of our experience that is eternal and timeless. These intimations of a larger knowing are found in the garden and in nature.

Horticultural therapy supports health and wellness by fostering engagement with our earth mother. This in turn catalyzes our connection to ancestral wisdom, archetypal knowledge, and spiritual understanding and provides access to the regenerative magic of natural cycles. Horticultural therapy teaches us respect and appreciation for the soul renewal possible when we are involved in the co-creation of life.

In closing I would like to share two stories that illuminate the magic and mystery of our interconnectedness. Last August, my wife, Rohana, and I attended a Beaver Festival in Martinez, CA just across the San Pablo Bay from where we live. The small business area that comprises downtown Martinez is situated along Alhambra Creek. The creek had become degraded over the years and was used as an unofficial dump site. A local environmental group took on a wetland restoration project in this area about 5 years ago. The following winter, a large rain storm brought a beaver couple into the creek. Seeing the neighborhood had improved, they decided to take up residency. Dams and a lodge were built, and the family quickly expanded. Some business owners became concerned that the dam was raising the water level and placing the foundations of their businesses at risk. They asked the town council to relocate or exterminate the beavers. This generated uproar in the community, and the organization Worth a Dam was born. They organized and attended meetings, had engineering studies done, and developed a win-win solution. A "Castor Master," flexible tubing, was placed through the main dam, to control the water levels. The beaver family expanded and did such a nice job with the area that a mink family moved in as well. Worth a Dam created the beaver festival that we attended. While we were waiting during the dusk hours for the beavers to appear, it occurred to me that horticultural therapists could develop community projects that restored natural habitats and helped to cultivate and reintroduce native (and in California and the Western U.S., drought resistant) plants. Clearly working to create a healthier natural environment will enhance the well-being of horticultural therapy clients.

I am grateful for the opening nature has afforded me and appreciative of the guidance I have received from Star Blanket and Stephanie Rainbow Lightening Elk while training in their mystery school. Rohana began her studies with them a year and a half before I did. She came back from a 10 day retreat in the Panhandle Forest of Northern Idaho and told me about a ceremony she participated in called *Walk of the Wolf*. Sitting around the campfire one moonless evening, the participants were asked to go out into the forest without flashlights and have an experience or communication with the non-human world to bring back to the circle. As I listened to her story, I could feel panic arise in me. Growing up in a well-built human city, Pittsburgh, I had a lot of fear of wild nature. I knew that there were lions and bears in Northern Idaho.

When I decided to pursue the same training, I knew that this walk of the wolf ceremony would come one night. I had almost two years to obsess and stress before it actually arrived. In a sense, I had more work and more opportunity because my fear had aged and grown in strength during this time. The last thing our teachers said to us as we were leaving the campfire was to remember to speak to the creatures and let them know we were coming into the forest for a ceremony, not to be anyone's dinner.

Let me step back for a moment. The area where we set up camp, Lightening Creek, was undeveloped; there were no bathrooms, or even outhouses. When nature called, we went out to secluded areas with shovel in hand. After a few days, I became skilled at looking for soft places in the earth out of the range of tree roots to dig my hole. The night of the Walk of the Wolf was dark, although the stars were glistening in their multitude. In an act of bravery, I left my glasses back at the camp because I could not see with them any ways. In fact, part of the design of the ceremony was to develop seeing not connected to our outer senses. The first thing I noticed was that the plants that grew in the areas between the trees where I had dug my holes possessed a luminescence in the dark. I was surprised to see that these plants I had been feeding (so to speak) were providing lit pathways to follow through the darkness. Most of the time. these plants guided me past the trees; on occasion I did take a dive over a tree root. I would get up, thank the tree for not killing me, and continue on. The further I went, the more I realized that the fear I had anticipated being a part of this experience was not there. I realized I was not all alone, perhaps a bigger fear than even meeting an animal. Rather I began to feel a presence. At times I could see glimmers of lights moving, and had the sense of consciousness, perhaps spirits of nature. Rather than feeling panic, I felt peace, connection and mystery.

In actuality, our minds are *of* nature and when we remain cognizant of this, we discover plants, as well as all of our other relations, are continuously sending us tweets that can illuminate our way in this world. We find this guidance expressed in the voice of an elder in the following poem by David Wagoner.

Lost

Stand still. The trees ahead and bushes beside you
Are not lost. Wherever you are is called Here,
And you must treat it as a powerful stranger,
Must ask permission to know it and be known.

—David Wagoner

From the book *Traveling Light: Collected and New Poems,* published by the University of Illinois Press in 1999

---

[1] This article is drawn from a keynote talk given on October 1, 2009 at the American Horticultural Therapy Association's (AHTA) annual conference Sustaining Health & Wellness Through Horticultural Therapy, in Pasadena, California. The American Horticultural Therapy Association was formed in 1973 to support the development and recognition of horticultural therapy as a unique treatment intervention. Gardens have been known to be curative and peaceful since ancient times. In the U.S., Benjamin Rush, a signer of the Declaration of Independence and the "Father of American Psychiatry," reported that gardens were curative for mental illness. In the 1940's horticultural therapy was utilized in the treatment of hospitalized war veterans. Currently, horticultural therapy is practiced in senior facilities, homeless shelters, prisons, rehabilitation hospitals, schools and hospices in the U.S, Japan, Australia, New Zealand, and Europe.

[2] I thank Meredith Sabini, Ph.D., for researching and gathering together all of Jung's writings on nature in The earth has a soul: The nature writings of C.G. Jung. (2002. Berkeley: North Atlantic Books.

References

Blanket, S., and Weaver, D. (2009). *Coyote goes global: A modern journey of forgotten ways.* Hampshire, England: O Books.

Cobb, E. (1993). *The ecology of imagination in childhood.* Dallas: Spring Publications.

Dunn, H. L. (1959). High-level wellness for man and society. *American Journal of Public Health*, 49 (6), 786-792.

Edwards, S. A. (2008, March 20). Eco-anxiety: An intelligent response. Article posted to http://eco-anxiety.blogspot.com

Etymology. (n.d.) In *Online Etymology Dictionary.* Retrieved from http://etymonline.com.

Frankiel, T. (2003, January 9). A review of Emanuel Swedenborg: The development of his thought. *The Global Spirit.* Retrieved from http://www.metanexus.net/magazine.

Heschel, A. J. (1951). *The Sabbath: Its meaning for modern man.* New York: Farrar, Straus and Giroux.

Hillman, J. (1996). *The soul's code: In search of character and calling.* New York: Random House.

Jung, C. G. (1960). Stages of life. In R. F. C. Hull (Trans.) *The collected works of C. G. Jung: Structure and dynamics of the psyche* (Vol. 8). Princeton, NJ: Princeton University Press, Bolligen Series XX. (Original work oublished 1947).

Jung, C. G. (1970). Civilization in transition. In R. F. C. Hull (Trans.) *The collected works of C. G. Jung* (Vol. 10). Second Edition. Princeton, *NJ: Princeton University Press, Bolligen Series XX..*

Marcus, C. C. (1990). The garden as metaphor In M. Francis, & R. T. Hester, Jr. (Eds.), *The meaning of gardens* (pp. 26-33). Cambridge, MA: The MIT Press.

McGuire, W. and Hull, R. F. C., (1977). C. G. Jung speaking: Interviews and encounters. Princeton, NJ: Princeton University Press.

Meade, M. (2008). *The world behind the world: Living at the ends of time.* Seattle: GreenFire Press.

Meltzer, D. and Williams, M. H., (1988). *The apprehension of beauty: The role of the aesthetic conflict in development, art and violence.* Perthshire, Scotland: Clunie Press.

Mitchell, J. (1970). Woodstock. *Lady of the canyon* [Album]. Burbank, CA: Reprise

Morris, W. (Ed.), (1981). *The American heritage dictionary of the English language.* Boston: Houghton Mifflin.

Pollan, M. (2002). *The botany of desire: A plant's eye view of the world.* New York: Random House.

Rice, J. S. (1993). *Self development and horticultural therapy in a jail setting.* Unpublished doctoral dissertation, San Francisco School of Psychology, San Francisco.

Rice, J. S. and Remy, L. L. (1998). Impact of horticultural therapy on psychosocial functioning among urban jail inmates. *Journal of Offender Rehabilitation*, 26 (3/4), 169-191.

Sabini, M. (Ed.), (2002). *The earth has a soul: The nature writings of C.G. Jung.* Berkeley: North Atlantic Books.

The Swedenborg Society. (N.D.) Writers influenced by Swedenborg. Retrieved from http://www.swedenborg.org.uk

Toksvig, S. (1948). *Emanuel Swedenborg: Scientist and mystic.* New Haven, CT.: Yale University Press.

Vital, C., (2008). *The tree of life: The palace of adam kadmon – Chayyim Vital's*

Introduction to the Kabbalah of Isaac Luria.(D. W. Menzi & Z. Padeh, Trans.) New York: Arizal Publications (Original work published 1910).

Wagoner, David. (1999). Traveling light: Collected & new poems. "Lost." Champaign, IL: University of Illinois Press, p. 10.

Winkler, G. (2003). *Magic of the ordinary: Recovering the shamanic in Judaism.* Berkeley: North Atlantic Books.

(Photo by Gary Newman)

Dreams Are Pure Nature

Meredith Sabini

Do we dream about the earth? We dream about our friends and family, our work and creative projects, so why would we not dream about this planet we call home? Perhaps because its scale is too big. We live in a certain town, a certain neighborhood, a certain hut or home. We Homo sapiens are rather small creatures, more comfortable when contained in proportionately small geographies. As a child, I used to stand under the night sky and wonder why I didn't fall off the earth; it doesn't take much to awaken that sense of fear and marvel, even now. Unless you happen to be an explorer seeking the source of the Nile or a world traveler frequently crossing borders from one continent to another, the globe itself would not be your daily landscape.

But something is happening today that challenges our former identification with a tribe, a culture, a country, inviting us to recognize the ways we are part of a larger interconnected whole. We now know, for instance, about the rain for-

Ocean sunset. (Photo by Gary Newman)

ests and ozone hole, the polar ice caps and loss of species. Whenever there is a common threat, our sense of identity tends to expand so that we can come into relation to the shared problem. Therefore we might expect dreams about the planet to be on the rise.

Our Western view of dreams itself has been too small, too confined by the dominant egocentric notion that we dream primarily about ourselves, a view not found in other cultures. We also refer to "having" dreams. I want to introduce a different possibility: that dreams *come to us*. We might speak about receiving dreams, witnessing dreams, being instructed by dreams. This shift in perspective will come into play when we look at dreams about the earth.

Some years ago, friends and I were looking for land in the country where we could settle. We'd had it with the modern world and sorely needed to live in a more natural locale, at a more natural pace. In addition to homes for ourselves, we were thinking of starting a retreat center for those in the helping professions. We looked at both vacant land and at properties with dwellings we could convert. After almost a year of searching, we found a place that seemed right: several forty-acre parcels on a remote mountainside two hours from the central Bay Area. No services were in yet. We drove out a dirt road, then hiked around. It was lovely.

That night I had a dream, in words: "*This* is how Western civilization spreads." I woke from it in shock. In the inimitable way of dreams, this stated the simple truth. By purchasing

---

Meredith Sabini, Ph.D., a Licensed Psychologist in the field since 1972, is founder and director of The Dream Institute of Northern California. She practices living sustainably, teaches Ecopsychology and Evolutionary Psychology, and is editor of *The Earth Has a Soul: Jung on Nature, Technology, and Modern Life*.

this land and building homes on it, we would be doing the very thing that we abhorred: extending the reach of civilization further into a wilderness area of the planet, fostering the cancer that has eaten up pasture land, open plains, and forested hillsides like the one we'd seen. I called my companions and told them the dream. I reaffirmed my preference to only buy something with existing structures we could remodel, and thus preserve.

Is this an "earth dream"? Surely it is. It is about the earth itself, about our attitude toward land, and how we live on it. The dream did not make any value judgment; it merely held up a reflective mirror in which the actual situation was depicted. The judgment call was mine to make. I could have said to myself, Well, it will be okay because we will build by hand, use soil from buildings' footprints to make adobe, put in solar, and not spread civilization as others have—or some such noble-sounding rationalization. But to do this lacked integrity.

The dream about spreading Western civilization could have come to others as well; it is what C. G. Jung called a "collective" dream. In a 1931 interview for the New York *Sun*, Jung gave an account of how collective concerns express themselves in dreams:

> We are awakening a little to the feeling that something is wrong in the world . . . We are suffering, in our cities, from a need of simple things . . . These things are being expressed in thousands of dreams. Women's dreams, men's dreams, the dreams of human beings, all having much the same collective primal unconscious mind—the same in the central African Negro I lived among and the New York stockbroker—and it is in our dreams that the body makes itself aware to our mind. The dream is in large part a warning of something to come (McGuire, 1977, p. 49).

Jung was far ahead of the times by recognizing that dreams are not limited to our individual lives but arise out of the cumulative experience of our species, which has been millions of years in the making. Based on contemporary neuroscience, it is now established that REM dreaming is a 140-million-year-old function in all mammals and associated with survival via the development of the nervous system and long-term memory storage. (See Parman 1979; Revonsuo 2000; Snyder 1996; Stevens 1993; Winson 2002.) Jung put this very clearly when he said,

> Dreams ... are pure nature; they show us the unvarnished natural truth, and ... give us back an attitude that accords with basic human nature when our consciousness has strayed too far from its foundation and run into an impasse.
>
> To concern ourselves with dreams is not our ego-consciousness reflecting on itself; rather, it turns its attention to the objective actuality of the dream as a communication or message from the unconscious, unitary soul of humanity . . . the trunk from which the ego grew (Jung 1970, par 317-18).

In it attempt to maintain homeostasis, the evolved dreaming mind will point out when we are out of balance with ourselves or at risk of jeopardizing the balance of other living systems, as it did in my dream of spreading Western civilization. It was as if the dreaming mind said to me, "You have a contagious disease and are about to introduce it into the new environment you've found." The dream placed me and the earth in an active and interconnected relationship, as if the earth were an extension of my body and I a part of its body.

I once met a woman who founded an environmental center and school where people could learn permaculture, survival medicine, tracking skills, integrated pest management, rainwater collection, urban food forests, and the like. My book of Jung's nature writings, *The Earth Has a Soul*, had just come out and she invited me to give a talk at the school. We met so she could show me around; she kept me waiting a moment while she finished a cigarette. Sitting face to face with her over lunch, I noticed the pallid, dry texture of her skin, evidence of the contraction of blood vessels that accompanies nicotine addiction. She alluded, embarrassedly, to her smoking. I responded, "*This* too is earth," touching my chest. She looked surprised, even puzzled, so I said more. "Everyone thinks nature is *out there*. But we're composed of the same balance of elements as the earth. Our bodies are our own small portion of earth." She admitted she'd never thought of it this way. Two years later, I learned through a mutual friend that she'd died of lung cancer.

I tell this story because it illustrates the dilemma I have: where does the "earth" end and the human being, I, begin? Stated like this, we can see the fundamental error of this kind of dualistic thinking. This is the theme of Jung's 1927 essay, "Mind and Earth," in which he gives this wonderful definition:

> archetypes are . . . the hidden foundations of the conscious mind, or, to use another comparison, the

roots which the psyche has sunk not only in the earth in the narrow sense but in the world in general (Jung, 1970, par. 53).

Do we dream about the earth in the narrow sense of the rocks and trees and soil? Perhaps, but not too often. We do dream about the earth in the broader sense of the world or life in general. Jung came back to the danger of dualism in his final essay for *Man and His Symbols*, saying that if we have *only* an image, "it is merely a word-picture, like a corpuscle with no electrical charge." But when the image—or dream—is charged with numinosity or meaning, "it is a piece of life," because the full archetype is "living matter" (Jung, 1976, par. 589).

One of my favorite earth-dreams features mushrooms as the main character. I don't have these dreams very often, but they always have the same form: I come upon a huge blooming of 'shrooms, not a single variety but many, though not species I recognize; sometimes the crop is as large as a field of poppies and other times they are tightly packed into a planting bed or around a tree trunk. The feeling in the dream is always the same: I am surprised to encounter the mushrooms and astonished they could grow so prolifically. The dreams have the combination Jung alluded to—a universal image plus a vibrant, meaningful emotion.

I have been an amateur mycologist—mushroom aficionado—for thirty-five years, initially having gotten intrigued during the daily route from my San Francisco apartment to a bus stop, which took me through a wonderfully unkempt urban park where, to my astonishment, I spotted lavender mushrooms! (They were Blewits.) Like termites, mushrooms occupy the unique and vital ecological niche of being recyclers. They do their job in the interstices of the living and the dying earth. By consuming the latter, they make possible the former. Mushrooms you see on a rotting log on the forest floor, for example, are transforming that decaying wood into humus. Most mushrooms are the fruit of an underground root system known as mycelium. The largest known organism on this planet is a mushroom, many miles in diameter (Paul Stamets, TED Conference, March 2008).

In light of these facts, what might dreams about mushrooms symbolize? I believe they represent the capacity of life to renew itself from unseen sources, from the ground up. My dreams about mushrooms seem to coincide with new phases in life, and I have come to think they signify emergence. Looked at with a limited lens, mushrooms are simply part of the earth in the narrow sense; but looked at more broadly, they take on the archetypal significance of a dynamic process of renewal found in the world in general.

There are other common dream motifs taken from nature that depict various life processes: flowing rivers symbolizing the force of life that carries us along; rains that wash away our mental fog or haze; earthquakes that coincide with a deep emotional upheaval. Tornadoes, floods, lightning, freezes, and other manifestations of nature may appear in dreams as metaphors for the ebb and flow of our emotional, mental, and spirited aspects: our tumultuous outbursts, gushings, sudden shocks of energy, cold withdrawal.

> Tornadoes, floods, lightning, freezes, and other manifestations of nature may appear in dreams as metaphors for the ebb and flow of our emotional, mental, and spirited aspects: our tumultuous outbursts, gushings, sudden shocks of energy, cold withdrawal.

Here is a dream about water that was shared at an annual dream retreat I lead: "I am at an artesian spring. I forgot to bring my camera, so I just try to sketch a picture of it." To understand the dream, we had to find out what distinguished this kind of spring from others. We learned that an artesian well is made by drilling through a dense layer of rock; the water below then rises to the surface like a geyser. The dream contains the classic storyline about how, at times, we have to dig down deep and penetrate our own dense layers in order to release the waters of life trapped below.

A recent earth-dream of mine concerned the melting of the ice caps. It was a plain, unelaborated scene of a polar bear standing on a tiny floe of ice, looking at me with helpless appeal. Is this an outward-facing dream about the actual melting of the ice caps or is it a subjective picture of some aspect of my own nature that has previously been frozen out of life, and now wants to join in? This question has to be asked about any earth-related dreams we have; we cannot assume they refer only to outer situations we are already familiar with.

The dreams cited so far—about mushrooms, artesian springs, and ice floes—seem to be most meaningful if they are viewed and interpreted subjectively as relating to the personal life of the dreamer, even though they do draw on motifs from nature that are factual and objective. In 1917, Jung distinguished between dreams that were subjective, or purely personal, and those that were objective and could be interpreted without the dreamer's own associations (Jung, 1966, par 130). A historically important objective dream that can speak to all of us comes from *The Lichtenberg Reader* (1959, pp. 118-21), an anthology of the writings of Georg Lichtenberg, an eminent scientist and philosopher in the 1700s who was a Professor of Mathematics and Astronomy at the University of Gottingen. His work combined a religious sensibility with a passion for empirical investigation. Though no longer well known, Lichtenberg was admired and quoted by Kant, Goethe, Kierkegaard, Wittgenstein, and Freud. His dream, from around 1780, foreshadows the way Western science has come to treat the physical world and is stunning in its relevance to the state of our planet today. It is lengthy, so I paraphrase sections but quote the central dialogue between Lichtenberg and the invisible figure who speaks to him.

The dream opens with Lichtenberg soaring over the earth. He encounters an old man whose glorious appearance fills him with awe. The man hands him a mineral, saying, "You love to investigate nature. Here you shall see something which can be useful to you … Test it and tell me what you've found." It is a bluish-green sphere an inch in diameter, and nearby are all the instruments Lichtenberg will need.

"I shook it and put it to my ear. I raised it to my tongue. I wiped away some dust … rubbed it on my sleeve to test for electricity. I checked it against steel, glass, and a magnet, and determined its specific gravity… All the tests showed me that the mineral wasn't particularly valuable, not very different from marbles I'd bought at the Frankfurt Faire for a farthing."

Lichtenberg finds it to be composed of clay, iron, silica, salt, and some unknown elements. As he finishes, the old man appears again, and asks, "Do you know, mortal, what it is you tested?" "No, Immortal, I do not know," Lichtenberg said, casting himself at his feet. "Then know: it was, on a miniature scale, nothing less than—the whole earth."

"The earth? Great, eternal God! And the ocean and all that dwell within it—where are they?"

"They hang there on your cloth, you wiped them away."

"And the sea of air and all the glory of the dry land?"

"The sea of air? That is probably left over in that cup of distilled water. And as to your glory of the dry land, how can you ask such a question? That was the imperceptible dust; some is clinging here to your coat sleeve."

"But I didn't find a trace of silver and gold, which rule the globe!"

"Know then: with your blade you cut away all of Switzerland and the finest part of Sicily, and you completely ruined a whole stretch of Africa . . ."

Lichtenberg was silent. He felt he would give nine-tenths of the life remaining him to restore his "chemically destroyed earth," and begs for another chance. "Oh great immortal being, whoever thou art . . . enlarge a mustard seed to the thickness of the earth and allow me to examine the mountains and strata till the germ develops." The wisdom figure answers that already on earth such a granule has been magnified; he informs Lichtenberg that "before your transformation, you will not reach that other side of the curtain which you seek."

The Immortal then hands Lichtenberg a pouch and tells him to test what is inside. Lichtenberg pledges to be more careful. He is surprised to find only a book with a simple binding. Its language is not known, but the title page has the same command: "Test this, my son, chemically, and tell me what you have found." Lichtenberg wonders what use it would be to chemically test a book, knowing that it is merely rag and ink: the contents of the book are its essence. He says,

"Suddenly, things became clear in my mind and an irrepressible blush of shame came over me. Oh! I called, more and more loudly, I understand, I understand! Immortal being, forgive me; I comprehend your kindly reproof, I thank the Eternal that I can comprehend it."

Lichtenberg was indescribably moved, and awoke in awe. The dream report ends here with no further comment.

What was it Lichtenberg understood? That breaking down the visible world into its physical properties does not yield its essence? That dissecting can destroy what it studies? From high above the earth, Lichtenberg was shown a larger perspective. Referring to himself as a "man of feeling," Lichtenberg was distressed over his destructive actions and wants to redeem them by tending a seed to germination. But the spirit guide or wisdom figure tells him that until he himself is transformed, he will not be able to see the spirit inside matter. But he is given a second chance. In examining the book, Lichtenberg realizes that the essence lies in its *meaning,* that is, its spiritual essence, not its physical composition.

This dream was three hundred years ago, at a time when the separation between heart and mind was not as severe as it is today. Like the visionary dreams Black Elk had as a youth, Lichtenberg's seems to describe developments that would unfold in the coming centuries. Perhaps we are now historically at the close of the first scene of his dream, discovering just how destructive our handling of the world's natural resources has been and hoping we have a chance to mend our ways.

I wonder what sort of dreams Audubon had as he killed hundreds of birds to make his fine drawings or the researchers today who infect chimps with AIDS to study the disease. Were there dreams that trouble the scientists who cloned Dolly or who developed the cell phones that have resulted in soaring rates of brain tumors in children? The Immortal who invited Lichtenberg to chemically test two objects and provided the tools for doing so was simultaneously testing the man himself. He failed the initial test, but his sense of morality led him to ask for another chance. He then suc-

> In initiation rites, failing some part of a task is what activates shame, remorse, and humility in a seeker and can thereby serve to transform them into maturity. The hubris of our Western ways is finally being called into question; perhaps more humble ways of treating our globe will emerge.

ceeded in solving the koan or riddle put before him. In initiation rites, failing some part of a task is what activates shame, remorse, and humility in a seeker and can thereby serve to transform them into maturity. The hubris of our Western ways is finally being called into question; perhaps more humble ways of treating our globe will emerge.

C. G. Jung had a waking vision of the earth and a spirit within it, which I include here because of its immediacy and his reaction to it. Jung does not give the date or location, but merely says:

> I once experienced a violent earthquake, and my first, immediate feeling was that I no longer stood on the solid and familiar earth, but on the skin of a gigantic animal that was heaving under my feet. It was this image that impressed itself upon me, not the physical fact (Jung, 1969, par 331).

Jung was standing on the earth as it shook, but what image was he simultaneously seeing? A nature spirit? In a brief essay published in 1945, Jung lamented the loss of nature spirits and suggested that the banishment of incubi, succubi, wood-nymphs, melusines, and "the rest that terrify and tease mankind" has resulted in an unfathomable change in our emotional life. "It was the triumph of the Enlightenment that such things as nature-spirits did not exist," he said. "But it was merely that what one *imagined* such spirits to be that did not exist" (Jung, 1976, par 1368). Jung brings a perspective to matter and spirit that brings them back into relation, as they have not been since the Enlightenment:

> There is nothing without spirit, for spirit seems to be the inside of things . . . Whether that is our own psyche or the psyche of the universe we don't know, but if one touches the earth, one cannot avoid the spirit. And if one touches it in a friendly way ... the spirit of nature will be helpful ... We never pay attention, so we probably offend the spirit of things all the time ... (Douglas, 1997, p. 459)

In the 1957 Houston films, Jung adds that this is not his own idea but can be found in Democritus, who spoke of a *spiritus insertus atomis*, the spirit inserted in atoms. Jung said that psyche, or spirit, is "a quality of matter . . . it is simply the world seen from within" (McGuire & Hull, 1977, p. 303).

This interior aspect seems to be appearing in contemporary dreams with renewed force, as in this next example:

> I see a face deep in the earth. It seems male and becomes female.

We are a very young species that has won over from the gods not only fire but information about nuclear, genetic, and psi processes—and we use this information often without adequate training, moral scruple, or guidance from a wisdom source.

> I put my head down and hear a sound like an ancient chant, faint at first, it becomes louder as I listen. "I am the ancient mother, voice of wisdom buried in the earth. No one has heard me for so many years. My sorrow is deep. The time is now to return to the surface, to give voice to the wisdom. Can you hear me?"

The voice identifies itself as a maternal wisdom buried deep in the earth not heard in many years, which now will return to the surface. To the question of whether we, as the collective dreamer, hear this voice, the implied answer is no, truthfully, we have not.

In the next example, a young man dreamed of being immersed in the percolation of the particles we call soil:

> I'm in the soil and *am* the soil, which is percolating. Tiny crumbs of dirt and air are in constant motion, mingling with each other. They are not building towards anything, but just moving around at a constant contained speed. I think, "This is what it means *to be*. This perpetuates growth."

The dreamer had an experience of the molecules in their constant, steady motion. Does this depict matter per se or does it hint at the movement of the spirit, symbolized as air? The thought he has in the dream suggests the latter. In our modern Zeitgeist, *being* is often misperceived as laziness or inertia, in comparison with *doing*, which is the preferred, more active mode. He is shown the mystery that *being* is the basis of growth.

Can we say that these dreams are mainly subjective or mainly objective? This simplistic distinction no longer seems appropriate for these contemporary dreams in which the dreamer as the initiate is taken below ground and shown something of nature's mysteries. Of course they carried significance for the dreamers; but they also have an emotional effect when shared with others, for they touch on universal life processes that we need to more fully understand. I think of such dreams as being in the postmodern mode we might call *participatory* or *engaged*.

The next dream is similar but involves a group of people participating in a mystery rite in which the earth is shown to be alive:

> Friends gather at my house for a sacred purpose. One woman prepares red oxide soil, tenderly raking and patting it. I show others how to use the soil, which is alive, to imbue a stupa with aliveness. The stupa is built out of stones and sticks, triangular, like a teepee. The woman says, "The soil is about ready." I kneel down and touch my face to the soil, like it is a dear, precious loved one. I prepare myself by gathering my energy. We take the soil and create the living shape. We shove the soil into the stupa from bottom to top. The soil begins humming, then the stupa, and then all of us are humming, connected together.

The dream identifies the group's activity as a sacred ritual. Movement takes them not upward into transcendence over the earth but downward into direct contact with rich red soil. Through the caring touch of human hands, the soil is enlivened. Soon it starts to "hum," and eventually the people too are humming, as if their aliveness has increased in pitch.

A stupa, traditionally, is a Buddhist monument, perhaps originally a burial mound, with a center pole that represents the tree of life or axis of the universe. Masses of earth are raised on a platform and then faced with stones. The structure is often surrounded by a processional path. Of varying dimensions and degrees of elaborateness, stupas are found in every country where Buddhism exists. The stupa in this dream is made with ordinary sticks, as if to suggest that in its "ur-form," this sacred structure could be constructed by anyone, anywhere. The tending of the soil is the main focus, and through it the earth comes to life. The spirit in matter is revived.

The dreams we've looked at comment on the crisis of our times: whether we can live in balance with this planet, this earth, this globe. We are a very young species that has won over from the gods not only fire but information about nuclear, genetic, and psi processes—and we use this information often without adequate training, moral scruple, or guidance from a wisdom source. In the fossil record, it is very unusual that one single species would predominate during any given era. We assume we are the only species extant; empirical data spanning a hundred years concerning creatures variously known as Sasquatch, Big Foot, and Yeti—possibly other primates—is chronically ridiculed and marginalized (see Bindernagel, 1998; Shackley, M. 1983). What if we took the advice from Lichtenberg's teacher and treated the earth as if it were a book to be read and contemplated rather than dissected? What if we ourselves are seeds that need proper tending in order to grow into our full and balanced humanness?

It's risky to turn to dreams or any other source for omens about the future, but it's understandable that we are looking for omens today, because things aren't going so well on our home planet. I have chosen especially inspiring dreams to illustrate my thesis that this thing we call "the earth" is not unidimensional, as often assumed, but multidimensional. I have left out dreams containing more predictable themes of disaster and destruction, but, at our monthly Culture Dreaming program at The Dream Institute, we do hear them: dreams of standing amidst post-apocalyptic rubble, of wading through city streets submerged in melted ice, of running from black goop falling from the sky. With both the inspiring dreams presented here and the dark ones not presented, we always have to ask, what does a dream tell us that we don't already know?

Having taken you high above the earth with Lichtenberg and below ground to the ancient mysteries of soil and water, I want to close with an exceptionally ordinary dream. We will go back in time not to the 1700s but the 1800s; the setting is the South during the era of slavery. The dreamer is Harriet Tubman, the brave woman who pioneered the Underground Railroad, a link of human hands, black and white, that joined to help those escaping the cruel and inhumane status of indentured servitude.

It was via dreams and visions that Tubman knew which routes to use for escorting her charges. It is conjectured that following a head injury inflicted by a slave-owner, she developed second sight; she often would fall into a trance for just a few moments and see a safe route. Once, Tubman was leading four men down a country road and fell into this brief sleep, during which she was shown a river to cross and a cabin in which to hide. Soon, they did come to a river, but it looked too deep to ford. Tubman walked right in, and found a shoal; the men followed. On the other side was a cabin where a black family was living; they took in the runaways, saving them from the men and dogs on their trail (Moss, 2009, p. 186).

This is not an ordinary night dream but a clear vision of the earth as seen from within, which Tubman had while lying on the ground in a trance. The problem it solved was how to get four people from one section of ground, where their lives were in danger, to another section where they would be safe. The dream-vision showed a route that actually existed. I called this an "exceptionally ordinary" dream; this is an intentional oxymoron. In exceptional circumstances, such as when someone's life is at risk, dreams and visions may occur that show the way out. The dream-vision may seem exceptional at the time, but there is ample evidence that they often occur at such moments and therefore they are "ordinary" and even predictable (see Dossey, 2009; Eisenbud, 1970; Jaffe, 1963).

In 1997, I had a dream that repeated twice which said, in words, that the manic speed at which we are living today is putting our species at risk; it said, in words, that we are at risk of extinction. We have become "slaves" to a way of life that is unsustainable. Many of us are dreaming about this, dreaming about a new path we could follow. Tubman's experience may be emblematic for our situation today.

It may be that we are unable to solve current environmental, societal, and health care problems because we've been drawing only on the limited range of our conscious, waking selves. The dreaming mind, millions of years older, has a much broader bandwidth and thus provides access to the full spectrum of our human capacities and to suprapersonal ones as well. Western civilization is entering into a phase of decay. Let us not be too afraid of the dying process; let us trust in our ability to compost former ways of living so that they are transformed into the fresh ground out of which new ways of living can mushroom.

> "We should regard dreams as an endangered species, a casualty of technological advance ... Dreams are an oasis of spiritual vitality ... they represent our primordial habitat, our last wilderness ... and we must protect them with as much fervor as the rain forests, the ozone layer, the elephant, and the whale."
>
> —Anthony Stevens,
> *The Two-Million-Year-Old Self*,
> 1993, pp. 122-23.

References

Bindernagel, J. (1998). *North America's great ape: The Sasquatch.* Courtenay, BC: BeachcomberBooks.

Dossey, L. (2009). *The power of premonitions.* New York: Dutton (Penguin Group).

Eisenbud, J. (1970). *Psi and psychoanalysis.* New York: Grune & Stratton.

Jaffe, A. (1963). *Apparitions and precognitions.* New York: University Books.

Jung. C. G. (1964). "Mind and earth." In *Civilization in transition*, vol. 10, *Collected works of C. G. Jung.* Princeton, NJ: Princeton University Press.

_____. (1964). "The meaning of psychology for modern man." In *Civilization in transition*, vol. 10, *Collected works of C. G. Jung.* Princeton, NJ: Princeton University Press.

_____. (1966). *Two essays on analytical psychology.* Vol. 7, Collected Works of C. G. Jung. Princeton, NJ: Princeton University Press.

_____. (1969). "The structure of the psyche." In *The structure and dynamics of the psyche*, vol. 8, *Collected works of C. G. Jung.* Princeton, NJ: Princeton University Press.

_____. (1970). "The meaning of psychology for modern man." In *Civilization in transition*, vol. 10, *Collected works of C. G. Jung.* Princeton, NJ: Princeton University Press.

_____. (1976). "Marginalia on contemporary events." In *The symbolic life,* vol. 18, *Collected works of C. G. Jung.* Princeton, NJ: Princeton University Press.

_____. (1976). "Symbols and the interpretation of dreams." In *The symbolic life,* vol. 18, *Collected works of C. G. Jung.* Princeton, NJ: Princeton University Press.

Mautner, F. and H. Hatfield. (1959). *The Lichtenberg reader.* Boston: Beacon Hill Press.

McGuire, W. and R. F. C. Hull. (1977). *C. G. Jung speaking.* Princeton, NJ: Princeton University Press.

Moss, R. (2009). *The secret history of dreaming.* Novato, CA: New World Library.

Parman, S. (1979). "An evolutionary theory of dreaming and play." In *Forms of play of native North Americans.* Norbeek, E., ed. West Publishing Co.

Revonsuo, A. (2000). "The reinterpretation of dreams: an evolutionary hypothesis of the function of dreaming." *Behavioral and Brain Sciences* 23, 793-1121.

Sabini, M. (2002). *The earth has a soul: Jung on nature, technology, and modern Life.* Berkeley, CA: North Atlantic Books.

Shackley, M. (1983). *Still living? Yeti, Sasquatch, and the neanderthal enigma.* New York: Thames and Hudson.

Snyder, F. (1966). "Toward an evolutionary theory of dreaming." *American Journal of Psychiatry.* 123: 121-142.

Stevens, A. (1993). *The two-million-year old self.* College Station, TX: Texas A&M University Press.

Winson, J. (2002). "The meaning of dreams." *Scientific American.* v.12: 1, pp. 54-61.

(Photo by Gary Newman)

Giving Voice to the Earth Dreaming

Kimmy Johnson

Slot canyon. (Photo by Gary Newman)

Out of the great void before the beginning, the Spirit of All that Is dreamed all that Is into being. At the center of All that Is, at the core of each particle, atom, each cell, is the Dream before the beginning, the Dream without end. We are expressions, emanations, of that Dream, dreamed and dreaming.

I dream of a landscape of bones – the bones of the ancestors of all the Earth's creatures scattered across the land under a dark sky. White bones against a black and grey landscape. Life has receded back into the depths, leaving only the rocky skeleton of the Earth's creatures. I am alone, a witness to what was and what has come to pass.

Kimmy K. Johnson, Ph.D., teaches courses and workshops in ancestral consciousness and healing, dreams as indigenous knowledge, shamanic traditions of our ancestors, and writing at St. Mary's College of California, John F. Kennedy University, and the California Institute of Integral Studies. She completed doctoral work in Traditional Knowledge at the California Institute of Integral Studies. Her scholarship, writing and teaching explores remembrance of who we are, recovery of relationship with the Earth, and reconnecting with place, ancestors and stories. Her medicine offers healing of our relationships with self, community and the land. Email: kimmykj@gmail.com.

I wake from the dream staggered by grief. I am aware that my kind has brought on this devastation – I stand in the wreckage of human greed. The Earth is showing me what is happening to her and where it will lead. Yet even amidst the devastation, I feel the gentle presence of the Earth. I am like a child being led gently by her mother. I feel the Earth's tender care of me, and I feel her sorrow.

There are personal dreams and dreams that come through from a greater knowing, a vastness that extends far beyond the boundaries of a human life. This dream of the Earth's body came to me from that greater knowing – it came and tore at my heart. When given these dreams, these visions of what is ahead or what has happened long ago in the beginning, we are overwhelmed by their power and mystery. They burst through the layers of ego and self-concern, immersing us in the vast expanse of being.

As a child I was given a dream of remembering, a dream of death brought on the native people of the land of my birth by the US Cavalry. The dream showed me a horrifying and tragic happening that had taken place almost one hundred years before.

> I watch in terror and anguish as men in dark uniforms carry off a woman who is my mother. They come from the south, riding hard. All around me is terror and confusion as the horses spin and screams fill the air.

Forty years later I learn about the massacre at Blue Water Creek in Western Nebraska. General Harney and his force of 650 soldiers, dragoons and Calvary attacked an encampment of 250 Brulĕ and Cheyenne men, women and children camped along the banks of the creek. The year was 1855.

The dream came to me in 1947 or 1948. We were living less than four miles from the site of the massacre. I knew nothing of this "battle," and yet a dream came to me from the land, showing me the horror of that morning a hundred years ago. The land remembers. It holds our blood, our bones, our memories. The land remembered that day in September 1855, ...and it gave me the dream to carry until I could join in the remembering. The dream came to me through the land, a remembering dream that called me to serve the memory it carried.

"The dream is in the landscape and the landscape is in the dream." Apela Colorado, my mentor and friend, told me this when I was in graduate school studying traditional ways of knowing. Her words gave meaning to the remembering dream, a dream intricately woven into the landscape of my childhood. The landscape held that memory and then brought it alive in me.

How different my life might have been had I been taken as a child to talk with a traditional medicine man or woman, a shaman able to see into the mystery of the dream. Would this shaman have freed me from the shadow of that remembering? Would she have cast out the terror and set my feet back on a good and true path? But there was no shaman available to my mother or to me, no one who could weave me back into a whole and present moment, free from the horrors of the past. The dream sank in to my soul, buried there, waiting.

Yet the dream would not leave me; it called to me to hear the voices of children and mothers who died, the families torn apart. The land held those voices – the rolling Sandhills, the prairie winds, the waters of Blue Creek. And I heard their cries and the voices echoed inside me.

Days, years, decades passed. Whenever dreams were talked about, that was the dream that came to mind, vivid, charged as lightening. The images, the power remained shrouded in mystery. Yet there was an insistence about it that never subsided.

> What are these dreams that find us and will not let us go? These dreams shape our destinies in ways beyond imagining. They are harbingers of suffering and founts of healing in an individual life. These dreams also call us to healing and reconciliation with the land and with the history of that place.

What are these dreams that find us and will not let us go? These dreams shape our destinies in ways beyond imagining. They are harbingers of suffering and founts of healing in an individual life. These dreams also call us to healing and reconciliation with the land and with the history of that place. My own journey of remembrance culminated many years later in a ceremony led by a Lakota Holy Man. After hearing of my dream, the spirits instructed him to bring me to Pine Ridge in order that the souls of his ancestors who had been at Blue Water might be released, and that I and my family might be freed from suffering. That ceremony continues to work inside me, weaving me back in to the great web of life. I give thanks to the land, to the dream, and to the Holy Man who gave so freely of his medicine.

Dreams of the future, dreams of the past – the Earth holds all in her body, in her stones, in her waters. The people of the land, the indigenous ones, listened and learned from the Earth and all her creatures. In dreams they were shown where to find game, where to fish, where to bury their dead, and where to gather berries. Their dreams even showed them the trail up through the stars to be followed after death. Dreams and visions came to them from the plants, the animals, the wind, and streams. They listened and learned.

We too must follow in the steps of our ancestors. We begin where we standing. We listen deeply to the Earth, and to the

> Dreams of the future, dreams of the past – the Earth holds all in her body, in her stones, in her waters. The people of the land, the indigenous ones, listened and learned from the Earth and all her creatures.

dreams that come to us from her body. Our dreams offer pathways through not-knowing. We must listen and learn how to live lives that are in harmony with All that Is.

---

[1] For a history of the Battle of Blue Water Creek related from the perspective of the US government, soldiers and white settlers, see R. Eli Paul's <u>Blue Water Creek and the First Sioux War, 1854-1856</u>, University of Oklahoma Press (2004).

Spiritual Intelligence and the Body

Karen Ann Jaenke

Definitions of spiritual intelligence, along with identification of its specific skills and capacities, vary across authors. In accordance with the theory on intelligence and multiple intelligences, there is a tendency to understand spiritual intelligence as "a set of mental capacities," downplaying or entirely ignoring the body's role in spiritual intelligence. It is argued here that just as we can develop a discriminating mind, so we can develop a discriminating body; moreover the integration of the body's perceptual capacities is essential to the development a truly holistic spiritual intelligence.

The literature on intelligence and spiritual intelligence is embedded in Western culture's long-standing spirit-matter, mind-body and self-world dichotomies, with a tendency to favor the capacities of the mind over those of the body. The mind-body split at the human level is derivative of the spiritual-physical ontological split in Western philosophic systems. Embedded in this dualistic framework is an implicit or explicit dissociation from the body; effectively, the body gets relegated to the unconscious (Goenka, 2000). Moreover, this commonplace but distorted view generates real-world consequences in the human relationship to matter, writ large in the ecological crisis, which reflects humanity's maladjustment to the requirements of embodied existence on planet Earth. Thus, this philosophical dichotomy, and the institutions that sustain it, translate into pragmatic real-world consequences.

The Japanese philosopher Yasuo Yuasa (1987) contrasts Western and Eastern approaches to the mind-body relationship. Whereas Western philosophy traditionally askes the abstract question, "What is the relationship between the mind-body?"—

Half Dome. (Photo by Karen Jaenke)

in the East one starts from the experiential assumption that the mind-body modality changes through the training of the mind and body by means of cultivation.... The mind-body issue is not simply a theoretical speculation but [originates as] a practical lived experience, involving the mustering of one's whole mind and body" (Yasuo, 2987, p. 18).

The theoretical then reflects this lived experience.

Influenced by the mainstream Western bias, the body's perceptual capacities are neither recognized nor incorporated into many understandings of spiritual intelligence. Yet in expansive states of consciousness, these Western dichotomies often dissolve into a holistic perception into the underlying unitive nature of existence. Don Johnson speaks of three ways that transformative body practices create openings to the transpersonal dimension: The dissolution of the fixity of the self; the dissolution of neuromuscular barriers that block a full and direct encounter with present reality; and the transcendence of ordinary awareness (Johnson, 2013, p. 484).

Any truly holistic approach to spiritual intelligence must intentionally include the body's remarkable yet generally dismissed perceptual capacities. Moreover, it seems that humanity's resolution of the mind body split and recovery of the depths of bodily intelligence will contribute to a respectful, empathic, and life-serving, rather than life-destroying, relationship with the Earth body and her many life forms.

the world around us [thereby conferring added meaning and value] (2000, p. 69).

Kathleen Noble (2001) defines spiritual intelligence as:

the ability to explore systematically the spiritual dimensions of our own being and to infuse what we learn into every aspect of our lives…it can only be achieved by expanding our psychological breadth and depth, living more deliberately, and functioning more wholly as individual and in the world (p. 122).

a set of mental capacities which contribute to the awareness, integration, and adaptive application of the nonmaterial and transcendent aspects of one's existence, leading to such outcomes as deep existential reflection, enhancement of meaning, recognition of a transcendent self, and mastery of spiritual states. Four core components are proposed to comprise spiritual intelligence: (1) critical existential thinking, (2) personal meaning production, (3) transcendental awareness, and (4) conscious state expansion (p. 56).

Michal Levin offers a far-reaching conception of spiritual intelligence: "a way to bring together the spiritual and the material, that is ultimately concerned with the well-being of the universe and all who live there" (Levin, 2000, p. 5). By uniting the spiritual and the material, and the human being with all other beings and the universe, her definition transcends the mind-body, spirit-matter and self-world splits long plaguing Western culture.

Not surprisingly, those authors who envision a dynamic unity between self and world as the ultimate outcome of spiritual intelligence explicitly address the body's role in spiritual intelligence. Their visions of spiritual intelligence are also the most expansive, not limiting spiritual development to the interior capacities of the individual, but explicitly naming how this internal development also translates into a radically transformed relationship between self and world.

> …humanity's resolution of the mind-body split and recovery of the depths of bodily intelligence will contribute to a respectful, empathic, and life-serving, rather than life-destroying, relationship with the Earth body and her many life forms.

Definitions of Spiritual Intelligence

Danah Zohar and Ian Marshall, coining the term spiritual intelligence in 1997, offer this expansive definition: "Spiritual intelligence, in essence, represents a dynamic wholeness of self in which the self is at one with itself and the whole of creation" (Zohar and Marshall, 2000, p. 124). For Zohar, the process of unifying the human self with the rest of creation constitutes the essence of spiritual intelligence. We will track the vital role of the body in this process of unification.

Zohar and Marshall identify transcendence as:

perhaps the most essential quality of the spiritual, [referring to] that which takes us beyond—beyond the present moment, our present joy or suffering, our present selves. It takes us beyond the limits of our knowledge and experience and puts these things in a wider context. The transcendent gives us a taste of the extraordinary, the infinite, within ourselves or within

Her conceptualization emphasizes psychological health an integral aspect of spiritual intelligence.

Cindy Wigglesworth defines spirituality as "the innate human need to be connected to something larger than ourselves, something we consider to be divine or of exceptional nobility";

Butterfly. (Photo by Karen Jaenke)

and spiritual intelligence as "the ability to behave with wisdom and compassion, while maintaining inner and outer peace, regardless of the situation" (2012, p. 8).

David King (2008) defines spiritual intelligence as

Criteria for Spiritual Intelligence

Moving from definitions of spiritual intelligence to the capacities, skills or criteria that make up spiritual intelligence, I focus on those authors who explicitly acknowledge or address the role of the body in spiritual intelligence: King, Zohar & Marshall, and Levin.

In offering criteria for spiritual intelligence, King follows the current general consensus in intelligence theory, as established by Gardner (1983), Mayer et al., (2000), and Sternberg (1997). Thus, for him, an intelligence should:

1. Include a set of interrelated men-

tal abilities (distinct from behaviours, experiences, etc.).
2. Develop over the lifespan (from birth to old age).
3. Facilitate adaptation and problem-solving in a particular environmental context.
4. Allow an individual to reason abstractly and make appropriate judgements.
5. Demonstrate a biological component or foundation in the brain. (King, 2010).

For King, "The first component of spiritual intelligence is referred to as critical existential thinking, defined as the capacity to critically contemplate the nature of existence, reality, the universe, space, time, death, and other existential or metaphysical issues" (2008, p. 57) The second component of King's model is personal meaning production, defined as "the ability to construct personal meaning and purpose in all physical and mental experiences, including the capacity to create and master a life purpose" (p. 61).

Transcendental awareness, the third component, is defined as:

> the capacity to identify transcendent dimensions of the self (e.g., a transpersonal or transcendent self), of others, and of the physical world (e.g., non-materialism, holism) during the normal, waking state of consciousness, accompanied by the capacity to identify their relationship to one's self and to the physical (p. 64).

King's last element of spiritual intelligence is "conscious state expansion, defined as the ability to enter and exit higher/spiritual states of consciousness (e.g. pure consciousness, cosmic consciousness, unity, oneness) at one's own discretion (as in deep contemplation, meditation, prayer, etc.)" (p. 72).

King makes several noteworthy comments on the potential role of bodily intelligence in relation to spiritual intelligence, which serve as valuable jump-off points for an expansion of spiritual intelligence theory, inclusive of bodily intelligence. First, King recognizes that both bodily control and cognition are necessary to attain conscious state expansion (2008):

> Gardner (2000) argues that the ability to enter higher states of consciousness simply reflects heightened control over one's physical body, and is therefore more reflective of bodily-kinesthetic intelligence. Although some physical control is necessary in most established methods of meditation and relaxation (e.g., controlled breathing; Cahn & Polich, 2006; James, 1902/2002; Maslow,

Calla lily. (Photo by Karen Jaenke)

1964; Vaitl et al., 2005), a cognitive component is quite evident as well (King, 2008, p. 78).

To this, I demur that control over the body is only one side of the equation. As we shall see, the ability of the mind to track, listen to and heed the body's autonomous sensations and perceptual capacities is vital for the development of mature, holistic spiritual intelligence.

King hastens to add that bodily intelligence may play a role in entering higher states of consciousness: "Just as Gardner's (1983) interpersonal intelligence requires aspects of linguistic intelligence, entering higher states of consciousness may involve some degree of bodily intelligence"; he contends, however, "that the cognitive capacities are paramount" (p. 79). I concur that cognition plays a role in bodily intelligence, as the mind must engage with the sensations present in the body in generating a more complex and nuanced body-mind intelligence, distinct from a merely mental intelligence that ignores or overrides the body's signals.

My proposed role of the body in spiritual intelligence differs dramatically from Gardner's Bodily-Kinesthetic Intelligence. Gardner (1983) identified two key operations entailed in bodily-kinesthetic intelligence: "the capacity to control one's bodily motions and the capacity to handle objects skillfully. Included in these capacities are the abilities to judge timing, force, extent of movements, and to subsequently make the appropriate physical adjustments" (King, 2008 p. 29), as well as a clear sense of the goal of a physical action and the ability to train responses. Those possessing high bodily-kinesthetic intelligence should be adept at physical activities, such as sports, dance and acting.

Both of these operations presuppose mental direction over the body, without consideration that conversely, the body may play a vital role of contributing its own perceptual data or feedback to the mind. Reversing the standard equation, the mind's ability to receive and be informed by the body's messages complexifies our conception of intelligence, suggesting a bi-directional rather than uni-directional process of knowing.

Moreover, the notion of bodily-kinesthetic intelligence counters commonplace notions that mental and physical activity are unrelated. "Neurobiological research indicates that learning is an outcome of the modifications in the synaptic connections between cells" (Brualdi, 1996); hence mental operations are intimately dependent upon the neurological circuits of the body.

Moving on to Zohar (1997), she offers 12 principles underlying spiritual intelligence:

- Self-awareness: Knowing what I believe in and value, and what deeply motivates me.
- Spontaneity: Living in and being responsive to the moment.
- Being vision- and value-led: Acting from principles and deep beliefs, and living accordingly.
- Holism: Seeing larger patterns, relationships, and connections; having a sense of belonging.

- Compassion: Having the quality of "feeling-with" and deep empathy.
- Celebration of diversity: Valuing other people for their differences, not despite them.
- Field independence: Standing against the crowd and having one's own convictions.
- Humility: Having the sense of being a player in a larger drama, of one's true place in the world.
- Tendency to ask fundamental "Why?" questions: Needing to understand things and get to the bottom of them.
- Ability to reframe: Standing back from a situation or problem and seeing the bigger picture or wider context.
- Positive use of adversity: Learning and growing from mistakes, setbacks, and suffering.
- Sense of vocation: Feeling called upon to serve, to give something back (2005).

King criticizes Zohar and Marshall for providing this list of indicators that are more likely outcome variables of a high degree of spiritual intelligence, and for avoiding a critical task: the establishment of a core set of mental abilities (p. 49). However, King also praises them for providing a model of intelligence that could result in the most integrative perspective on human intelligence so far. He finds Zohar and Marshall's model of spiritual intelligence resembles a holistic approach to psychology, which typically integrates factors on the physical, mental, emotional, and spiritual levels (Sultanoff, 1997). If Zohar and Marshall's (2000) model of human intelligence were expanded according to this holistic approach, some form of bodily intelligence would need to be [included]. The resulting model would by far represent the most integrative perspective on human intelligence to date (2008, p. 108-109).

I, too, find Zohar and Marshall's model of the Self and spiritual intelligence both compelling and useful in serving as a bridge to define the body's role in spiritual intelligence. Zohar and Marshall situate their discussion of the body by first explicating three layers of the Self. They adopt the image of the lotus as a map or mandala to depict "the layers of the human psyche from the outermost rational ego through the unconscious associative, [and emotional] middle to the [unitive spiritual] centre with its transforming psychic energy" (2000, p. 161). Spiritual intelligence encompasses the larger purpose of attaining knowledge of the self at all three levels and integrating them into psychic wholeness. Moreover, the three layers of the Self correspond to three basic intelligences "(rational, emotional and spiritual), three kinds of thinking (serial, associative, and unitive), three basic ways of knowing (primary, secondary and tertiary), and three levels of the self (a centre—transpersonal; a middle – associative and interpersonal; and a periphery – personal ego)" (2000, p. 126).

Moreover, Zohar and Marshall relate each layer of the self to specific brain functions, as required by intelligence theory. Ego, the most recently developed, rational layer of the self, "is associated with the serial neural tracts and programs in the brain, the neural system responsible for logical, rational thought and conscious, goal-oriented or strategic thinking" (2000, p. 127). Secondly, "the large middle layer of the lotus is the associative unconscious, that vast store of images, relationships, patterns, symbols and archetypes that sway our behavior and body language, shape our dreams, bind our families and communities together" and confer meaning to our lives deeper than rational thought (2000, p. 137).

Finally, the centre or innermost layer of the self, carries the unitive and integrative function; it "is the inspiring, energy-giving, meaning-giving unifying spiritual level of existence" (2000, p. 24). Moreover, in terms of brain functioning, "this centre is associated with the synchronous 40 Hz neural oscillations across the brain" (p. 126).

The brain's unitive experience emanates from synchronous 40 Hz neural oscillations that travel across the whole brain. They provide a 'pond' or 'background' on which more excited brain waves can 'ripple', to generate the rich panoply of our conscious and unconscious mental experience. These oscillations are the 'centre' of the self, the neurological source from which 'I' emerge. They are the neurological ground of our unifying, contextualizing, transforming spiritual intelligence. It is through these oscillations that we place our experience within a framework of meaning and value, and determine a purpose for our lives. They are a unifying source of psychic energy running through all our disparate mental experience (2000, p. 159).

Furthermore, Zohar and Marshall postulate that the Self has its source and origin in the evolution of the universe from the quantum vacuum—the still, ground energy state of the universe (2000). Thus the spiritually intelligent person "is attuned to the basic life forces of the universe" and, in serving the cosmic life force, naturally serves the groups of human beings with whom he or she interfaces (2000, p. 33-34). "Our spiritual intelligence grounds us in the

> ...the spiritually intelligent person "is attuned to the basic life forces of the universe" and, in serving the cosmic life force, naturally serves the groups of human beings with whom he or she interfaces.

wider cosmos, and life has purpose and meaning within the larger context of cosmic evolutionary processes" (Zohar and Marshall, 2000, p. 88).

For Zohar and Marshall, the body's role comes specifically into play through the Hindu chakras, which mediate between the associative layer of the self and the deep center. The chakras are "forces of energy linking this deepest middle layer of the unconscious with the source and centre of the deepest self" (2000, p. 150). "The Hindu chakras [are] energy patterns found in the unconscious middle layer of the self that, if used properly, can help to shift ego level personality traits" (2000, p. 130). For Zohar and Marshall, "this 'lotus ladder' of serpent-like, transforming energy, a set of seven vital locations within the body… represent stages of psychic development in the process of being and becoming" (2000, p. 142). The chakras are a dynamic energy exuding primal patterns of personal motivation. "In Hindu tradition, working one's way up the chakras is the key to personal transformation"; the chakras "contain universal structures and energies that are definitive of human being" and which must be engaged in developing spiritual intelligence (2000, p. 143).

Elmer Green (1999) offers a definition of transpersonal psychology based upon the Hindu chakra system. He differentiates the personal domain of the self, as denoted by the three lower chakras, from the transpersonal self, residing in the four upper chakras, while recognizing the interpenetrating nature of all chakras. At the personal level, "we are uniquely separate and closed to one another as personalities, but as transpersonal beings we possess, in spite of being 'ourselves,' a sense of being all other persons and all nature" (1991, p. 141). Moreover, the transpersonal and personal domains together make up "the planetary field of mind," roughly parallel to Teilhard de Chardin's noosphere—a field of mind surrounding the planet (1959).

According to Green, physiologically, "the brain and spinal cord are constructed of both 'dense physical' and 'etheric-physical' parts. The existence of etheric organs (for handling energy) is a basic hypothesis in all major systems of occult metaphysics," while being regarded as experiential 'fact' by practitioners of 'psychic' healing (1999, p. 142).

The etheric organs of perception and action are referred to in the East as chakras, and when perceived by mystics in the West, as auras. They were drawn in most medieval Christian texts as halos or other kinds of radiation, as from the heart of Jesus (Green, 1999, p. 142).

Abraham Maslow's hierarchy of needs also roughly corresponds to the levels of the chakras, with similar developmental challenges posed by the corresponding levels. Maslow (1954) identified the needs of "physiological," "safety," "belonging and love," "esteem," "self-actualization", later adding "transcendence" (1971) to describe the developmental stages of human motivations.

Pillars in surf. (Photo by Karen Jaenke)

In Green's theory,

> the brain is the interface mechanism that mediates between the physiological apparatus and the etheric organs. The etheric organs, or chakras, …are conceived as the direct sensors and effectors for all "higher" levels of mind, personal and transpersonal, when acting through the brain. Eccles' (1953) concept of the brain as the transducer of mind is essentially the same idea (Green, 1999, p. 142-143).

The etheric energies of the subtle body are parallel to the solid, liquid and gas of the dense physical realm, existing as progressive degrees of subtlety, and often visualized as forms of electricity, or as rarefied gaseous substances. In the classic oriental literature the etheric energies are referred to as pranas, with specific pranas serving as the agency through which one establishes direct conscious control of the heart, lungs, gastrointestinal tract, and other sections of the physiological machinery.

Similarly, Candis Best (2010) presents a model of lifespan development based upon the chakra system, outlining a lifelong path of transpersonal development. She defines the chakras in relation to their potential influence on psychological functioning, while adopting a transpersonal approach that goes beyond ego stability and functioning to include transcendence of egoic concerns in pursuit of reunion with divine consciousness. In her model, the chakras function as both stages of development and domains or energies that act as filters or prisms, influencing perception and behavior. Briefly, the root chakra is distinguished "by its focus on security and survival, sacral by sensations and individuation, navel by will and initiative, heart by love and affection, throat by creativity and nurturance, brow by intuition and wisdom, and crown by oneness with creation" (2010, p. 20). Like Green, Best associates the lower three chakras with the ego-coalescing aspects of personal development and the upper four chakras with the ego-transcending aspects of transpersonal development.

Best concurs with Emmons' (1999) view of spiritual intelligence, since "spirituality facilitates adaptive functioning [by supporting] goal attainment, self-congruence, and self-regulation" (2010, p. 21). For Best, the chakra system developmental model contextualizes spiritual intelligence by providing "a developmental sequence for the individual such that goal- directed activity is evaluated in light of both chakra stage attainment and the chakra domains which predominate an individual's perceptions at a given time" (2010, p. 21).

Lastly, we turn to the writing of Michal Levin, a former journalist with a deep existential ache who one day started meditating out of desperation. Meditation quickly opened the flood gates to vast spiritual dimensions, transforming her into an intuitive and healer sought out by many. Her understanding of spiritual intelligence is informed by her dramatic and expansive spiritual development, together with the experiences of her clients, rather than formal research. Her personal experience of radical transformation included the alteration of her body, especially the spine (2000, p. 19). While there is a certain imprecision in her intuitive writing style, her she contributes through direct experience to the role of the body, and the transformation bodily energies, in the development of spiritual intelligence.

Levin views spiritual intelligence as the combined essence of love and the gift of the heart together with the power of mental faculties.

The marriage of spirituality and intelligence [understood as the faculty for reason and intellectual skill] … offers a new way to bring together the spiritual and the material, using the language and concepts of our time to formulate its vision… Spiritual maturity, which is the product of spiritual intelligence, is [concerned] with the well-being of the universe and all who live there. At the same time it recognizes wider perceptual powers than the five senses… [learning] from contact with a greater reality (2000, p. 4- 5).

Levin deems that spiritual intelligence is the answer to the deepest cause of the modern person's pain, while spiritual reality is our "wider, greater further self—and its connection to the whole of the universe" (2000, p. 12). Spiritual intelligence begins with accepting that each individual must directly connect with spiritual forces oneself, not through guru or priest, embracing responsibility for our spiritual lives (2000, p. 96).

Similar to others, for Levin spiritual development is intertwined with emotional and mental development and hampered by unresolved emotional and mental issues. Moreover, Levin critiques the overemphasis of Western society on the functions of the brain and mental body, while asserting that the role of energy in spiritual development is absolutely crucial. "The development of spiritual intelligence is influenced by energy, a subtle quality, a spectrum of frequencies" that carries information (2000, p. 48-49). Like Zohar and Marshall, she recognizes that Western science does not yet possess sufficiently-sophisticated instrumentation to measure energy in the human body: "A key challenge facing science in understanding the functioning of the body is how to chart the relationship between energy, the information it carries and the matter it influences—our bodies" (2000, p. 50). Indeed, King also recognizes that "we cannot rule out human experiences simply due to a lack of scientific investigation, as this says nothing of their empirical value" (2008, p 71).

Regarding our bodies as "very sensitive instruments" that can be developed to be more sensitive still, Levin deems the cultivation of one's energy body as parallel to the development of spiritual intelligence. Spiritual growth implies the widening of our perception, which requires first cleansing or purifying the energy body. The clearing of the energy body entails removing obstructions within it, which cloud and narrow our perceptions. Progress in spiritual development occurs specifically through clearing one's energy, freeing chakras of obstacles, and purifying the energy body (2000). Furthermore, the development of the energy body extends to a sensitization to the energies present in the surrounding field.

Levin finds that the concept of the energy body obtains greater differentiation and precision through an understanding of the chakras. These distinct energy centers in the body are crucial to the development of spiritual intelligence. In fact, one's spiritual development can be traced through the chakras, which offer a route map developing for spiritual intelligence (2000).

The chakras are like junction boxes. They take in, send out and process energy. Each

> …as one develops spiritual intelligence, the perception of the world and its inhabitants is extended, and one's "connection to the greater whole, and joy in the process of life, will be greatly strengthened.

centre concentrates on a different range of the energy spectrum…generally getting 'higher' or 'finer' as you progress up to the crown chakra at the top of the head….The wider and more able to open the chakra, the greater [one's] perspective…. Also the more open the chakras, the more able [one is] to respond to the changing vibrations coming from the outside world (2000, p. 115).

As a chakra opens or widens, one's perspective on the issues that it governs increases, and with this enhanced insight, one's behavior also shifts in a positive direction. The purifying and strengthening of the chakras generally moves from the base chakra upwards, with the crown chakra playing a vital role in a widening perspective and the mastery of spiritual intelligence.

In addition to clearing the chakras and expanding one's perception is the accompanying challenge of balancing the chakras. "For spiritual and intuitive development, and physical health, the chakras must be as free of obstacles as possible, and as open as possible. And in balance" (2000, p. 115).

Most radically, Levin asserts that personal truth emerges when consciousness is aligned and merged with centerline of all chakras:

Your truth is a line through the center of each chakra. If your chakras are aligned and balanced, that line will be exactly through the center of you. Your truths will be consistent and you will be in balance. If, however, the chakras are each slightly out of balance, the lines will not join to make a straight line (p. 2000, 270).

Levin's centerline of the chakras and Zohar and Marshall's center of the Self both envision spiritual intelligence via a spatial orientation rooted in the central axis of the human being.

For Levin, as one develops spiritual intelligence, the perception of the world and its inhabitants is extended, and one's "connection to the greater whole, and joy in the process of life, will be greatly strengthened" (2000, p. 148). For her, there is a direct relationship, a throughline, between clearing one's energy body and relating effectively to the wider world. "Ultimately, the less obstructed your own energy, and the clearer you are in upholding your own perceptions, the easier it [is] to be aware of the forces of the universe, and to respond appropriately" (2000, p. 73). Moreover, spiritual intelligence leads to a deeper and wider participation in the processes of life: as "spiritual intelligence develops, it draws you back into life, insisting that you participate more and more fully, [while] connecting you with an ever widening circle" (2000, p. 206).

This healing of the self-world split is perhaps the crowning achievement of spiritual intelligence, becoming possible when the body's subtle perceptual capacities are fully engaged. The alchemical transformation of the energy body, activated when mind and body unite their distinct intelligences, leads to participatory consciousness, that is, "states of consciousness which are unobstructed by a delusionary sense of a separate self. Non participatory states of consciousness are adaptive to stressful and traumatic circumstances" and subsequently maintained through the constricting influence of the inner critic (Aftab Omer, personal communication, November 18, 2008).

Capacities of Bodily Spiritual Intelligence

King reminds us that "intelligence" refers to an interrelated set of mental abilities, as distinct from behaviors and experiences, and that intelligence develops across the lifespan as cultivated abilities. In applying these principles to the body, Don Johnson asserts the spiritual importance of cultivating one's sensibilities through long-term sustained practices that open up the deeper potentialities of the body, plus the intellectual importance of building theory from direct experience rather than speculative abstractions (2013).

A preliminary list of capacities that contribute to a holistic spiritual intelligence suggests how the mind's mental abilities relate to the perceptual capacities of the body in the cultivation of spiritual intelligence. In other words, the abilities given below reflect capacities of the mind directed towards the body and its depths of interiority and knowing. Several interrelated body-based capacities are identified as contributing to holistic spiritual intelligence, including: bodily awareness; tracking expansion and contraction in the body; accessing, clearing and balancing body energies through the chakras; and accessing internal and external flow states. The skills are listed in approximate developmental sequence, with more complex and advanced abilities following more foundational ones.

Dream waterfall. (Photo by Karen Jaenke)

Body awareness

Body awareness is a foundational skill within somatic psychology, also known as interoception, or the ability to perceive sensations in the internal organs and interiority of the body. Interoceptive signals are sent by body tissues to the brain via a diversity of neural pathways, allowing for the sensory processing and representation of internal bodily states, contributing to self-awareness.

- Ability to detect, listen to and appropriately act on, rather than deny and override, signals and perceptions arising in the body
- Ability to detect bodily symptoms in incipient stages through subtle body awareness and altered states of consciousness
- Ability to extend subtle perceptive awareness throughout the entire body, contributing to presence
- Ability to access and act upon the unified perceptions of body-mind

Bonnie Bainbridge Cohen recognizes that information from the body is always coming through viscerally from the proprioceptors, but normally "each person is selective in terms of what they choose to acknowledge" (2008, p. 64.) However people can be trained to systematically attend to the different systems of the body—the senses, skeleton, muscles, organs, glands, blood, etc.—consciously registering the information each offers.

Similarly, Eugene Gendlin speaks of the felt sense, a nonverbal, bodily awareness of the ongoing life process within the body (2007). He developed a way of measuring the extent to which an individual references the felt sense, and his research found positive outcomes among those who more regularly access the felt sense (2007). He then developed the focusing method to train people to access their felt sense, as a learned skill.

Gendlin expresses profound respect for the body's information-processing abilities:

The body is a biological computer, generating these enormous collections of data and delivering them to you instantaneously, when you call them up or when they are called up by some external event. Your thinking isn't capable of holding all those items of knowledge, nor of delivering them up with such speed…The equivalent of hundreds of thousands of cognitive operations are done in a split second by the body (2007, p. 34).

Interactive engagement between the somatic felt sense and mental concepts results in refinement of both. Gendlin's research discovered that when the felt sense, or implicit bodily knowing, interacts dialectically with conceptual understandings, each refines the other, through progressive deeper feeling and new formulation (Gendlin, 2007). The felt sense both disrupts existing conceptual models, and also provides fresh insights when there is a release of tension or shift in the body, indicating its rightness from a bodily perspective. "Thinking in the usual way, alone, can be objectively true and powerful. But, when put in touch with what the body already knows and lives, it becomes vastly more powerful" (2007, p. 165).

The skill of focusing can be applied to dreams, which surface the unfamiliar material of the unconscious. Dreams have a strong link with proprioception, both at the formative level and during interpretation, and serve as a means by which bodily processes or symptoms reach awareness (Garfield, 1001). Working with dreams offers a "way to approach the symbolic and meaningful aspect of our body-mind continuum," accelerating the mind-body connection (Deslauriers, 2000).

The Vipassana tradition of Buddhism also recognizes the necessity of learning to observe the body through its sensations:

> We each experience the reality of the body by feeling it, by means of the physical sensations that arise within it…. Without awareness of sensations there can be no direct knowledge of the physical structure…. Mind and matter are closely interrelated. Whatever occurs in one is reflected in the other…[As the Buddha expressed it,] "Whatever arises in the mind is accompanied by sensation." Therefore observation of sensation offers a means to examine the totality of one's being, physical as well as mental… Matter alone cannot feel anything if the mind is not present (Hart, 1987 p. 147-148).

One of the outcomes of cultivating body awareness is the unifying of mind and body. The Bodymind approach views the relationship between the human body and mind as a single integrated unit, an alternative to mind-body dualism. Body awareness is akin to the "transpersonal notion of presence, where the inner conversations, with their floodings of memories and images, lose their power and a person is simply available for what is here now" (Johnson, 2013, p. 486).

Tracking contraction and expansion in the body

While the literature on spiritual intelligence affirms expansive states of consciousness as a component of spiritual intelligence, a more encompassing perspective acknowledges the existence of contracted states and the ability to transmute them. Thus a broader view of spiritual intelligence includes the abilities to: a) track contraction and expansion within the body, b) release contracted states, as well as c) enter expansive states (Jaenke, in press).

- Ability to be aware of states of contraction and expansion in the body/subtle body
- Ability to attend to and clear contractions, tensions, wounds, shamed and numb zones in the body, shifting them towards openness, expansiveness and flow through mindful presence
- Ability to consciously choose and move into expansive states

Contraction and expansion arise as the dynamic expressions of the energy body, alternating modes through which the energy body announces its presence to consciousness, while simultaneously displaying its participation in the elemental dynamics of the universe. The energy body typically undergoes contraction from experiences of trauma and shame, while expansion is experienced through altered states of consciousness and spiritual practices like meditation. King includes conscious state expansion as a component of spiritual intelligence, implying the existence of contracted states of consciousness and the ability to transform them. Hence a fuller conception of spiritual intelligence entails the conscious ability to travel along the entire continuum from contraction to expansion (Jaenke, in press). Awareness of this continuum of expansion and contraction in the energy body emerges as a vital component of spiritual intelligence.

Trauma is a major source of contraction in the body. The response of living organisms to trauma can be seen in microcosm in the reaction of the single cell to environmental impingement. When a single cell is prodded with a sharp instrument, the cell contracts, recedes, shrivels. With the removal of the sharp point, the contraction releases, and the cell returns to its normal shape. However, if the prick is repeated several times, the cell retains a contracted state, even upon withdrawal of the intruding instrument (Judyth Weaver, personal communication). The response of the single cell highlights the entire organism's response to trauma. The primal response of living organisms to environmental impingement is to contract. Contraction entails a shift into a state of increased density or compression.

In human beings, these *densities of existence* that form following trauma are both somatic and psychological. Bodily tissue, especially the tissue most directly assaulted by trauma, contracts, just as the single cell organism does. The body forms places of holding or even armoring in reaction to external

> Contraction and expansion arise as the dynamic expressions of the energy body, alternating modes through which the energy body announces its presence to consciousness, while simultaneously displaying its participation in the elemental dynamics of the universe.

threats. To release this body armoring, Ida Rolf developed techniques to manipulate the network of hardened connective tissues (fascia, ligaments, tendons) that over time create an illusory sense of being a hardened object (Johnson, 2013, p. 484).

In trauma, not just the body but the also the human psyche contracts from its natural state of openness, trust, expansiveness, and participation, developing distrust, defensiveness, and alienation. Peter Levine developed the technique of somatic experiencing in order to release the contracted energy that becomes trapped in the nervous system during trauma, thereby returning the body to its natural openness (1997).

In order to shift contractions in the psycho-somatic system, consciousness needs to become capable of tolerating the densities of existence generated by trauma. Once the muscle of attention can meet these densities with unflinching awareness, a back and forth movement can occur, between the spaciousness of awareness and the dense sites holding compressed energies. Eventually a rapprochement takes place between the two, such that an interactive field between attentive awareness and the dense holdings is constellated. If engagement between awareness and density can be sustained, one eventually discovers its opposite—spaciousness—thereby unlocking the expansiveness and vitality hidden within the density. Expansive states of consciousness correct the tendencies of the body-psyche to develop contractions and stances of non-participation in response to life's inevitable onslaughts.

Awareness serves as the primary transmuting agent to transform contraction into expansion.

The capacity of conscious awareness can be cultivated to meet the sites of density in the body. The muscle of attention concentrates psychic energy and when applied consistently, carries power to shift densities in the body and melt frozen states of numbness. As the observing self extends pure presence to contracted zones in the body, a surprising quickening of energy occurs.

Accessing, clearing and balancing body energies through the chakras

Three distinct skills in relating to the energy body can be identified: first, accessing the energy centers in consciousness, becoming aware of their presence, for which the body awareness practices discussed above are key; second, clearing, purifying or opening the

Wildflower. (Photo by Karen Jaenke)

energy centers, so that the energy runs more clearly through them, rather than being stuck or blocked; and third, balancing the energy centers, so that energy flows more or less evenly through all of them. These abilities were discussed above in the work of Levin.

- Ability to consciously access each of the major energy centers (chakras) throughout the body
- Ability to clear, purify and open each of the major energy centers (chakras) in the body, releasing tensions and blockages in the energy body
- Ability to balance and harmonize the major energy centers (chakras) in the body

The conception of the energy body is consistent with the ontological claim of modern physics, namely that there is one primary form of energy from which everything else is derived.

In occult physics, however, it is postulated that the elaborated structure of the one basic energy includes not just physical substance but also emotional substance, mental substance, and other more rarefied materials, and that in the human being… all these materials are brought together. The early Greeks explained that this union of the substances (symbolized by earth, water, fire, air and ether) was what made man the microcosm (Green, 1999, p. 139-140).

In the Eastern traditions of Tibetan and Indian yoga, the basic manifestation of physical energy in man is through a power center in the "subtle" body, the etheric template of the physical body. The energy itself is called the kundalini… In both Integral Yoga and Tibetan Buddhism, all physiological energy in every organ is an expression of kundalini (Green, 1999, p. 146).

Ancient Eastern models and maps of the energy body inform us first that the energy body consists of channels, or meridians, through which energy ideally moves and flows but can become stuck and blocked. Secondly, the energy body possesses major energy centers, known as chakras in Hinduism. These major perceptual centers are associated anatomically with major organ systems, fed by complex neural networks. The high concentration of neurons found in the energy centers likely accounts for the special perceptual capacities located within the chakras.

Modern science has made some interesting discoveries that shed light on ancient intuitive understandings of the chakras.

The heart has been shown through measurement to produce forty to sixty times more electrical energy than the brain, and about a thousand times more electromagnetic energy. The electrical activity of the heart can be measured in every cell of the body. In other words, not only does the heart pump blood, carrying nutrients around the body, but it pumps patterns of energy, and therefore information to every cell as well (see *Advances: The Journal of Mind-Body Health*, Russell and Schwartz, p. 355) (Levin, p. 129).

The yogi Swami Rama states it this way: "the heart seen in surgery is only the physical appearance of the heart... the real heart is a large energy structure, of which they physical heart is only the dense section" (Green, 1990, p. 83).

Similarly, the digestive chakra located in the belly area has been recognized as "the brain in the bowel."

We now know that there is a brain in the bowel...It is the only organ that contains an intrinsic nervous system that is able to mediate reflexes in the complete absence of input from the brain or spinal column.... The brain in the bowel has evolved in pace with the brain in the head.... There are more than a hundred million nerve cells in the small intestine, a number roughly equal to the number of nerve cells in the spinal cord....We have more nerve cells in our gut than in the entire remainder of our peripheral nervous system. The enteric nervous system is also a vast chemical warehouse within which is represented every one of the classes of neurotransmitters found in the brain... The multiplicity of neurotransmitters in the bowels suggests that the language spoken by the cells of the enteric nervous systems is rich and brain-like in its complexity...the structure and component cells of the enteric nervous system are more akin to those of the brain than to those of any other periphery organ (Gershon, 1998, p. viii).

As Western neuroscience continues to advance in complexity, we can expect to learn more about the sophisticated neurological structures and biochemical operations associated with each chakra, as well as revise our theories of the mind-body relationship beyond simple dualism. According to Jack Schwarz, founder and director of the Aletheia Foundation, "It is an error to think of the body as a 'physical' structure rather than as a subtle energy structure, a part of the mind" (Green, 1990, p. 84). In yogic theory, "the body is a special case of the mind. Every cell of the body is a cell of the mind" (Green, 199, p. 83).

The mind-body dualism resolves experientially when the energy body becomes accessible and permeable to consciousness. Energy is the bridge concept between mind and body/matter. As the animating source of life, or spirit, energy is transmutable into matter.

Mind and matter are inter-transformable, an analog of the familiar $E=mc^2$ of physical science. Aurobindo, in considering this idea of transformability, says that one can think of the universe as all spirit, with 'matter' being its densest form, or one can think of the universe as all substance, with 'spirit' being its most rarefied form (Green, 1999, p. 140).

Bringing the normally hidden presence of the energy body's operations into awareness, the mind-body problem resolves at the level of immediate experience.

Intense spiritual disciplines such as meditation, special breathing exercises, asanas, or mantras are generally necessary to clear blockages in the energy body. "These are purifying practices that remove blockages to the free flow of energy through the subtle body" (Coward,1985, p. 383). Each individual chakra may require extended attention and engagement in order to generate a clearing.

Moreover, if subtle energy is not expended towards personal egoic concerns but instead focused toward cultivating awareness through meditation and various breathing exercises, "there will ensue an activation of specific chakras (etheric organs) which are especially sensitive to superconscious grades of matter" (Green, 1999, p. 146).

As awareness of the underlying subtle vibrations within the energy body increases to encompass each of the seven chakras, it becomes possible for the energies of the individual chakras to become joined and synthesized into a unified perception of energy flow throughout the body.

Accessing internal and external flow states

While Csíkszentmihályi's concept of flow states relates to the experience of oneness, attained through outward focus on a challenging and all-consuming activity, the experience of flow may also be accessed as an internal body state. This inner flow state is not activity-specific and can potentially be brought to bear upon any human activity. Internal flow is realized through the spiritual discipline of aligning and harmonizing consciousness with the body's subtle energies. The ability to access flow states relates to the realization of oneness between self and universe, regarded as the apex of spiritual intelligence by Zohar and Marshall.

Skills related to internal flow states include:

- Ability to access and attune to the energy body and deep life force energies
- Ability to regularly enter inner flow states in the body, as a source of natural joy and deep participation in life
- Ability to return to a state of flow as a baseline of inner harmony, enabling refined discriminations in judgment and action that generate outer flow or harmonies with the larger universal field

Csíkszentmihályi's flow concept relates to being at one with things through an outer focus on activity, undertaken with complete psychic immersion. Csíkszentmihályi and Jeanne Nakamura (2001) identified six factors involved in generating an experience of flow: intense and focused concentration on the present moment; merging of action and awareness; a loss of reflective self-consciousness; a sense of personal control or agency over the situation or activity; alteration in the subjective experience of time; and experiencing the activity as intrinsically rewarding.

Less prominent in the literature is the internal flow state, cultivated when the energies of the body exist in a state of vibrational flow. This internal flow may be attained through meditation practices directed towards bodily sensations. In vipassana meditation, as taught by S. N. Goenka, one first develops awareness of sensations throughout the body, without reacting to them.

> By remaining equanimous towards gross, unpleasant sensations, you will proceed to experience subtler, pleasant sensations. If you continue to maintain equanimity, sooner or later you will reach the stage described by the Buddha, in which throughout the physical structure, the meditator experiences nothing but arising and passing away. All the gross, solidified sensations have dissolved; throughout the body there is nothing but subtle vibrations. Naturally this stage is very blissful (Goenka, 2000, p. 63).

Internal flow states relate to the awakening of kundalini, as attested in ancient Hindu spiritual texts and the reports of modern persons, typically described as an electrical current running through the spine. In Hinduism, kundalini is pictured as a coiled snake lying dormant at the base of the spine but potentially awakened through various spiritual disciplines. The arousal of kundalini through the various chakras activates different levels of awakening and upon reaching the crown chakra, produces an extremely profound transformation of consciousness. Alternatively, due to its dramatic disruption of physiological patterns, meaning structures, and psychological functioning, the rapid arousal of kundalini in an ill-prepared person can result in a spiritual emergency.

Carl Jung, generally credited with bringing awareness of kundalini to the West through a lecture series given in 1932, examined the symbolism of each of the seven chakras, offering a psychological interpretation in terms of his theory of individuation (Coward, 1985, p. 380). Focusing on the symbolic meanings of the chakras, he viewed the chakras as psychic localizations, "highly complex psychic facts which can be expressed only in images," and as an Eastern spiritual system providing a transpersonal standpoint "to understand the psyche as a whole" (Coward, 1985, p. 384-385). He perceived that the chakras functioned in the East similar to Western Platonic thought, with both claiming that physical entities possess both an outer form and an inner idea (Coward, 1985, p. 385). Significant for our exploration of bodily spiritual intelligence, Coward notes that, "To its practitioners, Kundalini Yoga is not symbolism but an empirical experience" (1985 p. 391).

Conscious cultivation of the internal flow of subtle energies throughout the body increasingly makes possible a harmonization between self and world. As one becomes aware of the "organismic level of pulsating life force," one enters an interactive field with other species and environments that the more conventional self is unaware of (Conrad, 1997, p. 62). Similarly, Bonnie Bainbridge Cohen's (2008) Body-Mind Centering evokes "unfamiliar states of body-embedded consciousness that link individuals to the vast worlds of living beings" (Hartley, 1989).

The internal flow state shifts the alchemy of relating to the external world towards flow and harmony. William Sutherland, a pioneer in osteopathy, considers

> the work of enhancing the link between one's body and the energy forces of the cosmos as carrying on older esoteric European traditions. The key to that link is the cerebrospinous fluid, whose pulses throughout the body reflect our relationship with the larger fields of the universe…It involves the cultivation of the circulation of the cerebrospinous fluid and its awareness, resulting in profound experiences of harmony with the ancient fields of bioenergies (Johnson, 2013, p. 485).

This simultaneity of inner and outer flow produces a field of oneness both within and without, leading to a harmonizing of self and world, variously deemed the crowning realization of spiritual intelligence.

Conclusion

The addition of bodily intelligence to the spiritual intelligence discourse addresses the long-standing "tension between the transpersonal realm and the tangible worlds of body and earth" (Johnson, 2013 p. 489). Cultivating the various skills that make up bodily intelligence leads to a transpersonal consciousness in which the illusion of a fixed and boundaried self undergoes transformation, in favor of the dynamics of flow. From an internal flow state, one is empowered to participate differently, less oppositionally, in the network of living interactions that compose the surrounding environment. "In this revisioning of our intercorporeal origins, Western thought joins with the Buddhist notion of interdependence, realized in the flesh…[with an] easing of the boundaries between flesh, cells and higher states of consciousness" (Johnson, 2013, p. 489) The old conception of spirituality as an exclusively vertical and ascending movement is radically revised; "spiritual opening is not achieved through an upward 'evasion,' but rather through a careful plunge into one's body and the earthly, in a balanced and paradoxical movement of simultaneous ascent and descent" (Llamazares, in press).

This task—for transpersonal consciousness to descend into the depths of the body—is beautifully conveyed by the story of a physicist who during meditation saw two versions of himself, an intensely illuminated figure of himself which was upside down, balanced head-to-head on top of another figure of himself (Green, 1999). The lower figure was nonilluminated, depicting his normal self, yet he yearned to merge with the illuminated man. Merging with the illuminated, transpersonal self entails folding the upper figure down so that the feet come to the ground and the resultant figure is a completely integrated human.

This is, in essence, Aurobindo's idea of the necessity in modern times of bringing down the transforming power of the overmind and supermind so that the man and his environment both benefit. This is considerably different from the old yogic idea of escape into Nirvana (the Void) by lack of involvement in the world, without personal-transpersonal transformation (Green, 1999, p. 145).

Moreover, as Green suggests, the transpersonal self associated with the upper chakras connects with "the planetary mind, because awareness at these levels includes all other beings and humans of the planet" (1999, p. 145). Thus the fully integrated person, the perfected human or Bodhisattva, works in the world to hasten the evolution of consciousness in all other beings (Green, 1999). This "completely integrated being is developed through the voluntary control of subjective energies," the high mark of spiritual intelligence (Green, 1999, p. 146).

Accordingly, a second, and intimately related result of fusion of somatic perspectives and practices and transpersonal ones "is an enhanced capacity to deal with the great challenge of our time, the destruction of our ecosystem" (Johnson, 2013, p. 489). Our contemporary challenge "results from a cultural alienation from our soulful connection with flesh, for it is our skin, lungs and senses that interface our consciousness" with air, water, and earth (Johnson, p. 489). Exclusively ascendant conceptions of spiritual intelligence reinforce disembodied forms of spirituality in which too few people experience their consciousness, "minds, souls, ideals as intertwined with the earth in which we are embedded" (Johnson, 2013 p.489). A spiritual intelligence that encompasses this intimate and sacred intertwining between spirit and flesh, in addition to promoting a natural flow and joy in the individual, may well be necessary to avert planetary demise.

References

Best, C. K. (2010). A chakra system model of lifespan development. *International Journal of Transpersonal Studies.* 29(2), 11-27.

Brualdi, A. (1996). Multiple Intelligences: Gardner's Theory. Retrieved from: http://www.springhurst.org/articles/MItheory.htm

Cohen, B. B. (2008). *Sensing, feeling, and action: The experiential anatomy of Body-Mind Centering.* Northapton, MA: Contact Editions

Conrad, E. (1997). Continuum. In D. H. Johnson (Ed.), *Groundworks: Narratives of embodiment.* Berkeley, CA: North Atlantic Press.

Coward, H. G. (1985). Jung and kundalini. *Journal of Analytical Psychology.* 30, 379-392.

Deslauriers, D. (2000). Dreamwork in the light of emotional and spiritual intelligence. *Journal of Advanced Development,* (Vol. 9, 2000, 105-122).

Eccles. J. C. (1953). *The Neurophysiological Basis of Mind.* Oxford, England: Clarendon Press.

Gardner, H. (1983). *Frames of Mind.* New York: Basic Book Inc.

Gendlin, E. (2007). *Focusing.* New York, NY: Bantam Books.

Gershon, M. (1998). *The second brain.* New York, NY: HarperCollins.

Goenka, S.N. (2000). *The discourse summaries of S.N. Goenka.* Onalaska, WA: Vipassana Research Publications.

Green, E. (1990). Psychophysiologic self-regulation and human potential. *Subtle energies and energy medicine journal.* 1(1), 73-89.

Green, E. (1999). On the meaning of transpersonal: Some metaphysical perspectives. *Subtle energies and energy medicine journal.* 10(3), 138-156.

Hart, W. (1987). *The art of living: Vipassana meditation as taught by S. N. Goenka.* New York, NY: HarperCollins.

Hartley, L. (1989). *Wisdom of the body moving: An introduction to Body-Mind Centering.* Berkeley, CA: North Atlantic Books.

Jaenke, K. (2008). Earth, dreams, body. ReVision: Journal of consciousness and transformation. 30: 1&2, 10-12.

Jaenke, K. (In press). The physics of joy and trauma. *International Journal of Transpersonal Studies.*

Johnson, D. H. (2013). Transpersonal dimensions of Somatic Therapies. In *The Wiley-Blackwell handbook of transpersonal psychology.* Friedman, H. L. and Hartelius, G. (Eds.). San Francisco, CA: Wiley-Blackwell.

Jung, C.G. (1976). *Analytical psychology: Its theory and practice.* New York, NY: Routledge.

King, D. (2008). *Rethinking claims of spiritual intelligence: A definition, model & measure.* (Unpublished Master's Thesis). Trent University, Peterborough, Ontario, Canada.

King, D. (2010). My perspective. In Spiritual intelligence: A global emergence. Retrieved from: http://www.davidbking.net/spiritualintelligence/perspective.html

Llamazares, A. (in press). "Wounded West: The healing potential of shamanism in the contemporary world." *ReVision: Journal of consciousness and transformation. 32(2-3).*

Maslow, A. (1954). Motivation and personality. New York, NY: Harper.

Maslow, A. (1971). Farther reaches of human nature. New York, NY: The Viking Press.

Nakamura, J.; Csikszentmihályi, M. (20 December 2001). "Flow theory and research". In C. R. Snyder Erik Wright, and Shane J. Lopez. *Handbook of positive psychology.* Oxford University Press. pp. 195–206.

Noble, K. (2001). *Riding the windhorse: Spiritual intelligence and the growth of the self.* Cresskill, NJ: Hampton Press.

Levin, M. (2000). *Spiritual intelligence: Awakening the power of your spirituality and intuition.* London: Coronet Books.

Levine, P. (1997). *Waking the tiger: Healing trauma.* Berkeley, CA: North Atlantic Books.

Swimme, B. and Berry, T. (1992). *The universe story.* San Francisco, CA: HarperSanFrancisco.

Teilhard de Chardin, P. (1959). *The phenomenon of man.* (New York, NY: Harper & Brothers).

Wigglesworth, C. (2006). "Why spiritual intelligence is essential to mature leadership," *Integral Leadership Review,* Volume VI, No. 3.

Wigglesworth, C. (2012). *SQ 21: The twenty-one skills of spiritual intelligence.* New York, NY: SelectBooks, Inc.

Yasuo, Y. (1987). *The body: Toward an Eastern mind-body theory.* Albany, NY: SUNY Press.

Zohar, D. (1997). *Rewiring the corporate brain: Using the new science to rethink how we structure and lead organizations.* Oakland, CA: Berrett-Koehler Publishers.

Zohar, D. and Marshall, I. (2000). *SQ: Spiritual intelligence, the ultimate intelligence.* London: Bloomsbury.

*Indigenous peoples do not believe
  the world is ending.*

The world is changing, they say.

Even before the scientists named climate change

The shamans knew it

When they saw the snow caps melting

The earth quaking and tilting

Animals and birds leaving

The Ocean rising

*They say:
  The Earth is Changing. For the sixth time.*

* * *

*The Inuit ask:
  When all the ice melts, who will we be?*

*In Vanuatu they say:
  We have nowhere to go in this island.*

*The Kogi says:
  The Younger Brother is hurting our Mother*

*The Syrian refugees say:
  The war is caused by drought.*

*The Indian farmer says:
  I cannot pay my debts; I'd rather die.*

*The white man in Texas says:
  I will build me a bunker.*

*The white man in the White House says:
  I will build me a wall.*

*The Silicon Valley techie says:
  I will build spaceships to Mars.*

*The media mogul says:
  Let's make more reality tv spectacles.*

*The religious say:
  God will provide.*

* * *

In the meantime

*Fire says:
  I am hungry*

*Water says:
  I am thirsty.*

*Fish says:
  I am choking on plastic*

*Bees say:
  Your chemicals make me sick.*

*Monarch butterflies ask:
  Where s our habitat now?*

* * *

Chthulune, Anthropocene,

Biomimicry, New materialism

Agential Realism, Inter and Intrasubjectivity

Mental monocropping, Hybridity

Indigenous Cosmopolitanism

*Concepts roll off the brain
  but doesn t land on the skin*

* * *

Poetry at the end of the world is:

  Silence

  Elegant Disintegration

  Just. Be. Kind.

  Tender and Generous

* * *

Go barefoot often

Salute the Sun each morning

Say Goodnight, Moon.

Eat local and in season

* * *

I keep going because I belong to a village

*Pay my debt for the privilege of being here
  for a few moments*

Live poetically even if I am not a word poet

English is not my first tongue

* * *

Grieve now while you can

Build beautiful altars to Death

Sing and dance your prayers

Resist the temptation of bright-sidedness

Do not meditate away your grief

Do not write another self help book

Poems, yes.

—Leny Strobel

Book Reviews

Conversations with a World Ensouled
Edited by Craig Chalquist
World Soul Books, 2010

Reviewed by Marna Hauk

I belong to the land now
crawling along its story lines
recovering pieces of my lineage…
let it shiver you
let it loose all of the remembering
let it open up a space again

—from "Painted,"
Catherine Baumgartner, p. 275

Introduction

The field of Terrapsychology first budded with Craig Chalquist's ground-blessing book *Terrapsychology: Re-engaging the Soul of Place* (2007). The field has come to first flower with thirty terrapsychological explorations in a compendium just published called *Rebearths: Conversations with a World Ensouled* (2010)[1].

[1] Please note: In this review, all references without dates regard authors within the Rebearths (2010) anthology.

Marna Hauk is a doctoral student in Sustainability Education at Prescott College, and founding director of the Institute for Earth Regenerative Studies (www.earthregenerative.org), designing and offering graduate programs at the intersection of creativity and innovation, permaculture and ecological restoration, and earth wisdom. She conducts Terrapsychological research in the Pacific Northwest. Marna serves on the editorial board of the *Journal for Sustainability Education* (http://www.jsedimensions.org/) and helps with the nonprofit Moonifest (www.moonifest.org), providing micro-grants for women, arts, and earth regeneration.

Terrapsychology is a field that gives new depth to the idea of soul searching, "how the search for the soul can be understood as a deep longing for a healthy reconnection with nature" (Villaseñor-Galarza, p. 277). However, this study of the psyche of the planet goes further than relationship and connection, studying instead how the Earth (Terra) itself inter-permeates humans and "possess[es] a primal intelligence, sensitivity, and reactivity" (Chalquist, p. 2). "By uncovering their underlying forms, images, and reconnective motifs" (p. 5), "Terrapsychology closes the circle of inquiry by looking still deeper for place, creature, world, or thing that hosts the archetypal figure" (p. 7).

I first became aware of Terrapsychology in my desire as a qualitative researcher to interview the Earth as part of my research. I was pleased to discover this growing body of Terrapsychology literature from a wide intersection of geography, ecology, and place; poetry and dream; art and the imaginal; ethnography and geology; permaculture and sociology. As Chalquist encourages us, the terrapsychological movement of connections between self and world relieves pathologies along parallel dimensions of personhood and place. It is balm for the separation of industrial usury and colonization: "when we realize how deeply we belong to this lively world and to the cosmos glittering all around it" (p. 8).

Rebearths: Conversations with a World Ensouled is an Earth-wise treasure. The book answers the question, "What is Terrapsychology?" with examples across five domains and explorations of methods and ethics.

Wound and Root

Sometimes, the pathologizing influence of Western psychology can threaten to foreshorten the research findings within the field of Terrapsychology. George Kohn explains, "From the psychotherapeutic view used in Chalquist's dissertation, the place often takes the role of the traumatized victim, with the original European colonizers and developers seen as narcissistic abusers" (p. 306). Several pieces in the *Rebearths* anthology round out the picture, surfacing the underlying resourcefulness and wisdom of different place energies, which, though they might become distorted in response/relationship with the last millennium's place invasions and the violence of modern industry, still have essential, effective, generative capacity at their root.

as hope, because at other times it is revealed to its depth, "as the central methodology of choice for studying deep interactions with the soul of things, beings, place, and nature" (Chalquist and Rankin, p. 318).

Earth Healing in Terrapsychology

Some of the *Rebearths* research stretches back to the fertile, generative earth wisdom underlying place fields. Janet Bubar Rich's research on dew suggests "a reverence for natural events as animated conscious forces: living beings analogous to people but with more power" and connecting with them, nourishing our ability to "imagine a life lived in harmony with nature" (pp. 28-29). Bubar Rich draws on a mixture of personal experience, myth, and culture to understand how noticing earth-renewing dew and the sanctity of exquisite wildflowers can connect us with a capacity for close attention and caring, can awaken our imagination, restoring our capacity to "live together on earth, our organic home" (p. 29).

Soul of Place

Expressions from places themselves are the genesis of Terrapsychology, and its methods continue to deepen in the place realms. Möllers affirms, "the terrapsychological approach recognizes such a resonance of the indwelling spirit of place and its intimate connection with its inhabitants" (p. 85). She conducts Terrapsychological inquiry (TI) in Flint, Michigan, for "this place birthed me, has dreamed itself into me and lives in me" (p. 87). She includes dreaming in her work, finding that the integrative power of dreaming helped her understand the intertwined battered-woman abusive-husband archetype writ large in the city's excesses, and how "through openness and active participation in the inquiry, the heart and soul of Flint unfolded richly" in her. "Hardened prejudices regarding the city [melted…allowing] hidden dimensions of both [her]self and the city to emerge" (p. 84), to become an active and empowered collaborator for ecological solutions and personal empowerment: "as one of its chosen ambassadors…to summon the courage and the strength to act on her behalf" (pp. 87-88).

> The qualities of our culture that damage the Earth are also those destructive to the human soul.

As the place expresses, does its energy diminish? Or, is it that the pressures and distortions of the industrial utilization and domination need to be released in order for the underlying place strengths and wisdom to be able to be accessed? For example, can the defended-ness of San Diego at its heart be understood to have assets of enwombing and safety-creation when not distorted by modern humans' assault on the Earth and the Earth's defendedness in response to it?

Terrapsychology started out as "a pilot methodology for detecting and working with ecological complexes" and syndromes (p. 317) with terms such as ecotransference and ecoreactivity, assuming and focusing on trauma. It clarifies "the direct connection between environmental degradation and other forms of oppression: the qualities of our culture that damage the Earth are also those destructive to the human soul" (Möllers, p. 84), while also supporting healing these relationships:

> What would a psychology of homecoming look like? How can I be present to the trauma embodied both in me and in this place? How can I continue to tend the sources of trauma in ways that transform them from scary to remorseful? What skills and resources do I have to enable this deep healing to begin? (Möllers, p. 87).

This inquiry brings clarity as well

Laura Vogel explores presence and earth intimacy in her piece on dirt. She explores how to connect meaningfully and respectfully to place, the connections between the unique signature and taste—*terroir*—of each place, and the unique opportunity of presence available in each moment; intimacy with earth opens in us a capacity for deep presence:

> And I come to a new place, even while embracing my whole history and lineages, and take its soil in my hand, smell it, breathe it, and know that a universal and shared *terroir* is also here, in this soil, and here, within my body, and this is the most authentic intimacy available to me—this piece of earth at this piece of time in this piece of space—something utterly unrepeatable. The *terroir* of the present moment. (p. 24)

Rebearths also offers three inquiries into San Francisco. Michael Steiner connects the themes of transience and displacement in the Mission (p. 90), informed by race and class dynamics and a long history of cultural dislocation. He found the place itself provided a "profusion of energy which gives rise to the creative act of remembering," with the "remembering of cultural roots…a step…taken toward healing this displacement, pain, and suffering" (p. 96). Another Bay area researcher, Corey Hale learned through collaboration with a photographer and by deep "skin listening" how the Golden Gate Bridge, "with no barrier to protect…from the seductive appeal of the womb of the Bay," also acts as Hecate's Gate into the underworld (p. 103). Jane Tanner explores how Bay Area earthquakes provide an awakening to the inherent instability of our modern dependence on technological lines and bridge spans.

> Landscapes speak to us in feelings, sensations, emotions, images, sounds, scents, with all of our

senses. Communication between us and the land where we work and live is alive with meaning. This dialogue may be deeply healing and nurturing, or it may alert us to disturbances in the land and in our

> Landscapes speak to us in feelings, sensations, emotions, images, sounds, scents, with all of our senses. Communication between us and the land where we work and live is alive with meaning.

psyche. This way of perceiving the world is available to anyone who will take the time to be aware, to communicate with the land with openness and a sense of adventure. (pp. 117-118)

Further afield, Aviva Joseph finds in Jerusalem, a city shaped like a heart, a chance to rebuild communities in places of devastation and contested homelands. She feels the potential for wholeness. Regarding the warring factions within the city, "They no longer seem like 'sides,' but more like cells of a magnificent organ in confusion" (p. 138).

Stephanie Paidas-Dukharm learns how bears in the King of the Crown continental divide region allowed visiting humans to grieve their own displacement from wilderness, even when they were unable to see the impacts of colonization on indigenous peoples also occurring:

> We'd watch the bears pass as though royalty crossed before us. It was then that our discussions could turn to displacement, habitat destruction, and sheer will to survive and desire to thrive in places where encroachment is a dangerous, ever-present threat. …. It was as if the bears seemed to know, seemed to appear when we most needed them, as if they sensed, as I did, that they could really teach us what it means to roam a territory, cooperate, and build a culture firmly grounded in a sense of place. (p. 76)

The bears and the place, a collision of mountains and culture, can transform into a moment of coyote-bear-human contact, demonstrating how

> a potentially catastrophic situation had morphed into heartfelt connection on the road that links west with east, White with Red, humanity with the natural world. And like the land, the animal, the people, and the spirit of this place, the three of us had been transformed (p. 78).

Catastrophe and Transformation

Like the conflicting, the catastrophic can also offer terrapsychological wisdom for inner and outer transformation. Katrina Martin Davenport explores the power of the storm and hurricane and the pattern of cycles, circles, and spirals as intense bringers of change and renewal (pp. 40, 44). Danielle Neuhauser considers, "Can we mimic the landscape and its cyclical processes by integrating the outer eruption of wildfire with an inner dynamic of transformation?…[to] begin to cultivate diversity in psychic life by allowing new parts of the self to emerge and old patterns to subside?" (p. 54) His research suggests the disturbance of inner psychic fires may clear out a weedy or overgrown inner life, while the California landscape may be requesting a different response to fire disaster, "one of community, of relatedness, and compassion and respect" rather than an attitude of battle and heroic intervention (p. 54).

Even the radioactive can bring insight into how to connect with planet and place. Matthew Cochran's brilliant exploration of uranium, elementally and by the landscapes of its genesis and distillation, surfaces "*geologic soul … that permeable border or breathing boundary that fuses psyche and landscape*" (p. 231). He finds indicators in ancient petroglyphs, "a fighting *neikos*, a vibrating restlessness, a fury of sold out activity" (p. 238). Moab fatigues his body; "the body's extensive nuances relate the presence of place and can speak its subtleties" (p. 238). Methodologically, Cochran contrasts environmentalism and green technologies' "appropriation by the mainstream business and global economic machine [which] perpetuates a separate consciousness and a consciousness of separation" with the larger terrapsychological question: "What if we come to terms with the hidden wounds of place? What is the character beneath the wound and what transformation occurs in reconnection?" (p. 239). He says, "a geo-desire to be led by the land, to be fused with its consciousness, is the longing that leads" (p. 239). He finds uranium to be an intense tearing and refining of a part of ourselves "so complete that we've isolated the deadliest part of ourselves and made it into a weapon of geologic destruction" (p. 240). He finds the dynamics of "destruction and subsequent abandonment—the dark unrealized aspects of amplified disconnection: destroying the Earth in order to leave it" (p. 242). Even at the heart of the radioactive fire, and this intense displacement, throbs an intense and highly polished capacity, "a way through destruction to the creation nested within" (p. 245). He argues that uranium and its places direct us to connect with our own transmutative capacities, within the elemental energy and subtle orbits of the body, "where creative restoration catalyzes" (p. 246). He also shares other rich resources for addressing our nuclear inheritance, including Joanna Macy's Nuclear Guardianship Project, in which former detonation sites could "become well-tended shrines, verdant temples, places of prayer and contemplation, sanctuaries of awakening, and sites of a geologic ethic honoring both an outer and an inner condition" (p. 246). This is Terrapsychology at its strongest, combining autoethnographic, felt contact with place, mythological, and cultural resonances and liberation historical insight to surface and transform the torsions and possibilities of particular place-fields. [this sentence needs fixing – too many nouns in the highlighted phrasing}.

Earth Bodies

Terrapsychology also happens in human bodies and offers liberating ways of inhabiting limb and land. Laura Mitchell's nomadic awareness wakes up the senses as it follows the "'songlines' (the interlocked network of ways through the land)," deterritorializing our presence and offering a "new form of collective interrelatedness" (p. 151). Nomadic awareness includes both direct contact with place and diffuse contact with region in what she calls "nonlimited locality"; it offers "an acute sense of emplacement without appropriation" (p. 151).

Rather than wandering, Rebecca Wyse returns to her family home place to understand the terrapsychological dynamics of exile from homeland and body. She cites Jung's insight that it is the loss of contact between the body and the soil that drives loss of connection to homeland, exile, and resultant hunger to conquer other lands (p. 153). She chronicles parallels between an eating disordered relationship with the body and the loss of farming communities and old ways of land-tending and storytelling. Embodied Terrapsychology focuses on connection. Wyse's advocacy of

> Having a love affair with the earth, of being in a mutually satisfying relationship where we share quality time, feel joy in each other's company, feel a sense of being protected and nurtured by each other, feel heard and fed deep in our souls (p. 160)

...prefigures Kevin Filocamo's cultivation of erotic relationship with the natural world. Pam Greenslate advocates a return to living in a circular society rather than in boxes and grids, in order to increase connection and communication with each other and the living world: "The body of the place of our world is intricately connected to our human bodies and we back to that world" (p. 171). Greenslate makes a connection between circles, cycles, and spirals and being able to see more options and opening to unlimited possibilities (p. 170). She concludes, "The healthier our physical landscape…the more healthy grow our mindful bodies. They are forever connected" (p. 171).

Earth Dreams

> Dispelling the illusion of separateness, our dreams pull back the veil, revealing the hidden fields of energies into which our lives are cast. We are intimately part of the living splendor that spreads out continuously in every direction; dreams transport us into this seamless fabric of being (Jaenke, p. 188).

Dreaming and other messages from the imaginal realm are critical data points in terrapsychological inquiry. Karen Jaenke eloquently describes how "intimately interwoven" people and place become within the dreaming landscape (p. 189). Her essay identifies three kinds of dreams: earth-communing, earth-destruction, and earth-healing dreams. "Earth communing dreams bathe the dreamer in the same bath of

> Uranium and its places direct us to connect with our own transmutative capacities, within the elemental energy and subtle orbits of the body, "where creative restoration catalyzes."

animating energy that washes over the planet. Experiences in this participatory field serve to reawaken psychic kinship between dreamer and planet" (p. 197). Jaenke explains how dreams of earth destruction assist us psychologically to metabolize terror and catastrophic collective events, inviting us to presence and grounding (pp. 198-199). While they may be shocking, they also provide clues to earth healing, including healing the human-Earth relationship (p. 199). The earth healing revealed in dreams entails balancing opposites, which aligns with ancient indigenous wisdom regarding balance as a state of embodied aliveness and connection, embedded in the natural world. She expresses the promise for healing in terrapsychological dreaming: "our psychic kinship with the earth body can heal our planetary wounds" (p. 196).

Maturations and Extensions

The field of Terrapsychology is maturing, its practices expanding as dozens of researchers extend and respond to the calls of the land, including with places, dreams, and elements, as well as through bodies and things. In *Rebearths*, Terrapsychological research extends from homes and hives to rocks and corn.

Researcher Kathryn Quick found in her ancestral home an experience of reciprocal care. Plumbing challenges led to insights about having to dig deep to the roots for clear understanding (p. 272). Bonnie Bright engages with honey, bees, and nature to avoid the collapse of civilizations as well as bee colonies:

> By facing ecological anguish and reflecting on it, we begin to address the parts of ourselves that have been left arid, deforested, scattered, and alone. In fully engaging, we discover a song in the silence, the hum of longing to cross-pollinate a reciprocal relationship between bees and bodies, people and plants, humans and humus. We find ourselves opening, like a flower, to the wild (p. 215).

Ryan Hurd conducts his research on an ancient stone site in Nicaragua, loosening his Western perceptual habits to immerse himself in a sacred space and the spirit of place. He practices nature observation, lucid dreaming, and acoustic archaeology to connect with the stone wisdom of Ometepe, to cross the boundary markers from this world and the imaginal, to "walk into the sensing and intuitive realms" to access the "multidimensional language" of ancient peoples' place collaborations (pp. 260-261).

Chalquist's explorations of corn also reframe the heavy feeder plant to a point similarly expressed in Pollan's *Botany of Desire*: what if we look at it from the point of view of the corn plant? Chalquist argues corn's generosity and adaptability cannot be blamed for human farming excesses. Rather, Terrapsychologists trust the larger Earth system:

> Terrapsychology assumes an Earth that knows what it's doing. Just *how* it does it remains mysterious—manifestations of its latent animation? Emergent properties of natural systems?—but it is now clear that life here evolves into ever higher and deeper levels of complexity.

Research in ethology, ecology, and other fields has made relegating sentience only to humans highly problematic, suggesting that living qualities like purpose and intentionality do not reside solely with big-brained naked apes (p. 224).

In the final section of the book, researchers further extend Terrapsychology into related fields, such as land ethics, permaculture design, animal kinship, and Earth Keeping. The pieces model and explicate the methods, quilting an eloquent case for earth connection and showing the means of its surfacing.

Inquiry, Rigor, Methodology

Whereas most of *Rebearths* serves as a series of case studies, Chalquist kindly includes a section on methods and validation, which will enable Terrapsychology wider adoption in diverse communities of practice. In terms of methods, researcher Sarah Rankin supports the use of walking, sitting meditation, altar-building, and ceremonial work for Terrapsychological inquiry, all of which enable "deep listening...feeling more deeply in [the] body the crossing over to a different means of perception" (p. 290). She coaches humble participation rather than "intimidating grandness": "To know yourself as a listener to the land means that your ears must be attached to a great being, a being spacious enough to comprehend the voices of the forest" (p. 290).

In another essay, Kohn traces the intellectual family tree of Terrapsychology, seeing in it a fertile blending of geography and psychology, a confirmation of Jung's collective "background resonance of all humanity" with Sheldrake's morphogenetic field memory (p. 301). He identifies a triple weaving of Casey's intersubjectivity, Ellis's autoethnography, and Romanyshyn's imperative "that dreams, synchronicities, and other imaginal activities inform the research" (p. 311). Kohn finds lineage with David Abram's phenomenological hermeneutics, Roszak's ecopsychological continuum of planet and person, and Hillman's *Anima Mundi* (the soul of the world) in Terrapsychology: interbeing with "that wild otherness with which human life has always been entwined" (Abram, *Spell of the Sensuous*, quoted in *Rebearths*, p. 289).

One missing trunk in this family tree of Terrapsychology would be the thousands of indigenous wisdom traditions that have explicitly and continuously valued and integrated place-sourced connection and insight, generally avoiding the Western split between the planetary and personal, honoring sensorial embedment and information sharing in the emergent living presences of which humans are a part. Gregory Cajete's scholarship provides missing context for the indigenous roots of Terrapsychology. He articulates the indigenous wisdom of mutual experiencing: "the continual orientation of Native thought and perception toward active participation, active imagination, and active engagement with all that makes up natural reality... a part of the Earth mind" (pp. 27, 30). In reference to indigenous peoples, he writes:

They experienced nature as part of themselves and themselves as part of nature. They were born of the earth of their place...This is the ultimate definition of being 'indigenous' and forms the basis for a fully internalized bonding with that place (2000, pp. 186-187).

Citing traditions spanning more than 70,000 years, Gregory Cajete calls this Native "ensoulment of nature... a **geopsyche**,...the inner archetypes in a place...that interaction between the inner and outer realities" (2000, pp. 186-187). Other pieces in *Rebearths* better acknowledge this more ancient lineage of the work.

What about rigor and validity in TI (Terrapsychological inquiry)? Chalquist and Rankin offer great suggestions in "Enriching the Inquiry," including mixed methods approaches, validity, and reliability as Terrapsychology comes of age. Honoring TI's "flexibly transdisciplinary framework for organizing observations and impressions" (p. 317), the authors suggest its use in mixed methods approaches with consciousness and context-sensitivity to produce coherence, to avoid an unconscious extension of the fragmentation evidenced in the field of many place traumas in which the researchers will find themselves. The section on research validity for Terrapsychology is one of the most important sections in the entire tome. The authors review approaches for construct validity, internal validity, and external validity: "For TI, validity and reliability remain important criteria capable of being reimagined and reapplied from within its perspective" (p. 319). Adapting strategies from four Inquiries—Depth, Intuitive, Collaborative, and Liberation Psychology—TI does indeed offer a rigorous set of tools for deepening the research.

The descriptions of Rosemary Anderson's Intuitive Inquiry reminded me of my experience with Terrapsychology generally, that it speaks exactly to my actual deep and felt experience, without strange linear twists that Western academic approaches often involve. It is validating, therefore, to see academic research language placed on actual things of meaning and value in *Rebearths* in the form of eight types of validity that can be used in Terrapsychological research.

Resonance validity (from Intuitive Inquiry) involves the use of resonance panels of peers evaluating the research in progress from across multiple domains of experience, "'in a manner akin to poetry in its capacity for immediate apprehension and recognition of an experience spoken by another and yet be true to oneself, as well'"(Anderson quoted in Chalquist & Rankin, p. 320). **Efficacy validity** "has to do with whether research fosters creative jumps and insights and 'inspires, delights, and prods us into insight and action'" (Anderson in Chalquist & Rankin, p. 320). Together, in this qualitative frame, "both types of validity provide a qualitative measure of whether a study adds value to human life and promotes beneficial transformations in the participant's consciousness.

Additionally, Liberation Psychology offers **contextual validity** (fruitfulness of research frames and results for those involved in the research), **interpretive validity** (discussions across strata of meanings), and **catalytic validity** to the TI methodological rigor (p. 321). This last item, catalytic validity, involves a TI twist, not only "whether the research leads to creative, liberatory transformations in individuals who participate and in the world at large" but also "research that leads to transformations in the relationships of local residents to where they live" (p. 321).

Cycles of reflection and action are verified in Collaborative Inquiry. Unique to TI, ecoreactivity –"the felt sense of impingement or invasion by the terrain under study"—can serve as both construct validity and to demonstrate the researcher is avoiding projection (pp. 322-325). Projection is a key danger in Terrapsychological Inquiry. **Transformation validity** and **intragroup validity** can also offer validation of TI research, the depth of the perceived transformation between researched and researcher, and the confirmation of results with the use of multiple researchers (p. 322).

Finally, TI adds **community response validity** which involves both "How consistently do the people who live at the research site resonate to or recognize the findings, and to what degree does the study contribute to the aliveness, sustainability, and ecological integrity of the research site?" (p. 322). Finally, the authors suggest the main focus in reliability in TI is **generative reliability**, "the degree to which the study's clarity, resonance, and attention to detail allow other researchers to use it as a point of departure" (p. 323). This penultimate section of *Rebearths*, with its useful methodological guidance, including best practices regarding validation and rigor, will prove to be a bridge to future adoption of Terrapsychology by wider circles of researchers.

Concluding with the Earth

Terrapsychological work can hone a talent for using personal wounds to learn more about our surroundings, especially when they suffer ecological trauma. Properly tended, our 'inner' places of scarring, pollution, or barrenness can open doors into understanding and healing similar states in the terrain (p. 325, Chalquist & Rankin).

In order to avoid "forgetting, marveling at the landscape we overran, overlooking the fragmentation of our unearthed souls," Terrapsychology offers us "the openings to enter back into quiet contract with the Earth" (Cochran, p. 239). Terrapsychology teaches us "how imagination can be an organ of perception" (Villaseñor-Galarza, p. 281). The world soul comes alive in particular places, its strengths and resilience being freed from torsion and distortion by the empathic presence and process of the Terrapsychologist. We become more fully alive by opening to the spirit of place. "At the very least we must walk out under the open sky and let the beauty we encounter break our hearts and break us open to the work we are each called to do" (Wendy Sarno, p. 349). Terrapsychology offers a deeper path, to avoid being "mind-blinded to what is readily evident through emotional and intuitive lenses" (Karen Diane Knowles, p. 371). It answers the question, "How do we fire the forgotten synapse, live from the vitality of the senses, acting from common sense?" (Cochran, p. 230). Across panoplies of place, body, element, and thing, the Earth is living in us and we in the Earth, "not wholly inner or outer. It is both. By staying thoughtfully and heartfully within the overlap of the two, a realm of soulful interconnection and relationship emerges….despite corrosive criticism hurled by defenders of a dying paradigm" (p. 325, Chalquist & Rankin).

I have come to believe that the *genius loci* speaks directly to my psychological, spiritual, and physical state of being. The felt essence of a place and its natural features, whether conveyed by ancient geological faults and movements or more recent human accomplishments or catastrophes, finds its way through me, often by such a gracious path that I am unable to detect a solid boundary between it and me… (Villaseñor-Galarza, p. 284)

Terrapsychology shares specific methods and techniques for living and healing inside the larger body of the Earth. As David Abram so eloquently affirms in *Becoming Animal: An Earthly Cosmology*:

The world we inhabit…is our larger flesh, a densely intertwined and improvisational tissue of experience. It is a sensitive sphere sustained by a solar wind, a round field of sentience sustained by the relationships between the myriad lives and sensibilities that compose it. We come to know more of this sphere not by detaching ourselves from our felt experience, but by inhabiting our bodily experience all the more richly and wakefully, feeling our way into deeper contact with other experiencing bodies, and hence with the wild, intercorporeal life of the earth itself. (2010, pp. 143-144)

References

Abram, D. (2010). *Becoming animal: An earthly cosmology*. NY: Pantheon.

Cajete, G. (2000). *Native science: Natural laws of interdependence*. Santa Fe, NM: Clear Light Publishers.

Chalquist, C. (Ed.). (2010). *Rebearths: Conversations with a world nsouled*. Walnut Creek, CA: World Soul Books.

Chalquist, C. (2007). *Terrapsychology: Re-engaging the soul of place*. New Orleans, LA: Spring Journal Books.

Pollan, M. (2001). *The botany of desire: A plant's eye view of the world*. New York: Random House.

New from ReVision Publishing

THE LIGHT IN THE DARK: THE SEARCH FOR VISIONS

Ruth-Inge Heinze
Foreword by Stanley Krippner

Only $19.95
Includes shipping

264 pages

Order from:
ReVision Publishing • PO Box 1855 • Sebastopol, CA 95473

SHAMANS OF EURASIA

COMING SOON

New from
ReVision Publishing

$45.00
Pre-order Now

Mihály Hoppál

ReVision Publishing • PO Box 1855 • Sebastopol, CA 95473

ReVision Is ONLINE!

Visit us at
www.revisionpublishing.org